The Photoshop Toolbox

The Photoshop Toolbox is the key to editing your photos. Think of it as an art supply box: It holds all the brushes, erasers, paint colors, and tools needed to create your art.

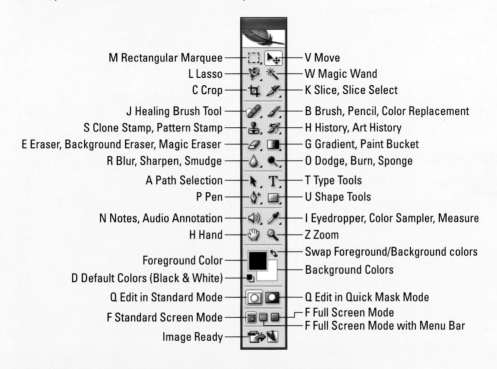

M Rectangular Marquee — V Move
L Lasso — W Magic Wand
C Crop — K Slice, Slice Select
J Healing Brush Tool — B Brush, Pencil, Color Replacement
S Clone Stamp, Pattern Stamp — H History, Art History
E Eraser, Background Eraser, Magic Eraser — G Gradient, Paint Bucket
R Blur, Sharpen, Smudge — O Dodge, Burn, Sponge
A Path Selection — T Type Tools
P Pen — U Shape Tools
N Notes, Audio Annotation — I Eyedropper, Color Sampler, Measure
H Hand — Z Zoom
Foreground Color — Swap Foreground/Background colors
— Background Colors
D Default Colors (Black & White) —
Q Edit in Standard Mode — Q Edit in Quick Mask Mode
F Standard Screen Mode — F Full Screen Mode
— F Full Screen Mode with Menu Bar
Image Ready —

Ten Must-Haves for Your Camera Bag

What	Why
Cell phone, healthy snacks, aspirin, and water	When venturing out on a photo shoot, especially to remote locations, make sure you always have these items in case the car breaks down or you get lost.
A tripod	A must for almost all types of photography, many newer tripod models are lightweight and sturdy enough for most digital cameras.
Lens cleaning paraphernalia	Always carry a bulb-blower (to blow dust off your lenses), lens-cleaning solutions, and a lens-safe cloth to clean off smudges.
Flashlight	Though most digital cameras have lighted control panels (for shooting in dark locations), a handy compact flashlight can help you adjust hard-to-read camera knobs or find that memory card in your bag.
Extra batteries	Keep an extra one or two digital-camera batteries, charged and ready to go, so you always have enough juice to get that shot.

For Dummies: Bestselling Book Series for Beginners

Camera Raw with Photoshop® FOR DUMMIES

Cheat Sheet

What	Why
Auxiliary lenses	You never know when you might need them, so always bring along your auxiliary lenses for your compact digital camera or dSLR.
Tools	Consider packing an all-in-one tool, just in case a knob on your tripod gets over-tightened.
Memory cards	Carry as many as you can afford, so you always have enough storage; download them when you get back, so they're ready for the next shoot.
Plastic bags	Self-sealing plastic bags protect your electronics and lenses from water and other elements.
Your camera's user manual	Most photographers don't know how to access *every* feature of their digital cameras. Your manual will come in handy for the 5% you don't know (which you may well need when you're out shooting).

Image-Management Workflow

Good practices: Keeping your images in organized folders, backing up all your originals, and using Bridge to check and organize your files. Making these habits into steps (and doing them in the same sequence whenever you add images to your collection) helps keep your images orderly and your work efficient. You can put all these concepts together in a step-by-step workflow by following these steps (detailed in Chapter 4):

1. **Organize your files around a plan to manage your images.**

   One folder can store additional subfolders that hold Original, Working, and Output subfolders to store versions of your images.

2. **Copy new images to their prepared folders on your computer.**

   Using a card reader (or by directly connecting digital camera and computer), download new images to your Original images folder.

3. **Back up your files to a backup device and optical media.**

   Make several backups and store them separately. Use external hard drives as backup devices and offline storage. For extra image safety, copy image downloads (the originals) immediately to CD or DVD, on premium optical discs that will be usable in the foreseeable future.

4. **Convert raw images to DNG format (optional).**

   DNG format is a new, versatile candidate for a standard raw-image file format.

5. **Add metadata to image files or sidecar files.**

   Descriptions of your files (including data from your camera) will help you identify, organize, access, and evaluate your images.

6. **Apply labels and ratings.**

   Adobe Bridge offers color-coding and rating functions that help you identify and retrieve the best of your image collection.

For Dummies: Bestselling Book Series for Beginners

Camera Raw with Photoshop®

FOR DUMMIES®

by Kevin L. Moss

Wiley Publishing, Inc.

Camera Raw with Photoshop® For Dummies®

Published by
Wiley Publishing, Inc.
111 River Street
Hoboken, NJ 07030-5774
www.wiley.com

Copyright © 2006 by Wiley Publishing, Inc., Indianapolis, Indiana

Published by Wiley Publishing, Inc., Indianapolis, Indiana

Published simultaneously in Canada

For general information on our other products and services, please contact our Customer Care Department within the U.S. at 800-762-2974, outside the U.S. at 317-572-3993, or fax 317-572-4002.

For technical support, please visit www.wiley.com/techsupport.

Wiley also publishes its books in a variety of electronic formats. Some content that appears in print may not be available in electronic books.

Library of Congress Control Number:

ISBN-13: 978-0-471-77482-2

ISBN-10: 0-471-77482-0

Manufactured in the United States of America

10 9 8 7 6 5 4 3 2 1

1K/QS/QS/QW/IN

WILEY

About the Author

Kevin Moss is a photographer, author, and expert in digital photography, personal computing, and the World Wide Web. An early adopter and long-time user of Photoshop, Kevin has specialized in combining traditional photography with the latest in computer and digital technologies. Kevin is also the author of *Photoshop CS2 and Digital Photography For Dummies,* and *50 Fast Digital Camera Techniques,* 2nd Edition.

Kevin specializes in fine-art landscape, abstract, and portrait photography. For more information about Kevin's photographic work, or to contact him regarding this book, visit his Web site at www.kevinmossphotography.com.

Dedication

For my wonderful wife, Amy, who has supported me all along in my new endeavors, and our children Amanda, Emily, and David. You have all supported me through this project, and helped me make it happen. Thanks for taking such good care of me while I spent all those days and evenings writing, taking naps, taking photos, and messing around with Photoshop. I love you all!

Author's Acknowledgments

Putting a book together is a large effort, and the author isn't the only one who spends a lot of time and dedication moving it toward completion. I have many people to thank for their hard work and dedication to this project. I especially want to thank Laura Lewin from Studio B and Bob Woerner at Wiley for giving me this opportunity. You are both a pleasure to work with, and I especially appreciate your professionalism.

I would like to personally acknowledge my Project Editor Nicole Sholly, who gave me tremendous support on a daily basis to help me through all the intricacies of writing a technical manuscript, plus helping me keep on schedule and always being available at any time when I needed some help.

I would like to acknowledge the copyediting work of Barry Childs-Helton. Barry's eloquent suggestions for tweaks to my otherwise-plain language have helped me take my writing to a new level. Barry worked extremely hard making sure words weren't a tangled mess, explanations were understandable, and humor was on–target. I think Barry worked as hard on this book as I did, and I am very grateful for the effort.

Any technical book, especially one written about complex software like Photoshop, needs a great technical editor. My special thanks to Ron Rockwell — whom I rely on to advise me about technical issues, offer great alternatives, and help keep my techniques correct. It's professionals like Nicole, Barry, and Ron that make the editing process fun and productive.

I would also like to acknowledge the rest of the team at Wiley who get things done behind the scenes, including Kevin Kirschner and Amanda Foxworth. Thank you all for your efforts to make sure my writing, images, and figures are all formatted, arranged correctly, and understandable.

Publisher's Acknowledgments

We're proud of this book; please send us your comments through our online registration form located at www.dummies.com/register/.

Some of the people who helped bring this book to market include the following:

Acquisitions, Editorial, and Media Development

Project Editor: Nicole Sholly

Senior Acquisitions Editor: Bob Woerner

Senior Copy Editor: Barry Childs-Helton

Technical Editor: Ron Rockwell

Editorial Manager: Kevin Kirschner

Media Development Manager: Laura VanWinkle

Media Development Supervisor: Richard Graves

Editorial Assistant: Amanda Foxworth

Cartoons: Rich Tennant (www.the5thwave.com)

Composition Services

Project Coordinator: Maridee Ennis

Layout and Graphics: Lauren Goddard, Denny Hager, Melanee Prendergast, Heather Ryan, Erin Zeltner

Proofreaders: Leeann Harney, Tricia Liebig, Dwight Ramsey

Indexer: Steve Rath

Publishing and Editorial for Technology Dummies

Richard Swadley, Vice President and Executive Group Publisher

Andy Cummings, Vice President and Publisher

Mary Bednarek, Executive Acquisitions Director

Mary C. Corder, Editorial Director

Publishing for Consumer Dummies

Diane Graves Steele, Vice President and Publisher

Joyce Pepple, Acquisitions Director

Composition Services

Gerry Fahey, Vice President of Production Services

Debbie Stailey, Director of Composition Services

Table of Contents

Introduction

· ·

*D*igital photography has come a long way in the last few years. When digital cameras broke the 3-megapixel barrier, I strongly considered jumping in and retiring my film gear. By the time 5-megapixel digital cameras hit the street, I was hooked. Then, just a few years ago, the raw file format started being offered, and Adobe Camera Raw was born. To me, this was digital heaven — to have full control over how digital images are processed, from camera all the way to print.

If you're shooting raw now, you've probably figured out the advantages of working in that format. Being able to correct image exposure and white balance is enough to sell me, but you can also make overall adjustments in color and tone without the danger of destroying valuable image data — and that's the biggest gift the format gives us. Camera Raw ties the process together, letting photographers bypass using third-party software so we can process raw files within the same software we use to edit our photos.

This book gives you a detailed explanation of the entire end-to-end process — from capturing raw images with your digital camera to organizing your files in Bridge, converting your images in Adobe Camera Raw, and then processing them in Photoshop. I explain each individual procedure as a *workflow* — a set of useful habits to develop in sequence. Okay, sure, the term has been a buzzword in photography trade rags over the past few years, but truly this concept is the path toward more consistent processes for getting your images from camera to print — resulting in more consistent quality. Your photography will improve just by following the steps provided in this book as you develop your workflows.

About This Book

I've spent the past few years perfecting my processes with Photoshop — which can be a very intimidating software program. The last few versions offered even more capability to master — the File Browser, the new Bridge program, and Camera Raw, now in its third or fourth version. This book gives me the opportunity to share that knowledge with photographers who shoot in raw format and want to get up to speed with these new Photoshop capabilities.

I've selected the content of this book based on what's most important to us as photographers. The chapters are also organized in a manner in which we use parts of Photoshop according to order, or in an overall workflow. Some of these topics include

- ✔ The importance of and implementing color management.
- ✔ The importance of and implementing workflows.
- ✔ Using Bridge and managing digital images.
- ✔ Understanding color.
- ✔ Using Camera Raw.
- ✔ Making overall color and tonal corrections in Photoshop.
- ✔ Making edits in Photoshop.

Mastering the skills in these areas of Photoshop and digital photography will help you organize and streamline your digital photography processes, making digital photography even more fun and gratifying.

Foolish Assumptions

This book is intended as a Camera Raw and Photoshop CS2 reference for those digital photographers who want to develop efficient workflows for processing raw images, organizing files, and making corrections and edits in Photoshop. If you have an advanced digital camera or digital SLR that can capture images in raw format, a computer (with a *lot* of memory and storage space!), Photoshop CS2, and even a photo-quality printer, you probably have all you need to get started!

Here is a list of things I assume you already have (or will be adding to your collection shortly):

- ✔ **Digital SLR or advanced compact digital camera:** For digital photographers who want to shoot in raw format, having a digital camera that can produce raw files is a pretty good idea. Most of the newer (and more advanced) compact digital cameras — and to my knowledge, all recent-model digital SLRs — offer the raw format. If your digital camera is a brand-spanking-new model (if so, congratulations!), it may take Adobe a few months to come out with an update to Camera Raw that includes your new model. One thing is certain: You're going to need some big-honkin' memory cards for your digital camera. Raw files can get pretty big — from *5 megabytes each* on up — depending on how many megapixels your digital camera can handle. So I'd also suggest a dedicated card reader to transfer those big files to your computer. Transferring files to your computer by attaching a USB cable from your camera can be a slow and tedious process; getting a card reader is a great investment, and they don't cost much (especially when you consider that your time is valuable).

✔ **Computer:** To work with Photoshop, you need a computer with enough memory and a decent monitor. Photoshop CS2 requires that your computer have *at least* 384 megabytes of memory. (And remember: As a rule, minimum requirements barely get the job done; try to exceed those specs whenever possible.) If you are shooting and processing raw files, I'd recommend *at least* 1 gigabyte of memory for your computer. Digital photo files, especially raw, gobble up disk space (I'd recommend at least 100 gigabytes for starters). You'll be surprised at how fast disk space gets used up.

✔ **Colorimeter:** Color management is a super-important part of your overall workflow. If you're not using color-management tools, I strongly suggest you look into purchasing a colorimeter and a software package that will allow you to calibrate your monitor. If you can ensure that what you see on your computer is what prints on your printer, you're better off; calibration makes it possible.

✔ **Photoshop CS2:** Photoshop CS2 is the central part of your digital darkroom. Just as Windows or Mac OS functions as your computer's operating system, Photoshop CS2 is your digital-photography operating system. New features in CS2 include Adobe Bridge for image management — and Camera Raw is included.

If you're still using Photoshop CS, don't fret! For the most part, the workflows in this book apply to you as well; the version of Camera Raw is very similar, and the File Browser concept of managing files is the same.

✔ **Photo-quality printer:** I'm assuming you're using Photoshop to process files for printing, but lots of folks use it for publishing in different media as well. Still, it's nice to have one of those superior new photo printers our manufactures have blessed us with. These days, for under $100, you can find a printer that will more than meet your needs. If you're making photos primarily for use on the Web, having a printer on hand helps if you want an actual *photo* you can hold, frame, or keep in your wallet.

How This Book Is Organized

This book is divided into parts that address general areas such as organizing photos, converting raw files, or working with Photoshop. I even include some fun chapters in The Part of Tens. Feel free to skip around, and if you have the time, read the book from beginning to end!

Part I: Getting Your Feet Wet

Okay, not all of us plunge right into digital photography (underwater or otherwise). So Part I offers an overview for the Photoshop and Camera Raw concepts covered in the rest of the book. It's a quick-start for shooting in raw format and getting your images into your computer. Chapter 1 briefly introduces shooting raw, using Bridge, and then using Camera Raw and Photoshop to process your images. Chapter 2 goes into more detail about the benefits of raw format, and takes a look at Adobe's new DNG file format. Chapter 3 speaks to a topic near and dear to my heart — color management. Chapter 4 explains the workflows covered throughout the book, and why they can improve your overall photography and your Photoshop skills.

Part II: Image-Management Workflow with Adobe Bridge

Adobe Bridge is what ties together all the Photoshop processes, your habits of image management, and the tweaks you make in Camera Raw and Photoshop. Image management, in essence, is keeping your digital files organized and backed up for safekeeping. After all, before you can use 'em, you have to be able to find 'em, and they have to be where you put 'em. So Chapter 5 shows you how to get around Bridge and take advantage of its file-management functions. Chapter 6 shows you how to add information to digital images to organize and reference them even better for future usage.

Part III: Working with Raw Images

Camera Raw is the program you'll use to process all your raw images, and Part III shows you how to do just that, in a smooth raw-image–processing workflow. Chapter 7 starts you out with understanding color, the basis of processing raw images. Chapter 8 gives you a tour of Camera Raw, while Chapter 9 shows you how to use all the tools and controls Camera Raw has to offer.

Part IV: Photoshop CS2 Image-Processing Workflows

All aspects of processing images in this book are presented in separate workflows that make up your overall image-processing activities. This part explains the workflows needed to process images in Photoshop after you've converted them in Camera Raw. Chapter 10 shows you workflows for correcting color and tone in Photoshop. Chapter 11 explains image editing as a workflow — you know, removing red eye, blemishes, and miscellaneous unwanted parts of your image (use your imagination). Chapter 12 is dedicated toward preparing images for output by correctly sizing them, applying color profiles, and routing them through an efficient printing workflow.

Part V: The Part of Tens

Always the favorite part of any *For Dummies* book, The Part of Tens provides you with a few chapters that add to your growing technical knowledge (and might enhance your reputation as a guru). Chapter 13 provides you with 10 cool things to do with your photos — such as creating abstracts, creating a photo Web site, and stitching panoramas. Chapter 14 shows you 10 cool Photoshop filters to use when you want to add special effects to your images. You know. The fun stuff. (Always my favorite subjects to show!)

Icons Used in This Book

What's a *For Dummies* book without icons pointing you in the right direction? This section shows and describes the five icons I use in this book.

This icon alerts you to some of the great new features available in CS2. If you're still using CS, you get a peek at the features that are waiting for you when you upgrade.

Use the text next to this icon as a guide for doing something *better* with your images. Often I add tips to the step-by-step instructions to give you some good ideas on the spot as you work with Bridge, Camera Raw, and Photoshop.

This icon is used to alert you to a topic that's important for you *not* to forget. Commit these to memory.

What you find next to this icon often helps explain technical topics in clearer terms. The information provided may not be critical, but the odd nice-to-know technical facts will make you look *real smart* in front of your friends.

When you see one of these, don't run; the sky is not falling! (Not yet, anyway.) It's simply a way to stay out of the way of potential trouble when hassles and glitches are lurking around the corner.

Where to Go from Here

This book isn't intended to be read from beginning to end like a mystery; it's a reference. Drop into it whenever you need a hand getting some pesky technique to work right. This book is organized to reflect the overall order in which you'd normally be working with digital images; feel free to look up any topic in the index and go right to that chapter to find out what you want to know.

To make things even easier, processes are broken down into step-by-step workflows (gotta love that word), with a bunch of actual Photoshop screen-shots and photos to provide visual cues. If you want to skip right to the part on using Bridge (Part II), go ahead! Want to see how to process images in Camera Raw (Part III)? You can skip to that step, too. I've also offered detailed workflows for making overall corrections, edits, and preparing images for output in Photoshop (Part IV). Consider this book an end-to-end guide for using Photoshop and Camera Raw to transform your raw images into exactly what you want to see.

Part I
Getting Your Feet Wet

The 5th Wave — By Rich Tennant

COSMETIC SURGERY

"This time, just for fun, let's see what you'd look like with bat ears and squash for a nose."

In this part . . .

Digital photography has offered old-school film photographers more tools and capabilities than you can shake a stick at! You have some great digital cameras, powerful computers that are afford-able, and some rockin' software like Photoshop CS2 that you can use to tweak, retouch, and even morph your photos. One rule remains true whether you shoot film or digital: Better photographs start with the photographer. True, software utilities and techniques help make a normal blah photo a little better, but images well exposed, composed, and focused make much better prints.

After you've taken some great photos, there's more fun to be had! Well, *some* folks have fun orga-nizing and downloading images, converting the raw ones, and making further corrections and edits in Photoshop. Okay, it's an acquired taste — a bit more complex than driving a roll of film down to the corner drugstore for processing! But think of the *control* you now have over how your images turn out. That's where some real creativity with digital photography begins — in the "digital darkroom" — and that's what this book is all about. The chapters in this part help get you started working with the tools and established processes of the digital darkroom: Bridge, Camera Raw, Photoshop, and the workflows that give you consistently impres-sive results.

Getting to Know Bridge, Camera Raw, and Photoshop

*R*emember the days (just a few years ago!) when digital photography consisted of having fun shooting photos, transferring them to your computer, and enhancing them using Photoshop? The choices were simple: shoot in JPEG or TIFF format. JPEG format is pretty good, but TIFF was supposed to be better (even though the resulting image files were huge). Before long, we figured out that JPEG quality was pretty close to TIFF quality; for the most part, shooting images in TIFF really didn't offer much advantage.

Discerning digital photographers have always wanted a file format that works like a digital equivalent of a traditional negative — giving the photographer total control over processing the image data captured by a digital camera. (Sure, you could skip the tweaking and leave it all up to the camera's internal processing software — but why settle for blah results?) In the past few years, new digital camera models have delivered just that — the *raw image format*. The software that gives you control of those raw images is called (logically enough) Camera Raw.

Shooting in the Raw

Well, no, you don't have to walk around wearing only your camera when you take photographs. I'm referring to shooting photos in the raw *format* with your digital camera. Today's digital SLR and advanced compact cameras (also called *prosumer* because their features are in-between "pro" and "consumer") can capture images in raw format, leaving the enhancements up to the digital photographer. That unprocessed image file — a *digital negative* — provides more artistic control. An example is the image shown in Figure 1-1.

Unprocessed raw image   Processed in Camera Raw and Photoshop CS2

Figure 1-1: Raw format gives photographers more creative control in processing images.

Why raw?

As a photographer, I shoot in raw format because it gives me better creative control over the image data captured by my digital camera. Raw format gives me an image file created exactly as the digital camera's sensor captured it. I can adjust white balance, tint, brightness/contrast, and hue/saturation exactly the way I want. I don't have to settle for what my digital camera's *firmware* (built-in internal software) does to the image.

As an added bonus, shooting images in raw format gives me a huge advantage over JPEG: I can correct nearly any incorrect exposure or off-kilter white balance I may have made while shooting. Don't get me wrong, getting the correct exposure and white balance is still just good photographic practice and well worth the effort — you have less tweaking to do later — but sometimes, when you're out in the field taking photos and (say) that bright green UFO lands *right over there,* you may have to shoot first and ask questions later.

Also, getting an accurate reading of the exposure is tricky if you're simply squinting at the images you've just taken (and their tiny histograms) on your digital camera's LCD screen — especially if you're shooting outdoors on a bright, sunny day. When you download those images to your computer and view them in Photoshop, you may discover that your image is either under- or overexposed. (It happens!) Raw format lets you use the capabilities of Photoshop to compensate for under- or overexposed photos *without degrading the quality of the image.* It's a nice backup if you ever need it.

Not all raw files are the same

Contrary to popular belief, not all raw images are the same; after all not all images — and not all cameras — are the same. The actual image data collected by a digital camera's image sensor can vary noticeably from one manufacturer to another; the electronics are different from model to model. For that reason, camera manufacturers offer their own proprietary software to process the raw images produced by their cameras.

If you purchase (for example) a Nikon digital camera such as the model shown in Figure 1-2, and that model offers the ability to capture raw images, you can process those raw files with a proprietary program, either Nikon Picture Project or Nikon Capture (advanced raw-conversion software available at an additional cost). If you also own a Canon digital camera that produces raw images, however, you won't be able to use Nikon's software to process them. For those images, you have to use Canon's proprietary software, Digital Photo Professional — but you can't process Nikon images using Canon's software. And if (like the pros) you *also* have other cameras by other makers . . . you get the idea. So did Adobe. That's why Camera Raw exists.

Figure 1-2: Newer advanced digital cameras can capture images in raw format.

I detail the advantages and disadvantages (yes, there are some) of shooting raw images in Chapter 2.

Though different camera manufactures have their own versions of "the" raw format, Photoshop CS2 provides a standard platform you can use to process just about *any* raw image, regardless of all that proprietary fuss. As an added bonus, Camera Raw can handle the whole process of adjusting and editing your raw images (called *workflow*) with no need to add other software programs. (Imagine that — *something* about photography has actually become simpler!) Adobe provides a list of the digital cameras with which Camera Raw is compatible at `http://adobe.com`. (For more about workflow concepts, spin through Part IV.)

Transferring Image Files to Your Computer

If you're already well versed in transferring images to your computer, feel free to skip to the next section. (I won't even be offended. Honest.) If you're still wrestling with transferring images from your camera to your computer, you can use any of several methods, but these two are the most common:

⌐ **Connecting your digital camera directly to your computer**. When you first get your digital camera home from the camera store, you have to unpack all those manuals, CDs, and cables that come in the box. The CDs include a software utility used to transfer images to your computer; one of the cables is for plugging your digital camera into your computer so you can transfer the images. (Refer to your camera's owner's manual to figure out which connection on the camera to plug the cable into. The other end of the cable connects to your computer's FireWire or USB port.)

Figure 1-3: Card readers are the fastest, safest way to download images to your computer.

⌐ **Using a card reader.** The fastest way to download images to your computer is to use a card reader. *Card readers* (such as the one shown in Figure 1-3) are devices that plug into your computer's USB port or (with some models) the faster FireWire port, providing an efficient way to transfer images — often from various cards with different formats such as Compact Flash, SD (secure digital), or memory stick.

Using a card reader to download images to your computer also offers added security. With a direct connection, there's often the worry that your digital camera's battery might go dead while the image transfer is going on. A card reader can be especially reassuring if you have a large batch of images to transfer, and want it to happen correctly the first time.

To download images to your computer, follow these steps:

1. **Determine where you want the downloaded images to go on your computer.**

   If you're a Windows user, the easiest place to put your downloaded images is in the My Pictures folder (opened by choosing My Computer➪ My Pictures). You can also create a new folder to hold your images. (More information on image management and creating image folders can be found in Chapter 4.) On a Mac running OS X, the Pictures folder is a convenient location for downloading your images to.

2. **Plug your digital camera into the computer, using the supplied USB or FireWire cable.**

Before you connect, make sure your digital camera is turned off. If you are using a card reader, make sure it's plugged into an available USB or FireWire port on you computer.

3. **Turn on your digital camera or insert a card into your card reader.**

Turning on your digital camera will automatically start the downloading process on your computer. If you're using a card reader, inserting a memory card into the card reader starts the downloading process automatically. Your computer recognizes the digital camera or card reader as an external device and displays the window shown in Figure 1-4.

4. **Copy images to your computer.**

Choose to open your folder, using Windows Explorer as shown in Figure 1-4. As your computer recognizes your digital camera or card reader as an external device (or drive), choose to open Windows Explorer to view your images. Copy all the images shown to a folder of your choice on your hard drive.

Figure 1-4: After your computer automatically recognizes your digital camera, you can choose how to download your images.

To better organize image folders on your computer, create a new folder to download each memory card to. Give each folder a name such as "Grand Canyon photos" to describe what's inside. It's a lot better than copying all of your images to the same folder every time (trust me on this one), and it helps you organize and find your original images later.

Never move images directly from your memory card to a folder. If you use the Move command, *the images will be removed from the memory card as they are copied* to the folder you chose to copy to. If the copying process is interrupted during copying, you can potentially lose images! Additionally, it's better to format your memory cards *in your camera* to remove old images, rather than erase them with your computer. By using your digital camera to format your cards, you'll ensure you are using the correct formatting algorithm your digital camera uses.

To help ensure regret-free image transfer, make it a habit to format your memory cards only after you've downloaded the images to your computer — *and* have made a backup to CD or DVD. (I cover backing up images in Chapter 4.)

Working with Images in Bridge

When you've successfully transferred that batch of raw images to a folder where they just wait for a good tweaking, they're in Adobe territory. Here's where some handy new Photoshop CS2 and Camera Raw capabilities come into play — in particular Bridge.

New to Photoshop CS2 is Adobe Bridge. Bridge is an upgrade to the File Browser we came to love in previous versions of Photoshop — but it's better! Bridge is now a standalone application that can be launched independent of the Creative Suite programs, or from within Photoshop CS2, Illustrator CS2, GoLive CS2, and InDesign CS2. Bridge provides better integration between the Creative Suite programs, but if you use only Photoshop CS2, it works great as your standalone or integrated program to organize, browse, or locate photos. Bridge also serves as the launching point to process raw images in Camera Raw.

Starting Bridge

Bridge can be started independent of Photoshop CS2. It's set up as any other program in Windows or on the Mac. The other way to start Bridge is through Photoshop CS2:

1. **Start Photoshop CS2 by either double-clicking the icon on your desktop or by choosing Start⇨Photoshop CS2.**

   You can also press Alt+Ctrl+O (Option+⌘+O on a Mac).

2. **From Photoshop, choose File⇨Browse or just click the Go to Bridge button**.

   The Go to Bridge button is located on the right side of the Photoshop CS2 Option bar shown in Figure 1-5. On a Mac, double-click the Bridge icon (located in the Applications/Adobe Bridge folder).

Option bar   Go to Bridge

Figure 1-5: To start Bridge, simply click the Go To Bridge button located on the CS2 Option bar.

Browsing folders and opening images

Okay, file management is always an issue when you're dealing with applications that generate scads of files and copies-of-files (as Photoshop does). Chapters 5 and 6 plunge into the details of file management and reveal the wonders using all the major features of Adobe Bridge. For the moment, I show you how to do a quick browse through the folders — and when you find an image you want, how to open it in Camera Raw and Photoshop CS2. So here's Square One: Figure 1-6 shows how the Bridge window looks right after you open Bridge.

Option bar

Folders tab   Look In menu

Menu bar   Thumbnails   Selected image   Close Bridge

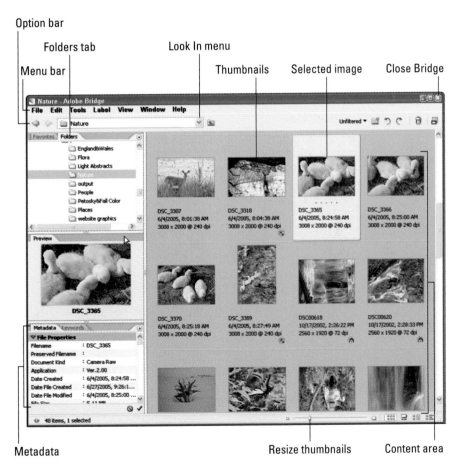

Metadata   Resize thumbnails   Content area

Figure 1-6: Bridge provides everything you need to view, open, and organize all of your photos.

To browse image folders located on your computer with Bridge:

1. **Click the Folders tab.**

   Clicking the Folders tab shows you your computer's drives and folders (as shown in Figure 1-7), enabling you to navigate your computer's folders to locate the folder you want to view — say, a folder you recently downloaded new images to.

2. **Choose the image folder you wish to view.**

   Figure 1-8 shows a series of folders I created to hold my images. Click a folder to view its contents in the Bridge Content area.

   Creating your image folders and downloading images to the same area on your computer makes it easier for you to locate images in Bridge.

3. **Select an image.**

   Single-clicking an image in the Bridge Content area shows you an image's metadata (information such as the camera settings you used when you shot the photo), in the Metadata tab, along with a thumbnail of the image in the Preview area.

   When you've selected a photo, slide the Resize Thumbnails slider all the way to the right to enlarge the thumbnail to get a better view of the image. You'll be able to see more detail of the image to better judge whether or not the image is sharp enough or focused correctly. Images can look great when they are viewed as smaller thumbnails, but when you view them at larger sizes, you can better judge whether the images are good enough

Figure 1-7: The Bridge Folders tab.

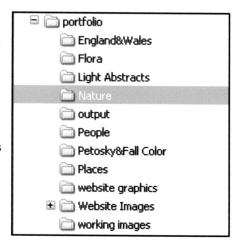

Figure 1-8: Clicking through folders allow you to locate your image files.

to use. Figure 1-9 shows a photo of little duckies. (Actually, these are baby swans, but I *like* duckies. Humor me.)

Those (ahem) duckies looked good in the thumbnail, but enlarging the thumbnail view gives me a closer look: Is the photo focused properly and is its overall detail sharp?

By the way, the reason I know they're swans is because the mother swan was only a few feet away and she would actually growl at me if I got too close to her babies. Lucky I was toting a 70-300mm lens for my Nikon D70 that day, so I could shoot the photo from a swan-safe distance.

Figure 1-9: Enlarge the thumbnails to better view and judge the quality of your images in Bridge.

4. **Open the image.**

   After you've browsed images in Bridge and have chosen an image to edit, double-click the thumbnail. If the image is a raw file, it opens automatically in Camera Raw. If the image is in another format (such as JPEG, TIFF, or PSD), it opens automatically in Photoshop. You can also right-click (Control+click a Mac) and choose Open from the menu to open the image.

Using Camera Raw

Adobe first introduced Camera Raw with Photoshop version 7 and has consistently improved this tool with the next versions, CS and CS2. Improvements such as *clipping warnings* (when Camera Raw indicates part of an image where over-/underexposure occurs, thus eliminating otherwise good image information), curves, and the addition of auto-adjustments have made Camera Raw a powerful tool to process your raw images. Camera Raw's seamless integration with Adobe Bridge and Photoshop makes it the tool of choice for many photographers who shoot raw and use Photoshop. No surprise there.

For me, Camera Raw is a powerful enough tool that I ignore the raw-image-conversion software from the manufacturers of the digital cameras I use. (Sure, I keep the discs — that's just a good practice — but I don't use them.) I like the idea of using one program that allows me to use raw files from different manufacturers' cameras and to work directly with Bridge and Photoshop CS2, so my choice is simple: I use Camera Raw.

I recently had the opportunity to photograph many historic sites and spectacular gardens in England and Wales. Figure 1-10 shows one of those photos, opened in the Camera Raw window — a scene photographed in a difficult lighting situation: bright, late-morning sun. Adjusting some exposure and color for this image in Camera Raw enables me to make overall color adjustments without degrading the information contained in the image.

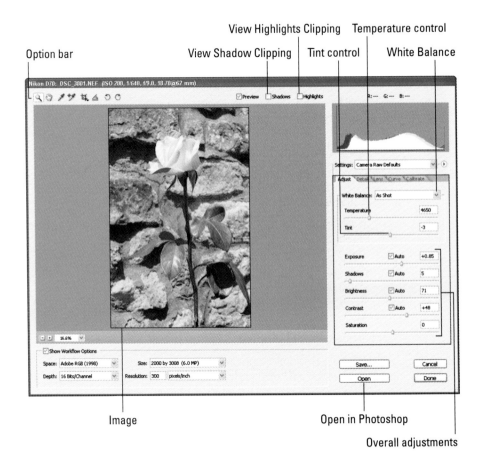

Figure 1-10: The Camera Raw window.

One advantage of making overall adjustments (also referred to as *tonal* adjustments) in Camera Raw is that doing so keeps the overall quality of the image intact. *Whenever you adjust the exposure, brightness, contrast, hue, and saturation in Photoshop, you actually destroy information in the image file.* The more adjustments you make to the image, the more information you potentially destroy, degrading the overall quality of the image. Making as many of these overall adjustments as you can in Camera Raw will guarantee that you retain the data that makes up the image file. Consider it a route to a higher-quality end product.

Becoming familiar with Camera Raw

The Camera Raw window is laid out simply. Commands aren't buried in a series of menus, and the Adjustment tabs are visible (refer to Figure 1-10) when you first open an image in Camera Raw. Commonly used tools are easily available to you on the Camera Raw Option bar, and the Image window is simple to operate (with zoom controls laid out at the bottom of the image). The Camera Raw window is made up of these sections:

- **Option bar:** The Option bar provides tools to help you move around, select a white point of the image (to correct white balance), crop, straighten, and rotate an image. The Option bar also includes check boxes you can use to toggle the image preview on and off — an easy way to switch between the original (unadjusted) image and the image as it appears while you're making adjustments.

- **Image window:** The area where you can view, zoom, crop, straighten, and rotate your image, using the tools in the Option bar.

- **Workflow options:** The area at the bottom of the Camera Raw window where you can modify the color space, size, and resolution of an image. (Chapter 8 provides more detail on workflow options.)

- **Histogram:** The histogram is the graph displayed in the upper-right part of the Camera Raw menu: a graphical view of how much red, green, and blue make up the image, and how each color is distributed.

- **Adjustment tabs:** The area to the right of the Camera Raw window contains tabs where Adjust, Detail, Lens, Curve, and Calibrate controls are located.

Adjusting images in Camera Raw

Camera Raw is a powerful enough tool that it's a good idea to get a handle on some of its new features before you go on a tweaking rampage. Here's the quick tour — followed by a small rampage.

One of the new convenient features of Photoshop CS2 is the addition of auto adjustments in Camera Raw. When you open a raw image in Camera Raw, auto adjustments for Exposure, Shadows, Brightness, and Contrast are automatically made. For some images, auto settings for these adjustments may be sufficient; however, I encourage you to look at each one and move the sliders to the left or right to see whether you can get a better result.

The steps to make overall adjustments in Camera Raw include these:

1. **Adjust White Balance and Tint.**

   White balance can be adjusted using either the White Balance selection box or the Temperature control. Both will adjust the white balance of the image if needed. Changing the settings in the White Balance selection box will adjust *both* the Temperature and Tint to match the Camera Raw pre-determined color conditions for that particular setting. As an example, the Daylight white balance setting changes the (virtual) Temperature to 5500K and the Tint to a setting of +10. For finer tuning of the white balance, you can adjust the Temperature and Tint separately by using the adjustment sliders for both of those adjustments.

This adjustment is best used on photos that used the wrong white balance setting when they were shot — say, a photo shot in bright sunlight while the digital camera's white balance was set to Florescent. (Yikes.) The wrong white balance setting results in odd color shifts, as in the photo shown in Figure 1-11. For this photo, I actually *like* the result I got as shot, where the Cloudy and Florescent settings show incorrect color for the photo. But strictly realistic it isn't.

| As shot | Cloudy | Fluorescent |

Figure 1-11: Adjusting the white balance.

2. Adjust Exposure.

The Exposure control is a digital camera user's best friend. I'm not one to abdicate the fact that all of your photos have to be properly exposed when you click that camera shutter. (Hey, we all know *that* doesn't happen in the real world! At least nowhere near often enough.) The biggest challenge for photographers is capturing images that are correctly exposed and sharp. You can't really correct unfocused images, but the Exposure adjustment allows you to correct an image that's under- or overexposed. As with other adjustments in Camera Raw, increasing or decreasing the exposure to obtain the results you want doesn't degrade the quality of the image file.

Click the Auto check box to let Camera Raw automatically adjust your exposure. Camera Raw will choose the optimum setting to the point at which the image isn't under- or overexposed, just shy of the point at which the shadows and highlights start to lose definition (called *clipping*).

Changing any of the control settings in Camera Raw can cause clipping. Clipping occurs when too much of an adjustment — such as adding too much brightness or contrast — renders parts of an image unusable by creating areas that are (for example) too light or too dark. Areas that are too bright and contain no detail are called *blown out*.

You can monitor if your changes are causing clipping by clicking the Shadows and Highlights check boxes located on the Camera Raw palette. Clicking these boxes will show you areas of the image that are too light or too dark. Shadow areas that are clipped appear in blue; highlight areas that experience clipping show up in red, as Figure 1-12 shows in an enlarged portion of the image.

Figure 1-12: Clipping in the highlight areas appears in red if the Highlights check box is checked.

3. **Adjust Shadows.**

   Camera Raw lets you adjust shadow areas (the very dark parts) of your image by increasing or decreasing the brightness in these areas while not affecting the highlight areas. Try the Auto setting for Shadows first, or you can move the slider to the left or right to get the effect you want. Make sure you keep the Shadows check box checked to limit and monitor clipping. If clipping occurs while you're making a Shadows adjustment, move the slider until the clipping in the shadowed areas disappears.

4. **Adjust Brightness.**

   The Brightness control allows you to increase or decrease how bright your image appears independent of the Exposure setting. The Brightness setting is best used in conjunction with other Camera Raw adjustments, such as Contrast and Saturation. Changing the contrast and saturation may require you to increase or decrease the brightness of the image slightly to compensate for the harsher changes.

5. **Adjust Contrast.**

   The Contrast control simply allows you to darken the dark areas of an image while brightening the lighter areas of an image. The Auto setting for Contrast may be the optimum setting for Contrast, but feel free to move the slider to the right to increase contrast in the image until you get the result you want.

6. **Adjust Saturation.**

Before you adjust a raw photo, it may appear dull and lacking in contrast. Don't worry! The color information is still in the file — all you have to do is increase the Saturation control to bring out the color. (Personally, the Saturation control is my favorite! I can't wait to get into Camera Raw, tweak my Exposure, Shadows, Brightness, Contrast, and then increase the saturation and watch my photos "come alive".)

There isn't an Auto setting for saturation. You have to do it by hand, increasing color saturation by moving the Saturation slider to the right. Figure 1-13 shows the original image and the image adjusted in Camera Raw.

As shot

7. **Click Open.**

Clicking the Open button will then open your converted raw image into the Photoshop window, where you can make further adjustments and edits to your heart's content. You can also click the Done button to save your Camera Raw settings for the image and return to Bridge without opening the image in Photoshop.

At this point, Camera Raw saves your changes, *but not to the original raw file*. Camera Raw leaves the original alone, but it does add your changes to a *sidecar file*, a file created to contain changes you've added to the original raw image. These files are small, and are given an XMP file extension.

Adjusted in Camera Raw

Figure 1-13: Original image, and the image adjusted in Camera Raw.

Hello Photoshop CS2!

I bet you were wondering when I'd get to Photoshop CS2! (Well, *back* to it anyway.) Thanks for being patient, but in this chapter, it's first things first; Bridge and Camera Raw are, after all, the first steps you take as you get into processing raw images. When you're familiar with browsing images, opening them, and then converting them in Camera Raw, you're ready to poke around in Photoshop CS2, check out the new features, and dive back into processing your images with a slew of new tools to use.

What's new?

The Photoshop version CS2 hasn't changed much from the past few versions (CS2 is actually version 9!), but a whole slew of new features have appeared under the hood.

I cover these features in Part III, but here are a few popular new ones:

- ✔ **New Exposure control:** Photoshop now includes a new control that lets you adjust exposure outside of Camera Raw that can be used for JPEG or TIFF images.

- ✔ **New Blur and Sharpen filters:** CS2 provides us with more Blur and Sharpen tools, I cover both in more detail in Chapters 11 and 12. Figure 1-14 shows the new Smart Sharpen filter — bound to be the new photographer's favorite CS2 sharpening tool for photos.

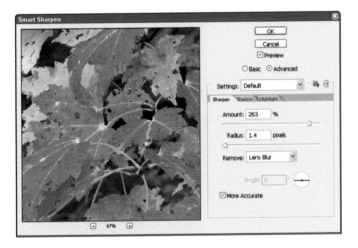

Figure 1-14: The new Smart Sharpen tool provides the photographer with more options for sharpening photos.

- ✔ **Vanishing Point filter:** This feature is tailored to advanced users who seek to edit images in perfect perspective.

- ✔ **Smart Objects:** Using these, you can make edits to an image file while linking the image to the original. Linking to the original lets you maintain the quality of an image; your photos remain sharp even after extensive edits because the linked original remains unchanged. I've found that even some older, low-resolution digital images can benefit from this feature, especially those I've edited extensively.

- ✔ **Lens Correction filter:** The new Lens Correction filter provides the capability to correct lens shortcomings such as barrel distortion and vignetting. Those of you who are familiar with those problems probably feel like cheering. Here's the gist: Some lenses at extreme settings create slight darkened borders around an image, called *vignetting*. Also, you can see visible distortion at extreme zoom settings, especially wide angle.

- ✔ **Red Eye tool:** The new Red Eye tool lets you easily correct the red eye effect that plagues so many snapshots of family and friends who really don't *want* to look like insomniacs or vampires.

✔ **Spot Healing Brush tool:** I use this tool a lot to correct blemishes on skin or get rid of stray gum wrappers on the floors of architectural images (such as the example shown in Figure 1-15). Nothing can ruin a photographer's mood like traveling a few thousand miles, taking photos of historic sites, and then viewing images littered with garbage on the floor! The Spot Healing Brush comes in handy for just those situations. (Too bad there isn't a real-life equivalent.)

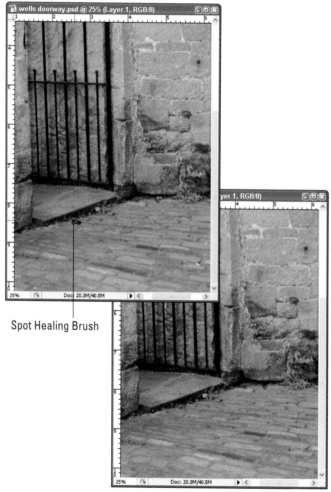

Spot Healing Brush

A cleaned floor

Figure 1-15: The Spot Healing Brush is a great tool to help clean up parts of a photo.

✔ **WYSIWYG fonts:** Great acronym, but what does it mean? (Just kidding. What You See Is What You Get has been around for a few years.) Photoshop now shows you exactly what the font will look like when you add text to a Photoshop document using the Text tool.

Getting around Photoshop CS2

Getting around Photoshop can seem a little intimidating at first, but after you get used to working with menus, palettes, and the Toolbox, you'll get comfortable pretty quickly. The trick is knowing what features are available and where to find them. So, by way of a little exploration, Figure 1-16 shows the Photoshop window and these essential areas:

✔ **Menus:** In the menu bar you'll find a whole slew of utilities, commands, filters, and settings. Familiar menus such as File, Edit, View, Window, and Help are there, and if you're used to working in Windows or the Mac, you'll be instantly comfortable with these.

✔ **Option bar:** The Option bar resides just below the menu bar and is reserved for settings related to tools chosen from the Toolbox.

✔ **Toolbox:** The Toolbox is (well, yeah) a collection of tools you use to edit images. Many of those tools are like camping knives; they have multiple tools inside them. Just right-click a tool and you'll see a flyout menu that shows you more tools.

I sometimes refer to these tools as "my little friends" — they don't talk to me, but I can talk to them. No, really: You can use one of these tools — the Audio Annotation tool — to record audio messages and attach the recordings to an image. Talking pictures, anyone?

✔ **Image window:** The Image window is where the image you opened in Bridge or from Camera Raw resides.

✔ **Palettes:** *Palettes* are control panels that provide information to you or enable you to perform specific editing processes to your image. For instance, the Info palette provides color information regarding specific areas of an image, where the Layers palette enables you to view, edit, and create the needed fill and adjustment layers.

Toolbox

Option bar

Menu bar

Image window

Go to Bridge

Palette well

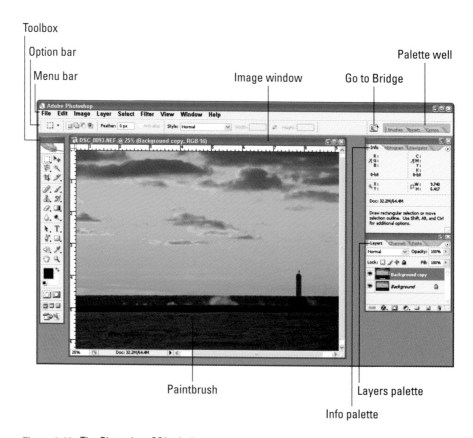

Paintbrush

Layers palette

Info palette

Figure 1-16: The Photoshop CS2 window.

Making adjustments

Though the goal with making overall adjustments in Camera Raw is to reduce the sheer number of overall adjustments needed in Photoshop, there is still much creative work to do! Photoshop is actually where you take the steps to *complete* the adjusting and editing of your image. The following overview of this process (known as "workflow") summarizes the steps for making quick tonal adjustments and edits to an image:

1. **Open an image in Photoshop.**

   Using Bridge, open an image in Camera Raw, make adjustments, and then click the Open button. The image opens in Photoshop.

2. **Save the image as a PSD file.**

   After opening an image in Photoshop from Camera Raw, the file is still in the digital format native to the camera that took the picture — for example, NEF for a Nikon digital camera or CRW for a Canon model. Additionally, you don't want to adjust or edit the original file; that process destroys some of the original data, and you should only do that with a copy. Saving the image to another folder in Photoshop format is the best method of keeping your images organized and your original image preserved.

   Figure 1-17: The Save As window.

   Select File⇨Save As, or press Shift+Ctrl+S (Shift+⌘+S on a Mac). The Save As window shown in Figure 1-17 gives you the choices to select a folder, change the filename if you choose, and most importantly change the file format. Select the folder you want to save your working file to, and then click the Format selection box to select Photoshop (*.PSD,*.PDD) as the file format. Click the Save button to save your working file.

3. **Duplicate the background layer.**

   As you'll discover, I'm a stickler for making backups and protecting original files — and *layers*. In Photoshop, images are adjusted and edited in separate layers. When you open an image, all the image information is contained in the background layer. Each adjustment you make should be made in its own layer. That way, if you need to correct an adjustment, you can always go back to that particular layer and make changes without affecting the other layers. You can also delete a layer if you don't like an adjustment you made — and keep the original image intact! When you've finished making changes to your image, you'll have a number of layers, each with its own adjustment or edit. (Working in layers gets the detailed treatment in Chapter 10.)

To back up and protect the original "background" layer, choose Layer⇨Duplicate.

4. **Adjust Color Levels.**

Create a Levels adjustment layer by clicking the Create Layer button located on the bottom of the Layers palette (see Figure 1-18).

Shown in Figure 1-19, the Levels adjustment window shows you a graphical representation of the color (red, green, and blue channels) distribution of the image, also referred to as the histogram. Under the histogram are three sliders. The slider

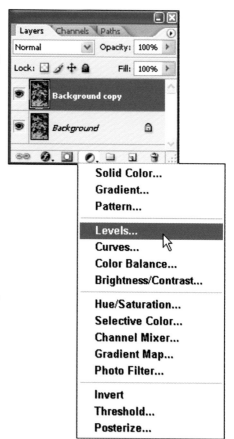

Figure 1-18: Creating a new Levels adjustment layer.

on the left controls the shadow portions of the image, the middle slider the midtones (also called *gamma*) of the image, and the slider on the right controls the amount of color in the highlight areas of the image. With the default Channel set to RGB, move the left and right sliders to the point of the histogram where pixels begin to show up clearly. Moving the middle slider to the right increases contrast in the image by darkening the highlight areas. Experiment with moving the sliders until you get the result you want.

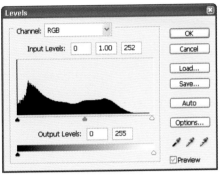

Figure 1-19: Adjusting Levels.

5. **Adjust Saturation.**

   My favorite adjustment can be found in the Saturation layer. Saturation
   allows you to increase color in your image. To make your images "pop"
   with some color, click the Create New Fill or Adjustment Layer button on
   the Layers palette and choose Hue/Saturation. In the Hue/Saturation
   window (shown in Figure 1-20), move the Saturation slider to the right to
   increase color in your image. Be careful not to add too much color; if
   you do, clipping can occur. Sometimes a little goes a long way!

6. **Save the image.**

   After making adjustments, save
   the image by choosing File⇨
   Save or by clicking the Save
   button on the Option bar.

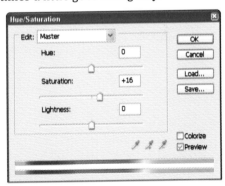

Figure 1-20: Increasing saturation in an image
with the Hue/Saturation adjustment.

Figure 1-21 shows you how making Levels and Saturation adjustments can dramatically change the appearance of an image. (Chapter 10 has the details of making overall adjustments.)

Original image   Adjusted image

Figure 1-21: Original image and the image with levels and saturation adjustments.

2

Enlightened by Raw

*L*uckily for shutterbugs, the technology of digital photography is always evolving. Earlier compact digital cameras were pretty advanced; their 3-to-5-megapixel capability produced pretty good JPEG images. But these cameras have now evolved to 7-to-9-megapixel sensors, bigger lenses (with vibration reduction), and greater ease of use. You can even shoot in automatic mode or set aperture priority or shutter priority to whet your creative shooting tastes. As a bonus, the macro capabilities of these cameras are phenomenal!

These advances mean you have more choices in equipment and capabilities. Today's affordable digital SLRs (and advanced compact "prosumer" cameras) boast capabilities we only dreamed of a few years ago — but their biggest advantage is that the latest models can shoot in raw format.

Raw format provides the photographer with more options for bringing out the best in digital images. You get more control over color, exposure, and sharpness — and if you're like me, the more control, the better. If you give a painter a greater selection of better paints, more brushes, and a bigger canvas to work with, you'll notice the difference in the paintings. Raw gives the photographer exactly that — a wider range of creative choices, more detailed control over color and tones, and a bigger canvas to work with.

What's Raw?

Quite simply, a raw file can be described in the same terms as a film negative that hasn't been processed yet — only without the chemical stink. The image data is there, but it needs to be developed. In effect, Camera Raw is the virtual equivalent of the film-development chemicals that were the only way to develop color images before digital cameras. You could say that shooting in raw is environmentally friendly, too! No toxic gunk to bite your fingers or pollute the environment — just you, your computer, and Photoshop CS2.

When you shoot a raw image, your digital camera collects data. The raw image file is just a recording of what the image sensor has collected. In raw mode, your digital camera doesn't do anything with the data, it just saves it to a file. No processing is performed like when you shoot in TIFF or JPEG format. The file doesn't become an image until the photographer processes it. Figure 2-1 shows just what a raw file looks like without being processed. It's dull, lifeless, and without vibrant color.

Figure 2-1: An unprocessed raw file, just waiting for you to develop it.

Because I brought up the topic of film, there is a huge difference between the chemical processing of film and the digital processing of raw-format files. With film, you get only one chance at processing the file. If the temperature of the chemicals are wrong, or the length of time in processing is wrong, the negatives get ruined. You can't go back and do anything to fix that. You only get one shot at developing film. If you make a mistake, your film — and the photos you shot on it — are (technically speaking) hosed . . . wasted . . . toast . . . *destroyed*. With digital raw files, you can process your images many times! Go ahead and make some mistakes, it doesn't matter! You can always go back to the original digital raw image and process the image again.

Being an old film guy who's developed many rolls of film in my old chemical darkroom, I think raw is a beautiful thing.

One of the reasons the raw photos first appear dull and lifeless is because raw files are for the most part captured in grayscale. Don't get me wrong — there is color information in a raw file, you can see some in the photo in Figure 2-1, which shows how the image looks when first opened in Camera Raw. Color characteristics are recorded *for each pixel* as red, green, or blue; a raw-converter program such as Camera Raw will interpret the color during conversion. That's why more color becomes visible as you make adjustments in Camera Raw.

Camera Raw converts a raw file by *interpolating* color information: The raw converter knows the color associated with a particular pixel, but "borrows" color from neighboring pixels to create the needed color. Additionally, Camera Raw opens a raw image with some automatic tonal adjustments made for you, however, saturation is not automatically added. Figure 2-2 shows the same image as in Figure 2-1, after color is extracted in Camera Raw.

Figure 2-2: The processed raw file shows the true color of the original image.

Raw versus Other Formats

Okay, raw format may not be ideal for *every* photographic situation. I shot thousands of images in JPEG format before the raw format made it into advanced compact digital SLR cameras. Many of those photos are permanent staples in my portfolio. And yes, I admit it: I still shoot JPEGs sometimes. I carry around a compact digital camera that produces great 7 megapixel images (Figure 2-3, for example). My compact camera is convenient for snapshots or interesting subjects I come across while driving around town — and it serves as a backup while I'm shooting nature photos. But for those images (as for all my more serious shooting), I use my digital SLR — in raw format, of course!

Though I have a nice collection of images from earlier digital cameras (and I still carry a compact around in my pocket), I often run into the limitations of shooting in JPEG or TIFF format — these, for instance:

Figure 2-3: Shooting in JPEG can produce great images, but you can't do as much to them.

- **Loss of image data while making adjustments in Photoshop:** Shooting JPEG, you can run into this problem a lot. Without the lossless overall color and tonal adjustments that you'd get in Camera Raw, you have to make those adjustments in Photoshop — and they'd better be right the first time. You lose image data every time you save, reopen, and readjust a JPEG in Photoshop. In essence, every adjustment affects the tonal range of the image; you're throwing away *bits* of information, leaving less data available for creating the image (a destructive effect).

When shooting in raw format, you have the advantage of making adjustments in Camera Raw to white balance, tint, exposure, shadows, curves, brightness, contrast, and color saturation — without the risk of losing image data (and some image quality along with it).

✔ **Limited white-balance adjustment:** When I'm out in the field shooting (with my digital camera, always!), I'll often set the white balance on the camera to best match the lighting conditions I'm faced with. I'll use the auto-white balance setting in some situations as well. If I'm shooting JPEG or TIFF and discover later when editing those images in Photoshop that the white balance needs adjustment, it will take a lot of work to make those corrections. If I'm shooting raw, I can easily adjust the white balance any way I need to.

✔ **Limited exposure adjustment:** I hear this argument all the time; "Good photographers should always get the right exposure when they shoot photos so they don't have to make adjustments in software later." That's good advice and should always be suggested as a goal — but in the real world, sometimes a perfect exposure just doesn't happen. Even the best photographers shoot photos that need some exposure adjustment in software. If I'm shooting in JPEG or TIFF format and I need to adjust exposure after the fact, I have to use Photoshop CS2 Exposure adjustment to do the job — and although this feature is a welcome addition for JPEGs, it can still degrade image quality.

Shooting in raw format means you don't have to settle for the exposure you get with the shot; you can fix under- or overexposed photos in Camera Raw, using its Exposure adjustment. Even better, you can do that without losing image data (which is what happens if you shoot in JPEG and use the Photoshop Exposure feature to tweak exposure later).

✔ **Limited image quality due to compression:** JPEG is a compressed file format. When you shoot a JPEG image, your digital camera processes the image, and then compresses it. One of the side effects of compression is the fact that you lose image data in the process. It's really not noticeable, but when you're using an 8-bit file format such as JPEG, you need all the image data you can get.

When you open JPEG images in Photoshop to begin adjusting and editing, make sure you save them *as a file format other than JPEG* when you import them into Photoshop. Converting the images to PSD or TIFF format will help avoid the image degradation that happens every time you save a JPEG file. Figure 2-4 shows the effects of resaving JPEG images while editing them in Photoshop: More artifacts creep into the image after it's been resaved a few times.

Figure 2-4: Resaving JPEGs reduces overall image quality.

Advantages and Disadvantages to Raw

Okay, even though this book is about shooting images in raw format and follow-ing the steps to completing your images for display by using Bridge, Camera Raw, and Photoshop, let's keep it real: There are both advantages and disad-vantages to shooting and processing raw images. Many pro-level photogra-phers don't mind taking the few extra steps that raw format entails — generally they get higher-quality images that way — but JPEG images are often faster to take if the opportunity to get a shot is fleeting. Bottom line: It's a three-way tradeoff. The individual photographer has to balance the speed and conve-nience of JPEG against the greater control and image quality that are possible in raw format.

Taking advantage of raw format

Of all the advantages that shooting raw offers compared to JPEG, the biggest is control. When shooting photos for my fine-art portfolio or for portraits, I want complete control over the tonal adjustments to my images. Even though the latest digital cameras are pretty handy at processing images, almost all need post-processing help in Photoshop. Shooting in raw format lets me judge and adjust color and exposure for each individual photo if *I* choose. I don't have to trust blindly that my digital camera automatically produces images that match my taste; I have the data I need to make them look right.

In addition to giving you control over the processing of your images in raw format, Camera Raw provides other advantages over JPEGs or TIFFs:

- ✓ **Full use of all the information captured:** Shooting in raw format gives the photographer all the data the digital camera's image sensor captures, thus providing the photographer with more data to work with to make adjustments, edits, and sizing later in Photoshop. You're not limited to the reduced data in a compressed 8-bit JPEG file (as detailed in the next section).

- ✓ **Easy exposure adjustment without losing image data:** Figure 2-5 shows a photo I shot at dusk (a difficult lighting situation) to capture the reflection of the sky on a pond. It was a tough task to get the right exposure for the image in a neutral part of the image. As it turned out, I was off a little in my exposure setting, but no problem: I used the Camera Raw Exposure control to increase the exposure by 1 1/2 f-stops.

Figure 2-5: Adjusting exposure "after the fact" is one advantage to shooting raw.

Some digital SLRs underexpose photos by about one f-stop when shooting in raw mode. That's by design; it prevents you from *blowing out* parts of the image (that is, overexposing certain parts of the image so no usable image data emerges). Such underexposure saves you from ending up with (say) unusable pure white as part of a sky. You could deal with extremes of exposure by using exposure compensation (if your camera has that feature) — or you could use Camera Raw to adjust the exposure after you shoot — and probably get better results. Keep in mind that it's often easier to compensate for underexposed areas than overexposed areas.

✔ **Easy adjustment of white balance:** *White balance* (or color temperature and tint, if you want to get real technical) is sometimes difficult to get right when you're out shooting with your digital camera. You can use the auto adjustment, but sometimes the color and tint of the images are slightly off when you view them in Bridge or Camera Raw. If I'm shooting raw, I'm not going to sweat too much; I can easily make a change in the white balance of the image later in Camera Raw. Figure 2-6 shows three versions of the same image displayed in Camera Raw, as shot in the digital camera using three settings (from left to right): Auto, Cloudy, and Shade. If I were shooting JPEG, I'd have to jump through hoops to make the same adjustments in Photoshop.

✔ **Non-destructive adjustment of tone and color:** This is the real kicker: By shooting raw — and converting the images later in Camera Raw — the photographer can make changes to brightness, contrast, curve tab, and color saturation without the risk of losing valuable bits of image data.

As shot   Cloudy   Shade

Figure 2-6: As Shot, Cloudy, and Shade white balance settings.

The 16-bit advantage

When you're shooting in raw format, you are essentially capturing all the data that your sensor can capture — and today's digital cameras can capture at least 12 bits per channel (that is, per each red, green, and blue channel) for each pixel. When you shoot JPEGs, you capture images at only 8 bits per channel for each pixel — you're already working with less data, and your digital camera had better process those 8-bit images *correctly*. Don't get me wrong, you can still get great photos working in the 8-bit world of JPEGs, but after you get them into Photoshop, you can do only a limited amount of processing before image quality starts to degrade.

When quality counts more than speed, shooting in raw format — and then editing the photos in Photoshop, in 16 bit-mode — gives you a large advantage over JPEGs. That's because JPEG quality is no more than what you get via your digital camera's software algorithms — results that are automatic and fast, but maybe not quite what you want. With raw format, you can make more accurate adjustments to the image, and have a lot of image data left over to give you more options. You can do more extensive edits, crop, or enlarge — while maintaining image quality throughout your image.

A few potential drawbacks

Even with all the great capabilities the raw image format provides, it actually does have a few disadvantages — not many — but a few are worth mentioning:

- **File size:** Raw images aren't compressed like JPEGs. The file sizes are much larger — and they take longer to download to your computer. A typical 8-megapixel raw image will be saved at a size of about 7 megabytes. The same 8-megapixel image shot in JPEG format will create a file less than half that size, around 3 megabytes. If you're cramped for memory-card space, you'll be able to fit at least twice as many JPEGs as raw files on your memory card. Just remember: JPEG compression loses some quality.

- **Extra step in processing:** Unlike JPEGs (which you can view immediately in Photoshop), raw images require an extra step: Opening them in Camera Raw and processing them. If your workflow is pretty close to the one explained in Chapter 4 — and you process raw images as shown in Chapter 9 — then the extra step will be worth the effort; the timesaving batch processes offered in Bridge can help you make up for lost time.

✒ **Slower processing in your digital camera:** Some older camera models that feature the raw format may take a few seconds to process the raw image before you're able to shoot another. Too, if you're shooting raw and JPEG (some digital cameras can produce two images for one shot), your digital camera will have additional work to do to produce both the raw and JPEG files.

✒ **Lack of raw-format standards:** Each digital camera manufacturer has its own version of raw format; proprietary formats reign right now. So far, those who shoot in raw have only one option that offers some versatility — Camera Raw, along with a new digital negative (DNG) format (see the next section) — currently endorsed by Adobe. It's not a big issue now, but some photographers worry about what might happen years down the road: Will future software be able to recognize current raw images? Adobe seems to be the only company addressing this issue right now.

The present drawbacks to shooting and processing raw-format images may not outweigh the advantages for many photographers. And why not? Cheaper, large-capacity memory cards can handle the extra card space needed to handle larger files. The extra step in processing really doesn't cost you much time — in fact, processing images in Camera Raw can save you from having to perform similar adjustments in Photoshop — *and* you can make adjustments without throwing away valuable bits of data. The final drawback to raw format (lack of firm industry standards) will most likely be overcome as technology develops and as more and more photographers use the raw format.

Introducing the Digital Negative (DNG)

Up to this point in the digital-photography era, raw file formats haven't been uniform. Each digital camera manufacturer that offers raw in its digital cameras maintains a proprietary format. (Imagine what it would have been like if *all* camera makers designed their cameras only to work with their own proprietary film. Or how about driving cars that only run on one brand of fuel? You get the idea.) Unfortunately, due to a lack of industry standards, camera manufacturers are forced to offer their own versions of raw images.

As if to add confusion for photographers, manufacturers package software with their digital cameras — and it only converts raw images shot in their version of raw format. Some of these programs work very well, but if you also shoot raw images using other digital cameras from other manufacturers, you can't use the software to convert those images. Camera Raw, at least, works with raw images from most makers' digital cameras — a step in the right direction.

Adobe has recently announced and released its attempt at coming up with one standard file format for raw images — *digital negative* (DNG). The introduction of DNG recognizes the need for an industry-standard format for raw images — and it is indeed a major step forward. But a true industry standard hasn't arrived yet; camera manufacturers as a whole have yet to buy in on DNG. But don't be too harsh on the industry. The technology is evolving rapidly, and leading manufacturers have done a terrific job delivering products that photographers want, and rather quickly. Until a raw-image standard is developed, Adobe's DNG format and the Digital Negative Converter software utility (shown in Figure 2-7) make a great first step. You can get a copy of the Adobe Digital Negative Converter at Adobe's Web site (go to www.adobe.com).

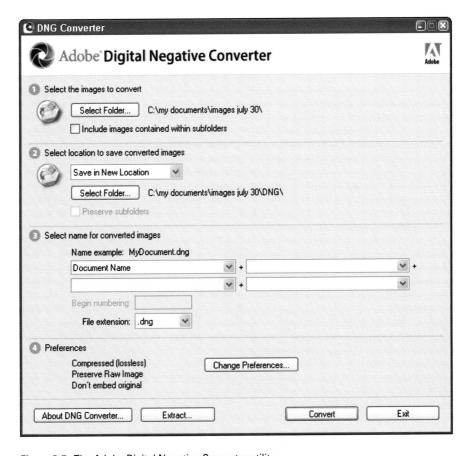

Figure 2-7: The Adobe Digital Negative Converter utility.

The potential advantages of using DNG include the following:

- **Common raw format:** If you're shooting professionally and need to submit images to publishers (or other clients who require raw images), DNG provides a common format for these images. DNG is a non-proprietary format, and it's publicly documented.

- **Changes and additions to the raw image are embedded within the DNG:** With other raw formats, when you make adjustments or add metadata to the raw files, those changes aren't saved to the actual raw file. Instead, they're saved to additional files called *sidecar files*. With DNG raw format, all changes and metadata additions are stored within the DNG file. This reduces the chance of the sidecar files not being copied or backed up with the original raw files when you move files around during image management.

- **Longer-term compatibility:** If it were easy to predict the future, we would all be millionaires! It seems likely, though, that software and computers will be able to read standard file formats (such as JPEG, TIFF, and possibly the new DNG) 10 or 15 years from now — maybe not so likely they'll be able to read the obscure (and proprietary) raw formats produced by some digital cameras.

  One vital capability — available now — is software that's compatible across all digital camera platforms, with no delays between updates for your digital camera equipment and software.

3

Applying Color Management

*D*igital photography costs a lot of money for one that wants to get serious with the craft. There's always the latest digital camera to buy, the next lens in your collection, memory cards, gadgets, and other gizmos. Ah, but there's more to contend with that will draw resources from your wallet!

If you do a lot of printing like I do, you're constantly running to the computer store or getting on to the Web to purchase inkjet cartridges and photo paper. I figure I'm spending at least a dollar per 8×10 print, plus a lot more when I'm printing up to 13×19 inch prints. Printing one series of prints can get quite expensive — and if you're not using a color-managed workflow, your costs can skyrocket.

When adjusting and editing images in Photoshop, you want to make sure that the images you print on your printer match exactly the image you've been viewing on your computer's display. Otherwise, you'll be throwing money out the window every time you make a "test" print that doesn't match, not to mention the level of aggravation you have to put up with during the neverending trial-and-error method of printing. To guarantee your sanity, you need to implement color management, and forever say goodbye to the expensive trial-and-error method of printing. As a bonus, you can buy some more of those gizmos with the money you'll save in ink and paper.

Coloring Your World

If you talk to digital photographers who have lots of experience shooting photos, working with Photoshop, and printing their images, you'll find one consensus among them: The hardest thing to accomplish in digital photography is managing color. When you think about all the steps involved — first shooting an image with particular light in mind, converting the raw file, making further adjustments and edits in Photoshop, and then sending the image to a printer — it's a miracle that the final print even resembles what was first envisioned!

One of the most difficult types of images to color manage is portraits. Let's face it (sorry about that), we human beings know the color range of skin tones — and if they're off just a little, we notice. Figure 3-1 shows a portrait as seen on a computer monitor and then shown as printed. Managing color helps you create prints that closely match what the colors should look like.

As seen on the monitor   As printed

Figure 3-1: Maintaining the correct skin tone in portraits reinforces the need for color management.

Color management is the process of producing images with the correct color, where color is predictable throughout the image capture, editing, and printing processes:

1. **Image capture.** This is a fancy way of saying "shooting photos." Making color space settings in your digital camera is the first step in your color-management workflow. Digital cameras actually have settings that determine the type of color they produce. This setting is known as *color space*. Many digital cameras operate in one color space: sRGB. sRGB is a color space intended for images to be viewed on your computer, not prints. This doesn't mean that images from most digital cameras won't make good prints; Photoshop will convert the images to any color space you choose. If your digital camera offers only sRGB as its color space, don't worry — you can always convert your files to another color space such as Adobe RGB (1998) when you open them in Photoshop.

   If your camera has the option of setting its color space to something other than sRGB, set your digital camera to Adobe RGB (1998). Doing so will ensure that you're shooting images in the same color space used for working with photos in Photoshop that are intended for printing.

2. **Applying color settings in Photoshop**. After you install Photoshop CS2 on your computer, it isn't exactly "ready to rock." You'll have a little work to do to make sure color settings are applied correctly.

3. **Viewing images on your computer monitor.** Most of your time is spent in the digital darkroom, working with images in Photoshop. The most critical element in implementing color management is calibrating your monitor. (I discuss that issue further in the "Getting Calibrated" section, a bit later in this chapter.)

4. **Printing.** In effect, it's the final destination for all your efforts — and printing can be considered an art in itself! During the printing process (explained in more detail in Chapter 12), color settings need to be precisely applied by you *Photoshoppers* (another one of my original technical terms) out there so that Photoshop is able to properly convert color that will correctly be applied by the printer when producing prints.

By applying the color-management processes described in this chapter, you get your images closer to digital-photography nirvana. Your prints will look more like what you originally envisioned while shooting your images and working with them in Photoshop. You'll save a bunch of time, money, and sedatives in the process! Color management is your guiding light (no pun intended) toward total inner peace and visual tranquility. About images, anyway.

Making Photoshop Color Settings

In addition to making monitor calibration part of your color management workflow, it's equally as important to make sure the Photoshop color settings are correct for the type of images you normally process. If you work with photographs that are meant for a variety of output methods, you need the custom color settings in Photoshop.

You don't want to expend a lot of energy shooting photos only to have them turn out wrong when you output your images to print or screen. Managing color properly can save you the hassle by getting your colors right — so make color settings the very first stop in your image-editing workflow.

Exploring (color and working) space

Color space is the range of colors available to you for editing your images. It's like the colors you used in your old paint-by-numbers set — only instead of 12 colors, you have millions! *Working space* is a Photoshop term used to describe which color space is assigned to an image. You'll find these two terms — working space and color space — used interchangeably in Photoshop.

CMYK (a working space for press-type printing) and *grayscale* (used for editing black-and-white images) are working spaces targeted toward specific purposes. CMYK is defined as a full-color representation of a printing press; the acronym CMYK defines cyan, magenta, yellow, and black inks for the printing press.

For photographers, the most important working space you use is RGB. Most of the photographer's work is geared toward printing on ink jet printers first, and going to press for magazine, book, or other types of publications (or to the Web) second. Digital photographers who incorporate a color-management workflow opt to use Adobe RGB (1998) first to edit images, and then convert to different color spaces if a particular output requires it.

The list that follows explains the differences and different uses of the working spaces available in Photoshop, while Figure 3-2 shows how using different color spaces for a photo affect how they look.

  ✓ **Adobe RGB (1998):** This color space is designed to match the color gamut of inkjet printers. Highly recommended for use with images to be printed on (well, yeah) inkjet printers.

✔ **sRGB:** This color space is designed for displaying photos on computer monitors, such as Web graphics and Web photos.

✔ **Colormatch RGB:** This color space is designed for a color gamut *between* sRGB and Adobe RGB (1998). Use for images with multiple purposes and output.

| Adobe RGB (1998) | sRGB | Colormatch RGB |

Figure 3-2: Different color spaces affect how color is rendered in an image.

As part of your overall color-management workflow, I recommend always editing your photographs in the Adobe RGB (1998) color space and saving that image as a master file. Adobe RGB (1998) provides the widest color gamut available when it's time to edit your images. For output destined for the Web or for special printing, save a copy of your master to an sRGB or CMYK version of the file for output later. Even while outputting your images in black and white, I recommend using an RGB color space for your master image.

Applying Photoshop color settings

In this section, I explain how to specify each setting in the Photoshop Color Settings window. This is one of the most overlooked steps in color management — and it makes a *huge* difference when used properly. Additionally, I explain when and how to assign a color profile to an image.

If most of your work involves preparing images for the Web, for printing, or for publishing, each of those tasks will need a different monitor setting. The first step after calibrating your monitor (which I show you how to do in the later section, "Getting Calibrated") is to set up your default color settings in Photoshop. Here's how:

1. **Choose Edit⇨Color Settings or press Ctrl+Shift+K (⌘+Shift+K on the Mac) to bring up the Color Settings dialog box.**

2. **Click the More Options button.**

   This expands the Color Settings dialog box so that you can see all the options, as shown in Figure 3-3.

3. **From the Settings drop-down list at the top, choose North America Prepress 2.**

   The default for Settings is the North America General Purpose 2, which isn't very good for photographers. Select North America Prepress 2 (as shown in Figure 3-4); this setting works best for photographers.

4. **Set the Working Spaces.**

   Change the Photoshop default for the RGB working space to Adobe RGB (1998), as shown in Figure 3-5. Adobe RGB (1998) is the best working space for photographers, providing the widest color gamut for color saturation. Make sure to leave the CMYK, Gray, and Spot selections set at the defaults.

   For most of your image editing, use Adobe RGB (1998) to edit your master images. If you need to, you can convert to the sRGB working space for the final output of Web images.

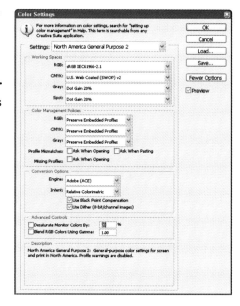

Figure 3-3: The Photoshop Color Settings dialog box.

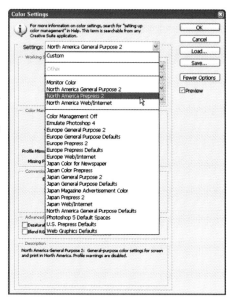

Figure 3-4: Changing the Settings to North America Prepress 2.

5. Set Color Management Policies.

Make sure to leave RGB, CMYK, and Gray set to Preserve Embedded Profiles. This ensures that color settings are maintained in images that you open in Photoshop.

Leave the three Profile Mismatches and Missing Profiles check boxes selected. These settings ensure that you're prompted to choose a color space to apply when you open an image in Photoshop that doesn't match your default working space.

6. Set Conversion Options settings.

I recommend leaving the defaults for these settings to Adobe (Ace) for the Engine and Relative Colorimetric for the Intent.

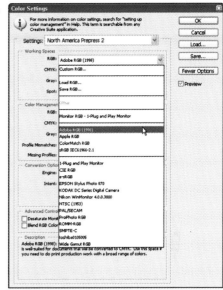

Figure 3-5: Setting the RGB Working Space to Adobe RGB (1998).

The *Engine* setting controls Photoshop methods used for converting colors from one profile to another. The *Intent* setting specifies what you want the rendering to accomplish for conversions from one profile to another. The bottom line? Adobe (ACE) and Relative Colorimetric are optimal conversion settings for photographs.

For editing photographs in Photoshop, you get the best results by leaving the defaults (Use Black Point Compensation, and Use Dither) selected. This option ensures the black point of your image matches the black point of your print (or output). I normally leave the advanced controls set to their default settings of *not* selected.

7. Click OK to save your color settings.

In the next section, I show you how to ensure that your color settings are properly applied to your workflow.

Assigning color profiles

The final step to ensuring a proper color workflow is to make sure that the images you open in Photoshop contain the correct color profile you've set up in the Color Settings dialog box (see the steps in the preceding section). When you open an image that doesn't match that default color space, you're prompted with the Embedded Profile Mismatch dialog box shown in Figure 3-6.

Figure 3-6: Setting an image that has the RGB Working space to Adobe RGB (1998).

In this dialog box, you can choose one of three options:

- **Use the Embedded Profile:** Select this option if you want to leave the image's working space as is.

  Remember that if you leave this option selected, you won't be working in the default color space you indicated in the Color Settings window.

- **Convert Document's Colors to the Working Space:** Select this option if you want to use your default color space. This is recommended for most images.

- **Discard the Embedded Profile:** Select this option if you don't want to use a color profile for the image.

Sometimes, when you're working on an image in Photoshop, you need to convert the image to another working space to get a task done. To get the best color workflow in a situation like this, first edit your images in Adobe RGB (1998) and then convert them later to meet your specific output needs. The combination of using *monitor* profiles (explained in the next section on calibrating your monitor) and assigning *color* profiles will help ensure an efficient color-management workflow.

The process to assign color profiles to an image is as follows:

1. **Choose Edit⇨Assign Profile.**

   The Assign Profile window appears.

2. **Select the Working RGB option.**

   Figure 3-7 shows the Working RGB set to Adobe RGB (1998). (Use the Don't Color Manage This Document selection *only if* you might want to submit your images to a

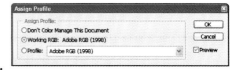

Figure 3-7: Assigning a color profile to a photograph.

third party, and you don't know how your images will be color managed.)

3. **Select another profile from the drop-down list provided by the third option (see Figure 3-8) if you desire.**

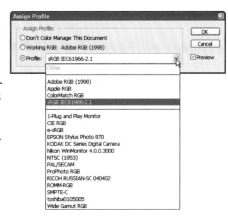

This choice is rare for most photographers, but you can use this option to assign a specific profile. For example, a printing company for press services may have supplied you with a required profile. You may also want to convert an existing image to sRGB if you are going to save a version of the image for viewing on the Web, but I usually use the File⇨Save for Web command for that.

Figure 3-8: Selecting another profile.

For most photographs, you want to select the Working RGB option, the same option I recommend you choose in the Color Settings dialog box as your default working space. (See the steps in the earlier section, "Applying Photoshop color settings.")

The PhotoDisc target image

The PhotoDisc Target image (also called the PDI test image) comes with a number of color-management products such as the ColorVision Spyder 2. It's also included in the Mac OS. It's an industry-standard test image used to give you a direct view of how accurately the colors displayed on your monitor match what you print or prepare for the Web.

Try using this image as a visual test to compare what's on your monitor and what's actually coming out of your printer. The image is royalty-free and can be easily obtained.

To get a copy, you can download the image from my Web site at `http://kevinmossphoto graphy.com/photodisctestimage.htm` or search for **PhotoDisc Target Image** on the Web.

Getting Calibrated

As a photographer, you have to visualize the changes you're making to your images — and the key component that allows you to do that is your computer monitor. It's also the only device that stands between the digital camera and your final print; displaying your images accurately on your monitor is critical. Properly profiling and adjusting — *calibrating* — your monitor ensures that what you see is what you're going to get in your final output of the image.

The most important step of implementing color management into your workflow is to calibrate your monitor. Calibrating on a regular basis is important because the colors, brightness, and contrast of your monitor change over time. Whether you use one of those big clunky computer monitors (called CRTs), one of those sleek new LCD monitors, or a laptop computer, the rule remains the same: Calibrate on a regular basis.

Most laptop (and some LCD) monitors won't let you adjust color balance and contrast; with some of them, only brightness can be adjusted. If you have an LCD monitor, you should still calibrate to ensure optimal brightness settings. Calibrating is important to ensure that colors are completely accurate; do as much of it as you can on your machine.

When you calibrate your monitor, you make adjustments to the brightness, contrast, and color balance to match what your calibration software uses as its standard. These adjustments are actual physical changes to the operation of the monitor (but not to the image files you are viewing). They're necessary to produce an accurate profile that your computer then uses to determine what prints out.

By calibrating your monitor, you are effectively setting the stage for a successful color-managed workflow. If you skip this step, you end up making adjustments to your digital files on the basis of *false* information. The resulting prints won't match what you see on your monitor.

Calibrating with Adobe Gamma

Adobe Gamma is a Windows software utility (included with Photoshop CS2) that you can use to calibrate your monitor and to create a profile that your computer will use. The Mac version of Adobe Gamma was available with previous versions of Photoshop and is no longer included with Photoshop CS2. Instead, Mac users can use the Apple Display Calibrator Assistant found in the System Preferences folder.

For best results, let your monitor warm up for 30 minutes before you start any calibration procedure.

To calibrate your monitor using Adobe Gamma, follow these steps:

1. **Open the Windows Control Panel by clicking Start⇨Control Panel.**

2. **Open the Adobe Gamma Wizard.**

   Double-click the Adobe Gamma icon located in the Windows Control Panel (shown in Figure 3-9) to start Gamma.

Figure 3-9: The Windows Control Panel and Adobe Gamma icon.

3. **Choose the Step-by-Step (Wizard) version (see Figure 3-10) and then click Next.**

   You are asked to choose either the Step By Step (Wizard) method or the Control Panel method. I recommend choosing the Step By Step method, as in Figure 3-10; it's a lot easier.

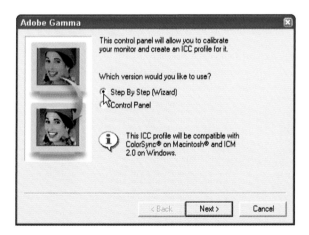

Figure 3-10: Choose the Step By Step (Wizard) version.

4. **Click Load (see Figure 3-11) to choose your monitor type, and then click Next.**

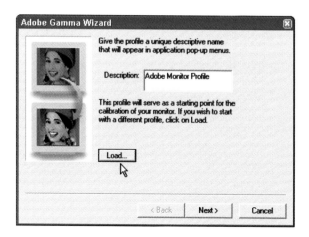

Figure 3-11: Click Load to choose your monitor type instead of the default setting.

You are presented with the Open Monitor Profile window.

5. **Choose a profile that matches your monitor or one that is similar to it (see Figure 3-12), and then click Open.**

This selection is used only as a starting point for the process. After clicking Open, you're sent back to the Adobe Gamma window shown in Figure 3-11.

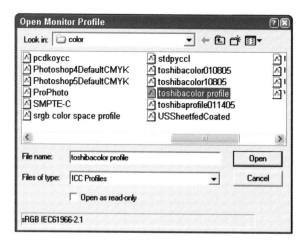

Figure 3-12: Select a Monitor Profile that matches your display or is a close match.

Select a profile that best matches the monitor you are using on your computer by clicking the display type name in the list of profiles shown in Figure 3-12. If your computer monitor is not listed in the profile list, you can always choose the default setting provided in the list of profiles. After your selection, click the Open button and you are sent back to the Adobe Gamma window shown in Figure 3-11.

6. **Type a unique description with a date and then click Next to proceed to the next window.**

   The profile you chose in Step 5 doesn't appear in the Description field. Don't worry: The monitor you chose in Step 5 is still associated with the process. Just type a unique name with a date, such as the name shown in Figure 3-13.

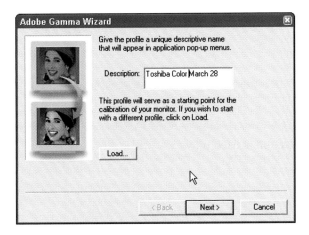

Figure 3-13: Include a date reference for your description.

7. **Adjust brightness and contrast and click Next to continue.**

   The Adobe Gamma window shown in Figure 3-14 instructs you to use the contrast adjustment on your monitor and set the contrast to maximum.

   Next, adjust the brightness control until the inside gray square is barely visible against the black surround. (Keep the lighting in the room as dark as possible.)

   Note that you can click Back at any time to make changes to a previous screen.

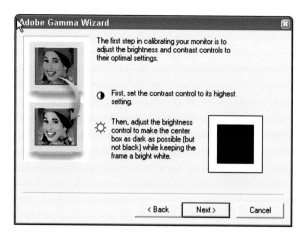

Figure 3-14: Adjust the contrast of your display in the Adobe Gamma window.

8. Choose the phosphor type for your monitor and then click Next.

If (in Step 5) you chose the type of monitor you're using, leave this setting as it appears. If you chose the default setting in Step 5, you can choose Trinitron, as shown in Figure 3-15. If you know the actual phosphor values of your monitor, choose Custom and enter those values. (You can look them up in your monitor's manual.)

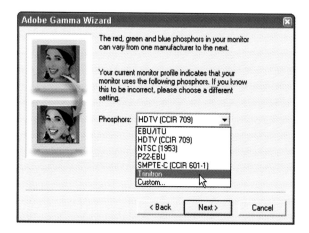

Figure 3-15: Most users can accept the default monitor profiles that appear in this step.

9. **Adjust gamma settings, and then click Next.**

   Keeping View Single Gamma Only selected (as shown in Figure 3-16), move the adjustment slider to the right or left until the center gray box begins fading into the outer box. This adjustment sets the relative brightness of your monitor. Make sure to choose Macintosh Default or Windows Default in the Gamma field. Before clicking Next, deselect the View Single Gamma Only check box.

10. **Adjust red, green, and blue gamma, and then click Next.**

    In this step, eliminate color imbalances by adjusting each RGB (red, blue, and green) slider, shown in Figure 3-17, until the color box in the middle blends in with the outer box.

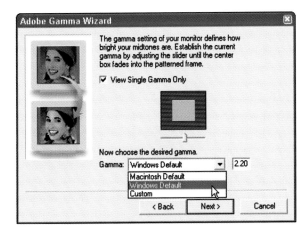

Figure 3-16: Making single gamma settings.

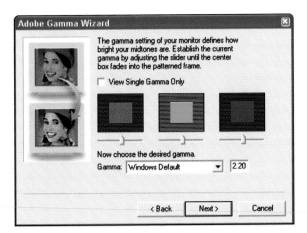

Figure 3-17: Adjust relative brightness.

11. **Set the hardware white point (see Figure 3-18) to 6500°K and then click Next to continue.**

   Most monitors are set with a native white point of 9300°K. For photographers, 6500°K provides the cleanest and brightest white point that matches daylight the closest.

12. **Set the adjusted white point (see Figure 3-19) the same as the hardware white point, and again click Next to continue.**

   I recommend that you set the adjusted white point to match the hardware white point. Choosing another setting can result in unpredictable results. For most applications, you can just leave this set as Same as Hardware.

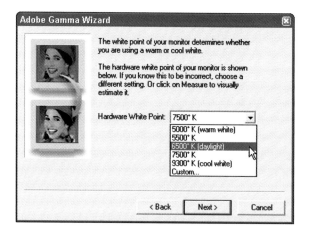

Figure 3-18: Setting the desired white point of your monitor to 6500°K.

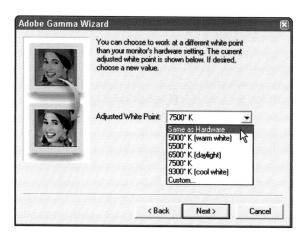

Figure 3-19: Setting the adjusted white point to Same as Hardware.

13. View your changes by clicking the Before and After radio buttons; click Finish.

You have adjusted the brightness, contrast, and color settings of your monitor to the optimum values. Clicking the Before and After options shown in Figure 3-20 shows you the difference.

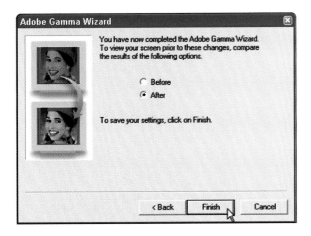

Figure 3-20: Use these options to view how the new adjustments look on your monitor.

14. Save your new profile by typing a new profile name in the File Name field (shown in Figure 3-21), leaving the file type as ICC Profiles; then click Save to complete the calibration.

This is an important step because — now that you've calibrated your monitor with Adobe Gamma — saving the information into a new monitor profile ensures that your computer and Photoshop CS2 can later use the profile correctly.

Keep the existing profiles intact by using a unique profile name you can easily identify. Make sure you include the date of the profile in the filename, as shown in Figure 3-21. This identifies your unique profile with a date so you know the last time you calibrated your monitor.

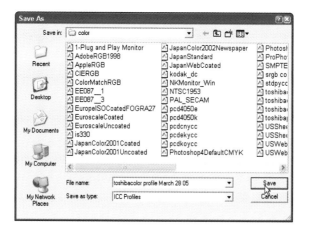

Figure 3-21: Saving the new monitor profile.

Adobe Gamma is a decent tool for calibrating your monitor if you're a casual Photoshop user and don't print a lot of photographs. If you're more serious about digital photography and regularly produce prints on a photo-quality printer, you should strongly consider purchasing a more advanced colorimeter and the software to go with it. You'll get significantly better results with this equipment, saving time, money, paper, and ink cartridges. The next section covers colorimeters and other such advanced calibration tools.

When you calibrate your monitor with Adobe Gamma, a color profile is automatically loaded into your Windows Startup Menu every time you turn on your computer. If you graduate to a more sophisticated colorimeter and use it to create a monitor profile for your computer, make sure you delete Adobe Gamma from your computer's Startup Menu to prevent Adobe Gamma from interfering with your new monitor-profile setup.

Calibrating with a colorimeter

The best solution for calibrating your monitor is specialized software used in conjunction with a *colorimeter* that reads the actual color values produced by your monitor. Today's top monitor-calibration systems include the ColorVision Spyder2, the ColorVision Color Plus, Monaco Systems MonacoOPTIX, and Gretag Macbeth Eye-One Display.

TIP

Prices for these products vary, but if you are on a budget, consider the ColorVision Color Plus. This software-and-colorimeter system offers good value for the money for most home systems; Color Plus provides much more accurate calibration than Gamma or Colorsync for the Mac. Professional or serious photographers may opt for the more high-end ColorVision (shown in Figure 3-22), Gretag Macbeth, or Monaco products.

Here are some important points to keep in mind when using a monitor-calibration package to calibrate your monitor:

Figure 3-22: The ColorVision Spyder 2 colorimeter attached to a laptop display.

- Colorimeters read color from your monitor much more accurately than you can when you look at your monitor; they provide a precise color profile.

- All the monitor-calibration products mentioned include colorimeters that attach to LCD monitors as well as to CRTs.

- The software programs are easy to use and provide step-by-step instructions while performing the calibration of your monitor. Usually the steps to calibrate your monitor with any of these products aren't any more difficult than using Gamma or Colorsync on the Mac.

- Most monitor-calibration solutions automatically remind you to calibrate your monitor every few weeks. This is important because monitor characteristics change over time; if you don't recalibrate on a regular basis, your settings start to look like bad science fiction.

- Calibrating your monitor every two to four weeks is recommended.

- Make sure the lights in the room you're working in are dimmed and the blinds are closed when you calibrate your monitor. (Lighting candles and incense can be cool, but keep 'em far enough away from the computer so the particles they give off don't gum up the works.)

Proofing

After making sure your color settings are correct in Photoshop — and that you've at least calibrated your monitor to give your computer a good profile to set your display to — you're ready to get into your color-managed workflow. (Part IV provides details of working with images in Photoshop.) While working with images, it's important to *proof* your images to make sure that what you're viewing on your monitor closely matches the type of output you intend for the image.

Proofing in Photoshop is actually a pretty simple process. First, you need to set up your proofing profile to match the exact output your image is intended for. When I use the term *output*, I'm referring to a printer, a specific type of paper you're using in the printer, or even output intended for viewing on the Web or a PDF presentation. Turn on proofing in Photoshop so the image you're working in is simulated as viewed on your monitor — and what you're seeing closely matches what should be printed. Here's how:

1. **Choose View⇨Proof Setup⇨Custom.**

2. **In the Customize Proof Condition dialog box that appears, select the output profile that best simulates the color on your computer's display, and then click OK.**

   Figure 3-23 shows the Customized Proof Condition with the Epson R1800 Printer Premium Luster paper profile selected. I chose that selection because that is the particular printer and paper combination I actually use. Your printer and paper combination will probably be different.

Figure 3-23: Selecting a profile to simulate on your monitor.

3. **Toggle Proof Colors on by choosing View⇨Proof Colors or press Ctrl+Y (⌘+Y on the Mac).**

Selecting the profile doesn't change your monitor display, which is why you must perform this step to get the right results. To view the difference between how your image looks on-screen and how it should look when printed (or saved as a Web image if you chose sRGB as a profile), toggle Proof Colors on and off (press Ctrl+Y [Windows] or ⌘+Y [Mac] to toggle). When Proof Colors is on, the image you're viewing on the monitor will closely match what should be printed.

4

Using Workflows to Process Images

*N*atural-born talent has always been an asset to the best artists, including photographers. Now that photography has transitioned to the technical realm of computers and software, however, talent alone won't get photographers through image management — or reveal how best to use Camera Raw and Photoshop. What will get you consistently good results, however, is a little practice with some of the techniques covered in the chapters of this book — and repeating them till they're second nature. Doing the same processes the same way every time reduces the effort required; the result is a consistent set of efficient habits called a *workflow*.

Workflow is the approach I take to every technique in this book. It works equally well whether you're managing images, using Camera Raw, or making adjustments and editing images in Photoshop. Okay, a step-by-step approach isn't rocket science, but if you stick to the steps that create each workflow — consistently — you'll notice improvements in your productivity *and* in the quality to your photographic work. Best of all, it isn't a gadget — workflow doesn't require you to spend more money!

Image Management as a Workflow

It's a familiar scenario: You go out and shoot some stunning photos and itch to get back to the digital darkroom so you can work 'em up. You can't wait to open Bridge, view what you've shot, and process the best ones. Before you know it, you've run a few images through Photoshop, made a few prints, and then maybe moved on to cruising the Web to check up on your fantasy football team, tomorrow's weather, or your bid on that Elvis coffee mug on eBay. The downloaded image is forgotten; it sits there . . .

If you've been using a digital camera for a while now and take photos frequently, you've probably noticed how quickly images pile up on your hard drive. Every time you download photos from a memory card to your hard drive, you can be adding *hundreds* of digital images to an already-crowded storage space. And they sit there . . . and pile up . . .

You've got potential trouble there. One of the biggest challenges digital photographers face is coming up with a system to *manage* all these files. It may sound about as exciting as watching reruns on TV, but image management *should* be exciting to the digital photographer — it means you can actually *find* your best work. Read on for helpful tips and a painless workflow that get you to this worry-free, image-organized state.

Organizing images

The *image-management workflow* isn't some industry-standard step-by-step requirement; it's yours to create. But don't panic. As a photographer, you'll have your own specific needs for managing images, and each reflects your work: categories, topics, clients, file formats, and so on, so that's where you start. How you organize your images depends (at least in part) on the type of photography you're into. A professional portrait photographer, for instance, may want to organize images by client; a fine-art nature photographer might organize pictures by topic.

You can — and should — tailor your image management to accommodate the specific work you do. The best tool for this purpose is a system of organizing images — creating one, following it consistently, and setting up a standard workflow for the images moving through it.

Creating an image-management system

Don't let that pile of miscellaneous images throw you. Implementing an *image-management system* starts with two straightforward tasks:

✓ **Planning how you want to organize your images:** Here's where your knowledge of your photographic work comes into play. A nature photographer might separate images into categories (say, plants, animals, and geographic features) or by region (American Southwest, Arctic tundra, tropical islands . . .).

✔ **Creating folders to hold the categorized images:** Whether you're using a Windows computer or a Mac, first create a master folder to contain all your original, working, and final output images. (I call mine Digital Images, but you can name it anything you want.) Then create subfolders within your main images folder — for example, classified by where they are in their development (working and output images).

Trust me — the shots will keep coming, so they'd better have a place to go. I shoot raw images — a lot of raw images — and I save every one that's downloaded to my computer from my memory card. I've planned my image folders in three basic areas (shown in Figure 4-1): Original Images, Working Images, and Output.

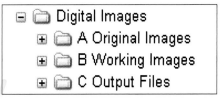

Figure 4-1: Folders set up for original, working, and output images.

I load each memory card into its own folder. Each "download" is given a sequential name, such as IMG0001 lake michigan, IMG0002 fall color, and so on. This system helps me organize original raw images by download, in a sequential order, while noting what's in the folder. See Figure 4-2 for an example of setting up and naming image folders.

Keep your original images original! I create a Working Images folder that contains all the images I'm working on in Photoshop. Whenever I open an image in Camera Raw, process it, and then open it in Photoshop, I immediately save the file as a Photoshop image (in PSD format) to

Figure 4-2: Name your folders so you know what types of image files are stored there.

one of my Working Images folders. You really can't mistakenly change a raw file, but you can a JPEG or TIFF, so by using this practice, you won't risk altering an original in any way.

Finding lost treasures while reorganizing

Recently, while using the new Photoshop Bridge feature to migrate images to new computers and external hard drives (for backups and offline image storage), I decided to go back to my old image files and reorganize them. I had stored CD after CD of older digital images, along with some of my favorite 35mm slides that I had scanned to digital files. I spent a few evenings viewing them, printing a few oldies-but-goodies of the family, and adding a few to my portfolio folder.

Just by viewing and organizing my old images, I discovered some great photos that I'd never had a chance to process or print — for instance, the photo of the creek during autumn a few years ago (shown in Figure 4-3).

Figure 4-3: Organize your older images and rediscover good photos.

When organizing your digital photos, don't forget to include all of the images you've downloaded to your computer in the past. If you had already archived these files to CD or DVD, take some time to view each disc, and copy the images that you never worked with before to your working images folder. If you take the time to review all of your older work, you'll be surprised how many gems you'll find.

Backing up images

One advantage to keeping all your original, working, and output images in a folder structure (also called a *directory tree*) is that they're easy to back up that way. Yes, you heard me right — back up your images! Digital photographers work in a digital world, and digital data is vulnerable. We rely on our computers and hard drives for the well-being of our images — and computers crash. As manmade things, machines are practically guaranteed to fail at a certain point. Computer techies like to say, "There are two kinds of people: Those who have lost all their data, and those that will."

To protect your images, back them up. The best method is to copy your image folder directly to a backup device such as an external hard drive (the device shown on the left in Figure 4-4). These devices are becoming very affordable, and easily attach to your computer via a USB or FireWire cable.

Figure 4-4: Back up all of your original images; you'll be glad you did!

Backing up your images to an external hard drive is a good short-term solution — but you still need to *archive* your images to make sure you can access them over the longer term. Computers today come standard with CD-writable optical drives (known casually as *burners*) that can write to blank CDs easily, storing more than 500 megabytes of data. DVD-writable drives (refer to Figure 4-4) are becoming popular. Now, a standard compact disc (CD) can store 700MB, but storing one 512-megabyte memory card per CD may be convenient. If archive CDs start to proliferate, remember: One DVD can store more than 4.5 gigabytes of files.

Whatever type of optical drive you have at your disposal, I strongly recommend that you *copy all your original images* to a CD or DVD immediately after you download those images to your computer.

Don't stop at one copy; make two. One copy should be kept close by, the other taken to your safety-deposit box (if you have one) or stored in a fire safe in your home or office. Making two copies of your original images will help guarantee that you can recover all that work in case your hard drive crashes, your computer fails, or a meteor lands on the office.

Protecting your images with quality media

You can purchase blank CDs or DVDs inexpensively now, and great bargains are available at your local computer or office supply stores. Whether you're using CDs or DVDs to archive your images, be aware that *optical discs are not all alike.* CDs and DVDs, like many things, are available in different levels of quality.

There are some cheap discs on the market, but they may be cheap for a reason: They may scratch easily, or may be susceptible to quicker chemical deterioration than other discs. When

buying blank CDs or DVDs to use for archiving your images, buy a name-brand premium disc (such as Delkin Archival Gold or Verbatim Datalife). These discs are said to hold up for many years, even decades if they're carefully handled and stored.

Managing images with Bridge

Bridge serves as your virtual light table, but also allows you to do much more with your images than view thumbnails. Bridge gives you the tools to get control of image management *before* you wind up with a mess on your hard drive. Integrating Bridge to view and retrieve photos (as shown in Figure 4-5) makes them a lot easier to keep tidy — especially down the road when you have accumulated *thousands* of images on your computer.

As a software program, Bridge doesn't just sit there showing you row after row of images, it gives you the tools to manage images by

- **Navigating image folders:** Use Bridge to view photos that you download. Use Bridge as your digital light table. You can even create folders — and copy images between folders — using the Edit menu in Bridge.

- **Loading photos into Camera Raw or Photoshop:** You can load raw images directly into Camera Raw just by double-clicking the thumbnails of the photos in Bridge. If your original images were in TIFF or JPEG format, your images will load directly into Photoshop.

- **Adding information with Metadata:** View technical information provided by your digital camera, and add additional information for each photo.

  This is your *cataloging* step in the image-management workflow.

- **Applying labels and ratings:** Color-code and/or apply ratings to your photos for easy retrieval later. The idea is to come up with a system of categorizing your images that makes them easy to find and evaluate.

- **Sorting and renaming photos:** By adding keywords, labels, and ratings to your photos, you can easily sort files at a later time.

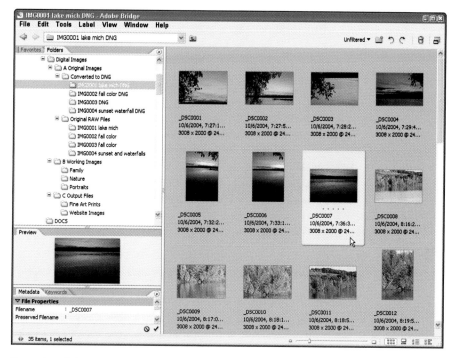

Figure 4-5: Bridge is your virtual light table.

Managing images with a workflow

Okay, suppose the basics are in place: You keep your images in organized folders, you back up all your originals, and you're using Bridge to further view and organize your files. What keeps all that working well is force of habit: Following the same procedure — every time you add images to your collection — is the best way to maintain your images efficiently. So here, without further ado, is the *image-management workflow*:

1. **Organize your files for image management.**

   The earlier section, "Organizing images," shows you how I set up one folder to store images in my Original, Working, and Output folders. Your work may dictate different needs for setting up working and output folders. For instance, if you're a portrait photographer or shoot commercially, you'll be setting up separate folders for each of your clients, and subfolders for the jobs you do for each client.

   However you decide to set up your folder tree, *always keep your original files separate from files that you work on in Photoshop.* You don't want to make a mistake and then save that mistake to your original file.

2. **Copy images to your computer.**

   Using a card reader (or directly connecting your digital camera to your computer), download your images to your Original Images folder. Get in the habit of creating separate folders for each download; create folder names that follow a numerical order in addition to providing a bit of information about the images you're downloading.

3. Back up your files to a backup device *and* to optical media.

You can never have enough backups. I use external hard drives as both backup devices and offline storage, but the first thing I do after down-loading my original images from memory cards is to copy them immedi-ately to CD or DVD. Use premium optical media so your discs are usable (as something other than coasters) in the foreseeable future.

Using a laptop in my travels puts a practical limit on how much disk space I have available. Using an external disk to back up images (and to store large image libraries) adds extra insurance for my images while providing convenient offline storage capacity.

4. (Optional) Convert raw images to DNG format.

I've recently begun converting my original raw files to Adobe DNG format as part of my image-management workflow. Though the DNG format is new and has yet to become a de-facto standard as a raw-image file format, it's the best we have right now.

I've also found that converting these raw images to DNG format and copy-ing the resulting files to CD or DVD gives me a little more protection, a little better chance that my images will be compatible with image-editing software in the distant future.

5. Add metadata to the files.

Adding descriptions to your files helps you identify them and provide practical information about your images for later use. I can look at an image that's a couple of years old and still know where I took it, the time of day, and what camera I used. If I view images that are 5 or 10 years old (before I developed the metadata habit), I may recognize where I took the photo, but probably not much else about it. Use Bridge to add descriptive information to your images. You'll be glad you did.

6. Apply labels and ratings.

Though you may have hundreds or thousands of images stored and archived offline, you can still have hundreds or thousands of photos on your computer that need managing. Bridge's color coding and rating functions can help you tell winners from losers in your image collection, applying color tags or numerical ratings to your images' metadata.

By following this workflow or modifying it to fit your particular needs, you'll be taking a huge step toward making your digital photography better orga-nized and protected — while saving yourself time in the long run because your organizing system will prevent unsightly file buildup as your image library grows. You'll be able to keep track of those old treasures, and have an easy way of finding images that you've taken, stored, and backed up.

When it comes to managing digital images, I don't really want to throw a cheesy cliché at you, but (ack! here it comes) "an ounce of prevention is worth more than a pound of cure (or, for that matter, cheese)."

Raw Conversion as a Workflow

Okay, suppose you've just downloaded and organized a slew of raw images — either in the native format from your digital camera or converted to the DNG format. You've beaten back the chaos with your image-management work-flow, all right, but chaos never sleeps. So the next step is to transform the process of raw conversion into a workflow. Details of using Camera Raw appear in Chapters 8 and 9; here, however, is the *raw-conversion workflow*:

1. **Open a raw image using Bridge.**

   Start Bridge by choosing File⇨Browse or by clicking the Go to Bridge button on the Photoshop Option bar. Choose a raw image you want to process by double-clicking the thumbnail of the image (or you can right-click the image and choose Open with Camera Raw from the flyout menu). Figure 4-6 shows the image loaded in the Camera Raw window.

The red indicates highlight clipping.

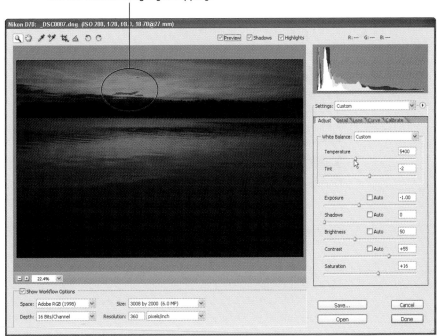

Figure 4-6: The Camera Raw window.

2. Click the Shadows and Highlights check boxes (next to the Preview check box) to turn on the clipping warnings.

Keeping these two check boxes checked is a good habit to develop: They call your attention to the parts of your image where shadow and highlight areas of the image are being *clipped* — that is, losing usable image data due to under- or overadjustment to exposure, shadows, or brightness. Such warnings help you adjust the image in Camera Raw.

When the Shadows and Highlights check boxes are checked, clipped shadow areas of the image show up in blue; highlight clipping is indicated in red, as shown in the portion of the sky in Figure 4-6.

3. Turn on Auto Adjustments.

CS2 brings us a new feature, Auto Adjustments in Camera Raw. If you use it, Camera Raw automatically adjusts color and tone to what it considers optimum for the image. Honestly, Auto Adjustments works pretty well. You just press Ctrl+U on a Windows computer or ⌘+U on a Mac, and you've got a good start in making adjustments. I use it when I first open raw images in Camera Raw.

4. Make overall tonal and color adjustments in the Adjust tab (see Figure 4-7).

When you open an image in Camera Raw, the Adjust tab is automatically selected. The Adjust tab contains all the controls you'll use to adjust White Balance, Temperature, Tint, Exposure, Shadows, Brightness, Contrast, and Saturation. Using Auto Adjustments in Step 3 will automatically assign values to Exposure, Shadows, Brightness, and Contrast — but you don't have to settle for the automatic settings. You can tweak till you get the result you want. (You'll have to set White Balance, Tint, and Saturation on your own; Camera Raw leaves those adjustments to the photographer.)

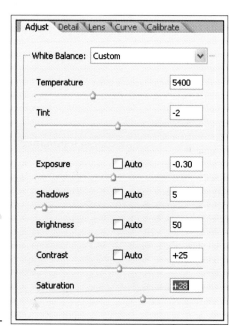

Figure 4-7: The Adjust tab contains controls for overall adjustments.

5. **Apply sharpness and luminance/color noise adjustments (see Figure 4-8).**

The Camera Raw Detail tab (shown in Figure 4-8) offers three controls for applying sharpness and noise reduction to both the luminance and the color of the image. Okay, what does that techno-babble really mean? Simply that you can sharpen the outlines of the image, and reduce those tiny messy bits in the grayscale areas, and get rid of the color-speckle thingies that show up in the color areas of the image. Both are referred to as *noise*.

The Luminance Smoothing slider is sheer death to grayscale noise, while the Color Noise Reduction slider is a hefty weapon against the color noise that can plague images shot in high-ISO settings or long exposures.

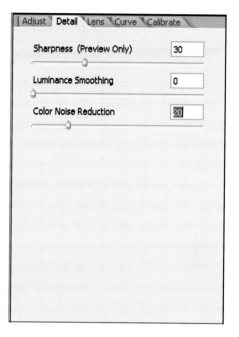

Figure 4-8: The Detail tab contains controls for sharpness and noise reduction.

Reducing luminance and color noise during the raw conversion workflow should be your preferred method for handling noise. Though Photoshop CS2 offers the new Reduce Noise filter, the goal is to be able to make as many adjustments as possible before you open images in Photoshop.

Save the sharpening of any image for the very last steps in your image-processing workflow. Use the Sharpness adjustment *only* for previewing images in Camera Raw. (There's more about sharpening images in Chapter 12; you might want to review it when preparing images for output.)

You can set Camera Raw Preferences to limit the application of sharpening to Preview Only. (I show you how to set Camera Raw Preferences in Chapter 9.)

6. **Fine-tune the tonality and contrast, using the Curve tab.**

The Curve tab (shown in Figure 4-9) lets you fine-tune an image's color characteristics (tonality). Unlike the Curves adjustment in Photoshop, the Camera Raw Curves adjustment works on top of the adjustments made in the Adjust tab; it works like an adjustment's own "fine-tuning." I find that making careful changes in the Adjust tab reduces any need to make changes in the Curve tab.

Though most of your tonal adjustments should be made using the Adjust tab, try using the Curve tab's Tone Curve selection box to view your image using the Medium Contrast and Strong Contrast preset adjustment. If you don't like the results of either, you can always leave the Curve adjustment set to its default (Linear).

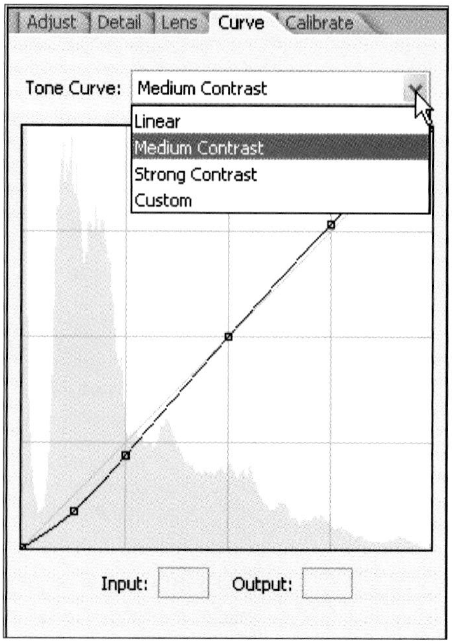

Figure 4-9: The Curve tab.

7. **Click Open to open the image in Photoshop CS2.**

You can also click Done, but that will just save the Camera Raw settings for that image you've just made, and then take you back to Bridge. Clicking the Save button will allow you to save the raw file (and its sidecar file with your adjustments) to a folder of your choosing. You can also specify another format for the file — raw, DNG, TIFF, JPEG, or PSD — but for the most part, you'll be opening the image in Photoshop for overall correction and image editing.

You may have noticed I didn't include the Lens or Calibrate tabs in the Camera Raw workflow described here. That's because normally these controls are used sparingly; you won't need them for most of your images. (Even so, I cover those tabs and their controls in Chapter 9.)

Correcting Images in Photoshop as a Workflow

I've found that the more practice I got making adjustments in Camera Raw, the fewer corrections I had to make in Photoshop. Better still, accurately adjusting white balance, exposure, shadows, brightness, contrast, and color saturation in Camera Raw isn't destructive. Making those same adjustments in Photoshop can destroy valuable image data that might affect the quality of my images, especially if I print them larger than 8×10 inches.

Unfortunately, not all images can be adjusted in Camera Raw — only (well, yeah) the raw ones! Let's not forget all those JPEGs and TIFFs that we shot in our misspent youth, or perhaps are even still producing. (Okay, I admit it: My everyday compact camera doesn't have raw as an option — only JPEG — and I take photos with that Nikon 7900 almost every day!)

But we can still make the best of the images we have. Behold: For fine-tuning images processed in Camera Raw — or photos shot originally in JPEG or TIFF format (such as the one in Figure 4-10) — I offer the *Photoshop image-correction workflow* (applause, please!):

Figure 4-10: A brand new JPEG image, just waiting to be adjusted!

1. **Open the image in Photoshop and evaluate the image to determine your plan of attack**.

   Does the image show an overall *color cast* (too blue, magenta, yellow, and so on)? Is the image too light or too dark? Do you want to increase the contrast? Do you want to add color satu- ration? Take a few moments to visualize how you want your image to appear; it'll help you determine which adjustments belong in the workflow.

2. **Create a Levels adjustment layer to correct color.**

   Use this layer to adjust the amount of color in each of the Red, Green, and Blue channels, using these levels to compensate for incorrect color. You can change the saturation or lightness for individual colors, or the entire color range at once (RGB). If you're just getting used to adjusting levels, simply make an overall correction in the combined RGB channel.

   I show you how to create adjustment layers in Chapter 10.

3. **Create a Curves adjustment layer to make finer color level adjustments.**

   Experiment with slight adjustments across the tonal range of the image. You can, for example, use the Curves adjustment layer to adjust the con- trast of the image — avoiding the Brightness/Contrast adjustment (which is a more destructive way to adjust contrast).

4. Punch up the color in your image using the Hue/Saturation adjustment layer.

As with Saturation adjustment in Camera Raw, you can move the Saturation slider to the right to increase the amount of color in your image. Figure 4-11 shows the adjusted image; the Layers palette shows adjustment layers created for Levels, Curves, and Hue/Saturation.

Figure 4-11: The adjusted image (and its adjustment layers) after image correction.

Consistently following the same steps — turning them into a familiar work-flow — as you make overall adjustments to images in Photoshop can vastly increase your efficiency — especially when you make those corrections in separate layers. Down the road, you can go in and change individual adjustments as needed instead of having to redo the entire image.

When you're making overall adjustments to your image, less is more. For many images, slight adjustments do the trick. Overdoing it can make your photos look fake and unrealistic.

Editing Images as a Workflow

Making adjustments to your images is a start, but editing images can involve a lot of small, specific changes to certain pixels — for example, removing red-eye, erasing chewing-gum wrappers or soda cans from the grass in a nature photo, or even making somebody's nose look twice as big (which can be fun, but be careful not to insult anyone!). Nailing down one procedure to handle image editing can seem as complex as mapping out an entire step-by-step process for life — it may sound impossible. Not so. Here are some basic steps to help you reinforce best practices; they make up your *image-editing workflow*, and they look like this:

1. **After you finish your overall adjustments in Photoshop, create a new layer and combine the previous layers into the new layer by pressing Ctrl+Shift+Alt+E (⌘+Shift+Option+E on the Mac).**

2. **For each edit you make, create a separate layer.**

   Creating separate layers for each edit enables you to go back to just that edit and remove or change it.

3. **Name each layer.**

   Click the layer name in the Layers palette and type the new name for the layer. Name the layer to indicate the type of edit made using that layer, (for example, **Healing Brush**, **Dodge**, **Burn**, **Black-and-White**, or **Red-Eye Removal**).

4. **Save the file in your Working Images folder.**

   After the overall adjustments and image edits are made to the file, you've created many layers. Save the image by choosing File⇨Save As and save the file in PSD (Photoshop) format. Saving the file in Photoshop format preserves the adjustments and edits you've made in layers. Saving the file in your Working Images folder is a good standard image-management practice.

By practicing these five basic steps for each edit, you'll find that your files will be more organized, making it easier to track changes for editing at a later time. (Handy if you get the itch to change your changes.)

Figure 4-12 shows the same image used to illustrate the image-correction workflow, with some new edits (courtesy of the image-editing workflow): I've added layers to provide selective blur (one of my favorite effects), and to clean up some spots using the Spot Healing Brush.

Figure 4-12: Create layers to add edits to an image.

Reviewing Workflows

As you use this book as a reference for converting raw images and using many Photoshop features to adjust and edit your images, use the workflows described in this chapter as your roadmap. Repetitive processes that use best practices create good habits, make you more efficient, and consistently boost the quality of your photos.

Figure 4-13 summarizes workflows for image management, Camera Raw, image adjustment, and image editing.

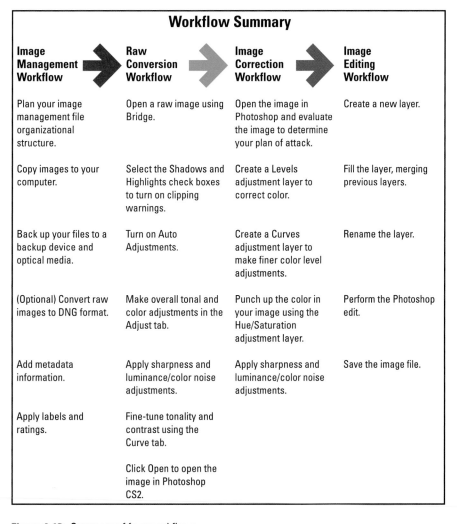

Workflow Summary			
Image Management Workflow	**Raw Conversion Workflow**	**Image Correction Workflow**	**Image Editing Workflow**
Plan your image management file organizational structure.	Open a raw image using Bridge.	Open the image in Photoshop and evaluate the image to determine your plan of attack.	Create a new layer.
Copy images to your computer.	Select the Shadows and Highlights check boxes to turn on clipping warnings.	Create a Levels adjustment layer to correct color.	Fill the layer, merging previous layers.
Back up your files to a backup device and optical media.	Turn on Auto Adjustments.	Create a Curves adjustment layer to make finer color level adjustments.	Rename the layer.
(Optional) Convert raw images to DNG format.	Make overall tonal and color adjustments in the Adjust tab.	Punch up the color in your image using the Hue/Saturation adjustment layer.	Perform the Photoshop edit.
Add metadata information.	Apply sharpness and luminance/color noise adjustments.	Apply sharpness and luminance/color noise adjustments.	Save the image file.
Apply labels and ratings.	Fine-tune tonality and contrast using the Curve tab.		
	Click Open to open the image in Photoshop CS2.		

Figure 4-13: Summary of four workflows.

Part II
Image-Management Workflow with Adobe Bridge

The 5th Wave   By Rich Tennant

"Room service? Please send someone up to refresh the minibar, make up the room and defrag the harddrive."

In this part . . .

*A*s you know, digital cameras offer photographers a huge advantage over film: You can shoot and shoot while reusing the same memory cards. You don't have to buy film anymore, just carry enough memory cards to do the job. On the flipside of all that uninhibited shooting at a greatly reduced cost, what are you to *do* with all those digital image files? The answer (drum roll, please): Organize your best practices into an image-management workflow with Adobe Bridge. This part shows you how.

If you want to avoid the nightmare of shooting more images than you can handle in Photoshop, Chapters 6 and 7 can help you make sense of it all. I show you how to set up folders to store your original images, and how to keep them separate from the images you're working on. Next, I show you around Bridge, introduce you to all its most useful functions, and apply those to managing your growing number of images. Organizing your images (and knowing how to take advantage of all the features Bridge offers the photographer) enables you to manage your images like a pro!

5

Getting Around, Across, Under, and Over Adobe Bridge

*B*efore digital photography, I would view my 35mm slides on a light table. I'd carefully take them out of their protective sleeves and view them a few at a time with a loupe (a little magnifying glass). Keepers went in one slide file, the rest were relegated to the other file. If it sounds archaic, it is, but that's how we viewed photos and organized them back then — with a light table and a file cabinet.

The timing couldn't have been more perfect when Adobe first offered the file browser in Photoshop 7, which has evolved into Bridge with the release of CS2. Now, working with thousands of digital files, I can use Bridge for almost all of my image management — including viewing my images on my virtual light table, the computer monitor. Many of my best practices from pre-digital days were easy to adapt. This book stresses the need for an image-management workflow, and Bridge is your tool for managing your increasing horde of digital images.

Introducing Bridge

Bridge is a standalone application that can be started in Windows or on the Mac independently of Photoshop. If you're running other software in the Adobe Creative Suite such as Illustrator or GoLive, you can use Bridge to manage files for all of them, including Photoshop — so it serves (aha!) as a bridge between them. You can use Bridge to perform quite a range of tasks as you organize your photos — including these:

✔ **Browse your computer for images:** First and foremost, Bridge is a great image-browsing program. You can easily navigate all the hard drives and folders in your system for images. Figure 5-1 shows the Bridge window with a thumbnail selected.

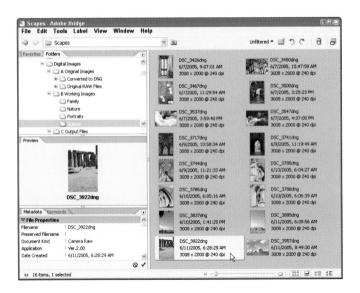

Figure 5-1: The Bridge window.

✔ **Open images directly into Camera Raw or Photoshop:** Bridge serves as file menu for both Camera Raw and Photoshop. Double-clicking raw-image thumbnails in Bridge will automatically open images in Camera Raw. If the image selected is another file format (such as JPEG, TIFF, or PSD), the image will be loaded directly into Photoshop.

If you have other raw converters loaded on your computer, double-clicking raw-image thumbnails might open your images in one of those other raw converters instead of Camera Raw. You can always click an image and then press Ctrl+R (⌘+R on a Mac) to open an image in Camera Raw.

✔ **Add metadata to images:** For my commercial work, one of the first things I do when first viewing a fresh download of images is to add *metadata* to each image — data about data (in this case, about images) that helps me organize the files. Your digital camera provides some metadata — for example, the date and shooting information such as shutter speed, aperture, and ISO setting. You can add more metadata in Bridge (say, copyright information and a text description of the photo).

Metadata information is stored in a *sidecar* file kept with your images. Whether you're viewing thumbnails in Bridge or editing photos in Photoshop, that metadata is retained. If you're using DNG format (which I discuss further in Chapter 2), metadata is stored directly in the image file (no sidecar file).

✔ **Add ratings and color labels to images:** One cool feature of Bridge is the convenient way to rate, rank, and label your images. You can indicate a rating to an image of one to five stars and even apply a color code to an image. Both ratings and color labels are good tools to use in conjunction with Bridge's image search features, which allows you to search for images based on ratings and labels.

✔ **Rename a bunch of images at once:** Bridge offers the ability to batch and rename images, giving you the choice to both rename those images and then store the renamed images in a folder of your choosing. This feature comes in handy when you have a number of images you'll want to send to a client (or a friend for that matter), but don't want to use the same filename for the images that your digital camera provides.

✔ **Choose workspaces:** Depending on what you're doing with your images, you can use Bridge to switch between *workspaces* — different working views of Bridge. If, for example, you're creating a filmstrip-style presentation, you can use the Filmstrip workspace shown in Figure 5-2. For other tasks, you can change workspaces easily by choosing Window⇨ Workspace (or by clicking the Workspace icons in the lower-right corner of the Bridge window).

✔ **Run Photoshop automation features from Bridge:** These automatic features that can be run directly from Bridge include creating a PDF presentation, creating a Web photo gallery, and stitching together panoramas (using Photomerge). But the crown jewel of these features is the powerful and time-saving Image Processor, where you can batch-convert any number of images from one format to another while choosing a separate destination folder for those files.

With all the image-management functions that Bridge offers the photographer, it's worth taking some time to get to know. If you read up on using its features, play around with it some, and fit it into your workflow; you'll save a lot of time in the long run, and your images will be a lot better managed and organized. Just as Windows or Mac OS is the operating system for your computer, consider Bridge the operating system for your images and Photoshop.

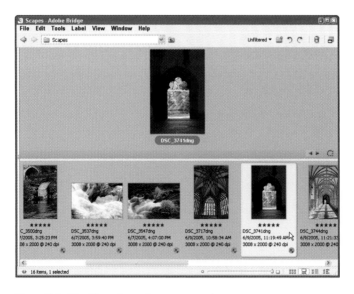

Figure 5-2: The Filmstrip workspace, one of many.

Getting Acquainted with Bridge

The Bridge window is the gateway to where all the goodies are, but there's one immediate piece of business to take care of: How do you start Bridge? (Oh yeah, that . . .) There are actually three ways to fire it up:

✓ **Start Bridge from your computer.**

Bridge is an independent software program just like Word, Excel, or Photoshop. From a computer running Windows, choose Start➪Adobe Bridge. From the Mac Desktop, double-click the Bridge icon (Applications➪Adobe Bridge).

You can start Bridge by pressing Ctrl+Alt+O (Windows) or ⌘+Option+O (on the Mac).

✓ **Start Bridge from the Photoshop File menu.**

From Photoshop CS2, simply choose File➪Browse shown in Figure 5-3.

✓ **Start Bridge from the Go to Bridge button.**

From Photoshop, just click the Go to Bridge button on the Option bar shown in Figure 5-3.

Go to Bridge button

File menu   Option bar

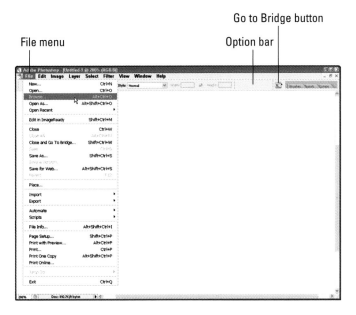

Figure 5-3: Starting Bridge from the File menu or the Go to Bridge button.

Getting the lay of the land

Bridge is indeed a powerful standalone program — complete with menus, tabs, work areas, and a range of specialized views to fit your work. Before you jump into the details of how to manage images, however, take a look at the components of the Bridge work area shown in Figure 5-4:

- **Menu bar:** Contains Bridge commands within the File, Edit, Tools, Label, View, Window, and Help menus. Just about everything you want to do in Bridge is found in these menus; I sum up those commands in the next section.

- **Option bar:** Contains the Look In menu, Go Up a Folder, the Filtered/Unfiltered Images button, the New Folder button, Rotate Left/Right, Trash, and Switch to Compact Mode buttons.

- **Look In menu:** Displays the folder hierarchy, favorites, and the folders you've used most recently. It's a fast way to locate folders that contain images.

- **Favorites panel:** Gives you fast access to folders, Version Cue (used to manage the versions of files throughout the Adobe software suite), Stock Photos, and Collections.

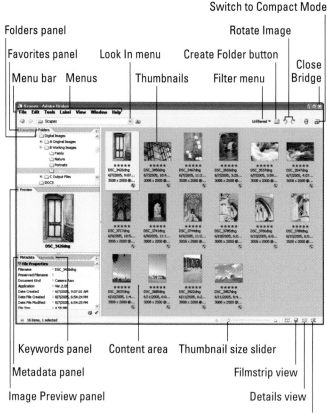

Figure 5-4: The Bridge window.

🖉 **Folders panel:** Shows folder hierarchies and lets you navigate folders.

🖉 **Preview panel:** Shows a preview of the selected image.

🖉 **Metadata panel:** Contains information about the selected image (including data from your digital camera on how the photo was shot, aperture, shutter speed, ISO settings, and such). You can add various types of information about the file in multiple areas.

🖉 **Keywords panel:** Lets you add keywords to the image information so you can organize images by keyword (which really eases file searches).

🖉 **Content area:** Displays resizable thumbnails of images and basic file information.

Would you like to see a menu?

As with any typical Windows or Mac program, Bridge comes equipped with a full set of menus — offering just about every function you'll want to perform (except maybe brewing coffee). For example, if you want to open an image, click the thumbnail, choose File⇨Open, and *voilà!*

You could also just double-click the thumbnail to open the document. Often you have many ways to perform the same or similar functions in Bridge — and, for that matter, in Photoshop. The functions you choose from other parts of Bridge can also be found in the menus:

- **File menu:** If you're used to working with Windows or Mac programs, the File menu should be familiar to you. Shown in Figure 5-5, the File menu is where you can open a new Bridge window, create a folder, open a file or choose which program to open it in, close Bridge, or send a file to the Recycle Bin/Trash. You can also add information about the file (metadata) to an image via the File Info command.

- **Edit menu:** I'm a frequent visitor to the Edit menu (see Figure 5-6), mainly because that's where the Undo command is. Sure, the Bridge menus show you the keyboard shortcuts, but for casual users, using the menus is easier than memorizing all those keyboard commands, such as Undo Ctrl+Z (⌘+Z on the Mac). You'll also find the familiar Cut, Copy, and Paste commands here in the Edit menu.

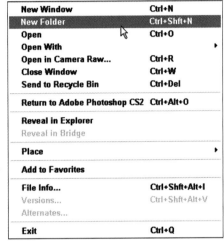

Figure 5-5: The Bridge File menu.

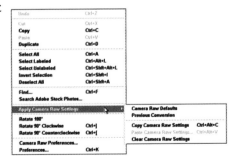

Figure 5-6: The Edit menu.

One command I use frequently is Apply Camera Raw Settings. It copies the exact Camera Raw settings made to one image and applies them to multiple images — a great timesaver! (There's more about that technique in Chapter 6.)

An especially nifty Edit menu command that I use often is Duplicate (Ctrl+D [Windows] or ⌘+D [Mac]). Using it, you can easily make an exact copy of an image — handy for creating more than one version to work on at the same time. The Duplicate command is also the very thing when you want to create a "working" version of an image while leaving the original in pristine, untouched condition. Bridge automatically adds copy to the filename of the newly created duplicate.

↙ **Tools menu:** The Tools menu (shown in Figure 5-7) is home to many of the Bridge and Photoshop automation features. Batch Rename (for example) is a huge timesaver — you can reuse it to rename any number of files you've selected in the Content area, and save those files to another folder. And the Photoshop Services command links you to Web resources where you can upload your images to have them printed — as proofs, or in book, calendar, or greeting-card format.

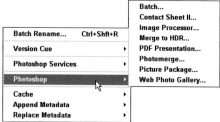

Figure 5-7: The Tools menu.

Choosing the Photoshop command will take you to Photoshop's automation features, including:

- **Batch:** Run Photoshop Actions on any number of images selected in the Content area.

- **Contact Sheet II:** I'm sure you're curious to what happened to Contact Sheet I, but I'm *sure* II is better! Here's where you can select any number of images in the Content area, and almost instantly create contact sheets from those images.

- **Image Processor:** Yet another great timesaver! If you want to convert a number of images from one format to another (say, PSD to JPEG), the Image Processor is the Photoshop automation tool for you.

- **Merge to HDR:** Using this new feature in Photoshop CS2, you can merge a number of images into one HDR (high dynamic range) image. It's an advanced command that can be a powerful technique. Combining different versions of a same image, taken at different exposures, can help you compensate for difficult lighting situations. Merging underexposed and overexposed versions of an image *together* (using Merge to HDR) would give you a single image from two or three — maybe with striking results!

- **PDF Presentation:** After selecting images in the Content area, use PDF Presentation to create presentations of those images that you can post to a Web site or e-mail to friends, family, or clients.

- **Photomerge:** Stitching together images to create panoramas is easy using Photomerge. I show you that feature in more detail in Chapter 13.

- **Picture Package:** If you remember school pictures from back in the day, or currently have your own kids in school, Picture Package is where you can create your own 8×10-inch print; it includes various sizes of your chosen photos.

- **Web Photo Gallery:** This is one of my favorite automation features of Photoshop. Quickly and easily create your own photo Web site. As a guy who's developed many Web sites over the years, I can tell you this utility really works well! You can choose a Web site template, select photos to display by selecting thumbnails in Bridge, and there's your gallery. Hey, it's so easy — and this Web site doesn't even have to send development offshore to be completed! Using Web Photo Gallery is a no-brainer way to share, admire, or just show off your photos.

✔ **Label menu (see Figure 5-8):** The Label menu provides all the options for applying ratings and labels to images. (I show you how to use these features in Chapter 6.)

✔ **The View menu:** The View menu is where you find the options that control how Bridge displays itself on-screen. The commands to display your thumbnails in Thumbnail, Filmstrip, or Details mode are in this menu as well. You can also sort your thumbnails or show only certain types of images (such as all files, graphic files, or Camera Raw files only) by using this menu.

Rating	
No Rating	**Ctrl+0**
*	**Ctrl+1**
**	**Ctrl+2**
***	**Ctrl+3**
****	**Ctrl+4**
✔ *****	**Ctrl+5**
Decrease Rating	**Ctrl+,**
Increase Rating	**Ctrl+.**
Label	
✔ **No Label**	
Red	**Ctrl+6**
Yellow	**Ctrl+7**
Green	**Ctrl+8**
Blue	**Ctrl+9**
Purple	

Figure 5-8: The Label menu.

One neat feature I recently discovered while playing with the View menu is Slide Show (Ctrl+L, ⌘+L on a Mac). Starting Slide Show allows you to view your thumbnails in full-screen mode (as in Figure 5-9). Slide Show can be another way to view and evaluate images in Bridge, or simply to show off some cool photos on your computer.

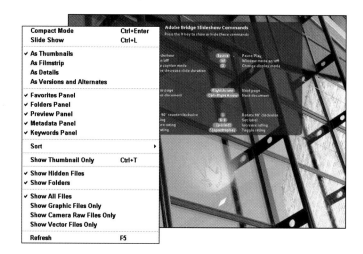

Figure 5-9: The Label menu and Slide Show.

 Window menu: The Window menu contains all the different *workspaces* (different views of Bridge; see Figure 5-10) that you can choose while working in Bridge. Let's face it — digital photographers have different personal tastes when it comes to working in Bridge and Photoshop; the Window menu accommodates them by letting you specify different working conditions:

- **Default (Ctrl+F1, ⌘+F1 on a Mac):** The Default workspace provides the best of everything Bridge has to provide. The Favorites, Folders, Preview, Metadata, and Keywords panels are displayed along with thumbnails.

- **Lightbox (Ctrl+F2, ⌘+F2 on a Mac):** The Lightbox workspace changes your Bridge view to Thumbnails only. You still have access to all Bridge menus, but the panels are gone.

- **File Navigator (Ctrl+F3, ⌘+F3 on a Mac):** The File Navigator workspace shows you thumbnails in the Content area and the Favorites and Folders panel. This view allows you to view thumbnails in folders that you can navigate in the Folders panel.

- **Metadata Focus (Ctrl+F4, ⌘+F4 on a Mac):** The Metadata Focus workspace presents Bridge with a smaller thumbnail view with the Favorites, Metadata, and Keyword panels displayed.

- **Filmstrip Focus (Ctrl+F5, ⌘+F5 on a Mac):** The Filmstrip Focus workspace provides a thumbnail view of your images, with a larger preview of a selected image in the main portion of the Content area. No panels are displayed.

Default workspace   Lightbox workspace   File Navigator workspace

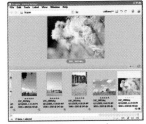

Metadata Focus workspace   Filmstrip Focus workspace

Figure 5-10: The Window menu.

✔ **Help menu:** The Bridge Help
menu gives you links to
Photoshop's updated Help
program, and the convenient
Updates command. Bridge
doesn't really have its own
help section, but Bridge Help
(F1) does link you directly to
the Bridge section of the
Photoshop Help application
(shown in Figure 5-11).

Figure 5-11: Bridge Help.

The Updates command in the Bridge
Help menu links you directly to the
Adobe Photoshop updates area of
adobe.com. This useful feature makes getting software updates for
Photoshop, Bridge, and Camera Raw easy. I recommend checking for updates
every month.

Using Bridge panels

Located below the menus and Option bar is the panel area. The default workspace of Bridge will show the Favorites, Folders, Preview, Metadata, and Keywords panels. Each panel has a specific function:

Figure 5-12: Favorites panel.

✔ **The Favorites panel:** The Favorites panel shares the same space in Bridge as the Folders panel. Shown in Figure 5-12, Favorites is an "area" browser. Instead of rummaging around in one folder at a time, you can browse specific areas — say, your computer, Adobe Stock Photos (Adobe's new stock-photo service), Version Cue, and Collections. (I show you how to customize Favorites in the next section, "Customizing Bridge.")

The Favorites panel saves you time by letting you just drag a folder in from the Content area when you want to create a Favorites shortcut. If you work mainly from a few image folders, you simply click My Computer, find the folder you want to drag to the Favorites panel, and drag it. Finding that folder becomes a lot easier as you work in Bridge (or when you first start it up) — not a drag at all.

Figure 5-13: Folders panel.

✔ **The Folders panel (see Figure 5-13):** As a user of multiple image folders, I rely on the Folders panel to navigate — and it's where I manage the folders on my computer. Similar to Windows Explorer, the Folders panel lets you click through drives and folders or move them around by or dragging them to other folders or drives.

You can make just as many mistakes in the Folders panel as you can in Windows Explorer. Be careful when you move folders around, or send folders or files to the Recycle Bin or Trash. You can inadvertently delete folders and files you want to keep.

✔ **The Preview panel:** The Preview panel displays an image that is selected in the work area. Right-click (⌘+click a Mac) to show the preview image (and all the options shown in Figure 5-14) on-screen, much the same as when you preview an image in the work area.

Open
Open With   ▶

Reveal in Explorer
Add to Favorites
Batch Rename...

Rotate 180°
Rotate 90° Clockwise
Rotate 90° Counterclockwise

Send to Recycle Bin

File Info...
Label   ▶

Preview

DSC_3500dng

Figure 5-14: Preview panel.

✔ **The Metadata panel:** You can view information about a selected image in the Metadata panel. Figure 5-15 shows basic image metadata, but you can also add EXIF information (data your digital camera saves with the image — aperture, shutter speed, ISO, and such) and other important professional tidbits such as copyright.

The IPTC section is the place to add copyright and other information (for instance, more about the photographer and the images) following IPTC standards. If you're wondering who the heck the IPTC is, it's a London-based press-and-telecommunications organization that sets standards for news-media data. You can check out this organization at www.iptc.org.

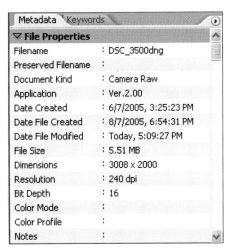

Metadata	Keywords
▽ **File Properties**	
Filename	: DSC_3500dng
Preserved Filename	:
Document Kind	: Camera Raw
Application	: Ver.2.00
Date Created	: 6/7/2005, 3:25:23 PM
Date File Created	: 8/7/2005, 6:54:31 PM
Date File Modified	: Today, 5:09:27 PM
File Size	: 5.51 MB
Dimensions	: 3008 x 2000
Resolution	: 240 dpi
Bit Depth	: 16
Color Mode	:
Color Profile	:
Notes	:

Figure 5-15: Metadata panel.

✔ **The Keywords panel:** A good image management process that I recommend in Chapter 6 is adding keywords to your images using the Keywords panel. (I guess I'm recommending it here, too.) Adding keywords to your images makes all the difference when you're organizing them (or searching for them later). Getting in the habit of associating keywords with images gives you a powerful image-management tool; you'll thank yourself in the future.

Figure 5-16 shows a keyword I've added to indicate where the selected image was taken.

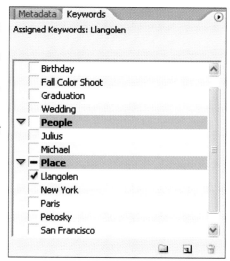

Figure 5-16: Keywords panel.

Customizing Bridge

One of my favorite things about Photoshop and Bridge is that they let me easily customize my view of the software. Sure, a lot of computer programs let you add toolbars, change fonts, or fluff the cosmetics, but when you're crafting an image, you may want to change the look of Bridge entirely to fit the work in hand.

Bridge gives you power over how it's displayed when you choose and tweak your workspaces. Many programs don't let you customize panels and work areas, but Adobe has gone out of its way to make Bridge customizable to fit your tastes or needs. Changing the background color of the work area is kind of cool (your only choices are black, white, and grayscale); you can put a lot of detailed information in metadata — and manage it with Bridge — or even specify which metadata fields are viewable. Bridge is a tweaker's paradise; you may not use even a fraction of the options, but you have 'em if you need 'em. If the designers and developers at Adobe wanted to ease the artist's mind, well — congratulations on a job well done!

Changing workspaces and views

Photographers can be picky; I guess it's the nature of an artist who demands perfection down to the slightest detail. Bridge workspaces and views offer enough options to reasonably satisfy the most discerning taste. (Okay, maybe most digital photographers don't *really* get that finicky about Bridge workspaces, but having options sure is nice!)

This list highlights some of the ways you can change the way Bridge and its sections appear:

✔ **Change your workspace:** The Window menu offers a useful range of workspaces, but the one I use most is the default, shown in Figure 5-17. It includes the Favorites/Folders section, a small preview, Metadata, and Keywords panels — everything I need for my work.

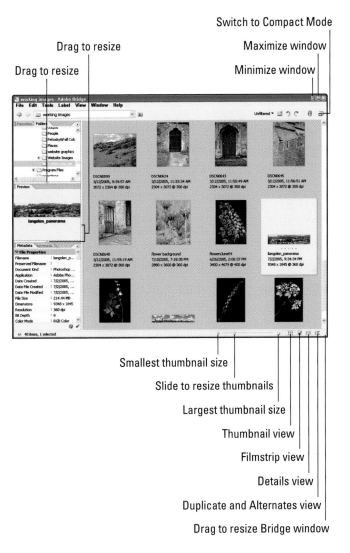

Switch to Compact Mode

Drag to resize — Maximize window

Drag to resize — Minimize window

Smallest thumbnail size

Slide to resize thumbnails

Largest thumbnail size

Thumbnail view

Filmstrip view

Details view

Duplicate and Alternates view

Drag to resize Bridge window

Figure 5-17: Customizing the Bridge workspace.

✔ **Resize panels and the Content area:** You can easily resize your panels and the size of the Content area by dragging the borders (refer to Figure 5-17).

✔ **Resize the Bridge window:** In the bottom-right area of the Bridge window, you can drag the corner to resize the entire Bridge window (unless you've maximized it already by clicking the Maximize button in the upper-right corner of the window).

✔ **Change to Filmstrip view:** If you like the default workspace (the way I do) but you'd rather look at your thumbnails in Filmstrip view shown in Figure 5-18, click the Filmstrip view button at the bottom-right of the Bridge window.

✔ **Change to Details view:** If you're comparing and analyzing your images, you'll want to view them with more image data displayed. The Details view provides a view of each image in the work area, showing more file properties than are displayed in the other views.

✔ **Change to the Versions and Alternates view.** If you're working with images in Version Cue, you can use this view to compare the different versions or alternatives that were created.

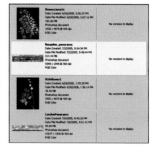

Changing Bridge preferences

Just when you thought it was safe to go back to your computer, there's more customization to do! Bridge gives you some detailed options for changing window colors and specifying which metadata fields to display with thumbnails. To change Bridge preferences, follow these steps:

Figure 5-18: Filmstrip, Details, and Versions and Alternates views.

1. **Start Preferences by choosing Edit⇨Preferences, or press Ctrl+K (⌘+K on a Mac).**

   The Preferences window gives you various ways (in the left column) to modify your preference settings: General, Metadata, Labels, File Type Associations, Advanced, and Adobe Stock Photos. The default choice is General Preferences, shown in Figure 5-19.

Figure 5-19: The General Preferences window.

2. Change the Content area background to black, white, or gray.

One cosmetic change you can make to Bridge is to change the background of the Content area. You can't specify a color, but you can use the Background slider in the Thumbnails section to adjust from black (at left) all the way to the right for white.

A neutral gray background is actually best for viewing image thumbnails — and that's true whether you're viewing images in Photoshop, Bridge, or even prints on your desk. Your eyes can best judge colors without the interference of a white, black, or color background. For most images, leave the background of the Content area gray.

3. Modify information to be displayed under thumbnails.

By default, thumbnails appear with the filename, date/time the image was taken, image dimensions, and keywords. Figure 5-20 shows a fourth line change to show copyright information, which I specified using Additional Lines of Thumbnail Metadata in the third selection box.

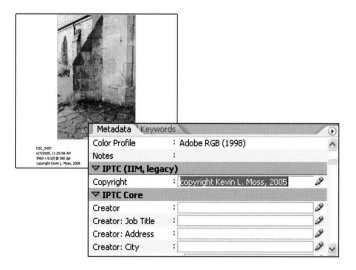

Figure 5-20: Changing thumbnail-image information in Preferences.

4. Customize Favorites.

Remember the Favorites Panel? You can specify the areas of your computer that appear in Favorites by selecting what you want in the Favorite Items area of Preferences. Figure 5-21 shows how selected Favorite Items appear on-screen in the Favorites panel.

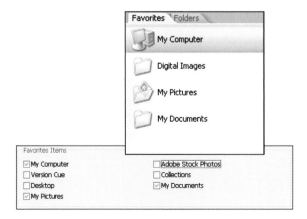

Figure 5-21: Changing what's displayed in the Favorites panel.

5. Customize Metadata Preferences.

Click Metadata in the Preferences window to show the available meta-data selections. There you can select and deselect the metadata fields you want to appear in the Metadata panel.

Review that slew of metadata default fields carefully. Decide which fields you will and won't be using — and then select or deselect them accordingly in Metadata Preferences (shown in Figure 5-22).

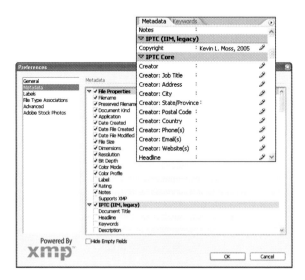

Figure 5-22: Changing what's displayed in the Metadata panel.

6. Modify Label definitions.

Chapter 6 shows you how to apply color labels to your images, but you can customize the descriptions of your color labels in the Labels section of Preferences (shown in Figure 5-23). The default for each color label is simply the color name, but you can customize these names any time you want to fit your own labeling system. Knock yourself out!

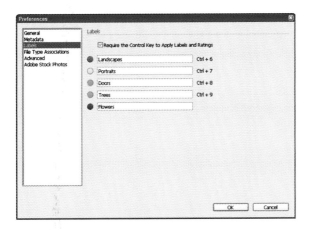

Figure 5-23: Changing what's displayed in the Metadata panel.

7. Modify File Type associations.

You may want to leave this section of Preferences as is. Though you can change the software programs associated with file types, why do that if you're happy with the way things are working on your computer? You're unlikely to need this section unless something unusual is going on. For example, if your JPEGs are opening automatically in Word instead of Photoshop, you can change that setting here.

8. Change miscellaneous settings.

The Advanced preferences are further ways to customize how Bridge works. You can set the largest file you'll let Bridge open, how many recently viewed folders the Look In pop-up shows you, and whether to use double-clicking to edit Camera Raw settings. I tend to leave these settings alone, but some are like parachutes: When you need them, nothing else does the job. For example, if you work with Bridge in a language other than English, you can select from many languages by clicking the Language selection box shown in Figure 5-24.

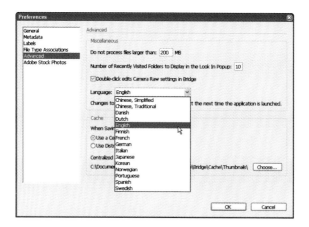

Figure 5-24: Changing the language setting in Preferences.

6

Managing Images

*I*f you went through Chapter 5, you got a look at how powerful Bridge is for working with images. I've been using only Bridge — ever since it was in beta — to manage my images, until now it's my primary tool for keeping my ever-growing image library under control. Windows Explorer used to be my tool of choice for organizing and managing my images; for one who's been using Windows for more than a dozen years, it took a program like Bridge to get me to break old habits.

If you're new to digital cameras and Photoshop, you may have only a few hundred photos to manage. So far. But if you take a few weeks' vacation to that exotic island you've always dreamed about (and if you do, congratulations!), you could come home with *hundreds more* digital images. Those images add up quick — and can fill up your hard drive in a hurry. Solution: Manage your images with Bridge. Then go take a vacation!

Managing Images with Bridge

In Chapter 5, I show you just about every menu, command, panel, and change to workspaces and preferences to Bridge, now it's time to put this software to work managing images. As with every process covered in this book, I take the same approach: setting up and using a workflow (in fact, the same one mentioned in Chapter 4) for image management.

Here's the image-management workflow you can implement with Bridge, step by step:

1. **Navigate and create image folders.**

   You can view photos that you download directly from your digital camera or card reader. This is a lot better than the old light tables that used to be used to view those little negatives and slides.

2. **Organize images.**

   Organize your images into Original, Working, and Output folders. Use the Folders panel and the Edit menu (Copy and Paste commands) to move images into their designated folders — or drag and drop images from folder to folder.

3. **Add information with the Metadata panel.**

   You can view the information provided by your digital camera — in particular, technical data for each photo — and add information about each image in the Metadata panel.

4. **Apply labels and ratings.**

   You can color-code your photos for easier retrieval later — and rate your photos (from one to five stars) and save the ratings so you can get to the best ones quickly.

5. **Sort and rename photos.**

   By adding keywords, labels, and ratings to your photos, you can easily sort files later. Renaming files is a snap using Bridge: Double-click the filename and then type a new name.

6. **Load images to Camera Raw or Photoshop.**

   After you've properly organized your image files (and viewed their thumbnails in the Content area) is the time to load your raw images into Camera Raw or your other images directly into Photoshop.

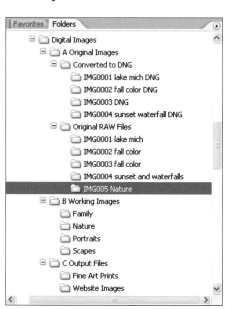

Figure 6-1: Viewing folders in the Folders panel.

Navigating and creating image folders

Using the Bridge Folders panel is just like navigating folders via Windows Explorer, My Computer, or the Mac Finder. The Folders panel gives you an Explorer-like view of your computer and your storage devices (such as a CD-ROM drive or an external hard drive). Figure 6-1 shows how you can view folders using the Folders panel.

TIP

Another way to view folders and their contents through Bridge is to use the Look In menu on the Option bar, as shown in Figure 6-2.

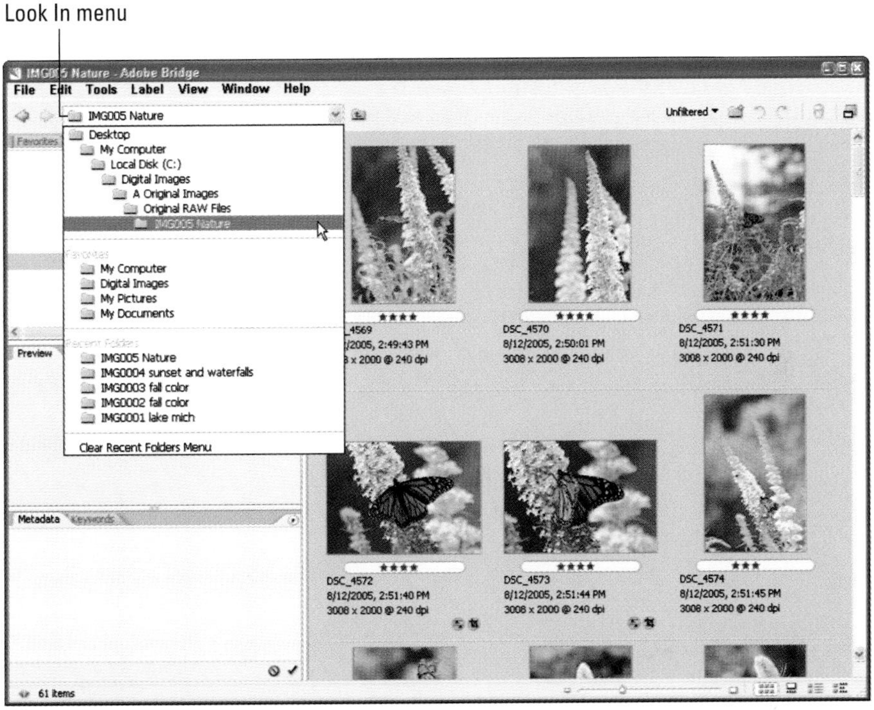

Look In menu

Figure 6-2: The Look In menu.

The Look In menu gives you a hierarchical view of the folders contained in your Desktop, Favorites, and most Recent folders. Click a folder in the Look In menu, and the contents of that folder are displayed in the viewing area.

Creating folders

If you haven't yet created your Original, Working, and Output folders, here are the steps that create these folders using Bridge:

1. **Using the Folders panel, select the drive where you want to create the new folder.**

2. **Create a new images folder.**

   Choose File⇨New Folder or press Ctrl+Shift+N (⌘+Shift+N on a Mac). You can also click the Create New Folder icon on the Bridge Option bar.

3. Name the folder.

Figure 6-3 shows you the newly created folder in the Content area. Type a folder name over the highlighted text New Folder. This is where your creativity comes into play; you can name the images folder anything you want. Just don't get *too* silly. (Personally, I call my main images folder by the boring but practical name "Images.")

4. Create working and output folders.

Click the new Images folder just created and repeat Steps 2 and 3, creating subfolders within this folder. You've just taken a huge step toward getting control of that unruly horde of images!

Figure 6-3: Naming a new folder.

Digging for lost treasures

While you're busy implementing a workflow to manage your images, take time to organize some of your older images as well. If you're like me, you have years of valuable photos that need to be organized and archived. Not only is going back and viewing older images fun, it can be productive.

Currently, I'm in the process of scanning my older 35mm slides. Some of those photos match or exceed my quality expectations today, but were never processed and printed for a variety of reasons (but none of them very good excuses!). The same story goes for some of my early digital photos. It's a long process, but with a solid image-management strategy, you can probably identify many of your older images to add to your portfolio.

Go ahead and start digging for lost treasures; Bridge makes it fun and easy!

Organizing images in folders

After setting up folders for storing your digital images, you can get down to business organizing your images into those folders. You may have many folders already, in various areas of your hard drive, but take this opportunity to move those folders into the new structure you've set up for image management. Organized folders are great for peace of mind. As I've demonstrated, I set up three basic areas to store my images. Here's how:

1. **Copy your original images to your Original Image folders.**

    I always leave my original images *as* originals. I don't like to make changes to these files; I want to keep them intact, as you would a film negative. I simply download images from memory cards, each one into its own subfolder in my Original Images folder, and then back up the new image folder to DVD.

Give each folder a name that combines chronological sequence with a few descriptive words so you have a clue to its contents (as with the folders shown in Figure 6-4). Such folder names make it easier to recognize folder contents later when you view them in Bridge. When your number of original image folders grows to the hundreds, the chronology and descriptions included in folder names will come in handy.

- Img0037 still lifes
- Img0038 printers&portraits
- Img0039 emily eye&tripod
- Img0040 Still lifes
- Img0041 natpreserve&orchids
- Img0042 Orion and Squirl
- Img043 Somerset
- Img0044 racoon
- Img0045 sunset at nat preserve
- Img0046 equipment
- Img0047 duckies
- Img0048 CBR
- Img0049 pianos
- Img0050 7900
- Img0051 7900 tiger stadium

Figure 6-4: Assigning chronological and descriptive folder names to your original image folders.

2. **If you have some unfinished "images in progress," save them to your "working" image folders.**

    Create your working image folders to match the targeted purpose of your images. If (for example) you do mostly personal work such as pictures of family, nature, or pets, then create a working folder for each category. If you're taking photos professionally, create a separate folder for each client or job you're working on.

When first you open images in Camera Raw and Photoshop, get into the habit of immediately saving the image file to a working image folder, in Photoshop's PSD format. That way the saved image becomes the one you're working on, and resides in the working folder. The original stays intact, and you eliminate the risk of altering the original accidentally.

3. **If you have images you want to print or publish, save them to "output" image folders.**

   When you've finished adjusting and editing your images, you'll want to save specialized versions of them to specific output folders — say, for print, Web, or publication — with each version sized differently and quite possibly assigned a different color space. (I cover creating output images in more detail in Chapter 12.)

Adding Information to Images' Metadata

Metadata is information that describes an image file — and it can encompass not only the information provided by your digital camera, but also such tid-bits as author information, your copyright, and keywords. Normally metadata isn't stored inside your image file, but instead in a standard Extensible Metadata Platform (XMP) format, in a separate *sidecar file* — unless you're using DNG files (which store metadata along with the image).

You can use metadata information you add to an image later to organize and keep track of files and versions, as well as search and sort images. The more images you have, the more valuable this information becomes as a tool to help manage your image library. This is one of the features that makes Bridge so powerful.

You add metadata information to images by typing the information in the Metadata panel in Bridge, as shown in Figure 6-5.

File Info offers you an easier and more efficient method for adding metadata information. You can access File Info by choosing File⇨File Info or by pressing Ctrl+Shift+Alt+I (⌘+Shift+Option+I on the Mac). The File Info window (the Pictures–Adobe Bridge window on the Mac) appears, as shown in Figure 6-6.

The Description window is the first to show up on-screen. On its left side, you'll see a number of pages in which you can view or add metadata.

Metadata	Keywords	
▽ **File Properties**		
Filename	: DSC_4572	
Preserved Filename	:	
Document Kind	: Camera Raw	
Application	: Ver.2.00	
Date Created	: 8/12/2005, 2:51:40 PM	
Date File Created	: 8/15/2005, 10:20:47 PM	
Date File Modified	: 8/12/2005, 2:51:42 PM	
File Size	: 5.26 MB	
Dimensions	: 3008 x 2000	
Resolution	: 240 dpi	
Bit Depth	: 16	
Color Mode	:	
Color Profile	:	
Rating	: 4	
Notes	:	
▽ **IPTC (IIM, legacy)**		
Copyright	:	🖉
▽ **IPTC Core**		
Creator	:	🖉

Figure 6-5: The Metadata panel in Bridge.

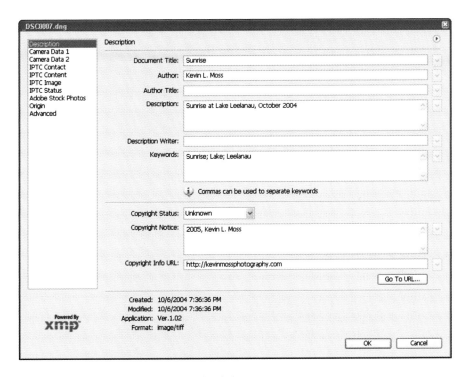

DSC0007.dng

Description

Document Title:	Sunrise
Author:	Kevin L. Moss
Author Title:	
Description:	Sunrise at Lake Leelanau, October 2004
Description Writer:	
Keywords:	Sunrise; Lake; Leelanau

ⓘ Commas can be used to separate keywords

Copyright Status:	Unknown
Copyright Notice:	2005, Kevin L. Moss
Copyright Info URL:	http://kevinmossphotography.com

Go To URL...

Created: 10/6/2004 7:36:36 PM
Modified: 10/6/2004 7:36:36 PM
Application: Ver.1.02
Format: image/tiff

Powered By
xmp

OK   Cancel

Figure 6-6: Entering data into the File Info window.

As you click through each page of the File Info window, adding or viewing data, you can always click OK to save your added information (or click Cancel to quit).

The different File Info metadata pages include these:

✔ **Description:** You can add general information about your image here.

✔ **Camera Data 1:** Displays information provided by your digital camera.

✔ **Camera Data 2:** Displays more information provided by your digital camera (some models are just pickier about details).

✔ **Categories:** You can enter information based on Associated Press categories.

✔ **History:** Displays Photoshop history information if the image was previously edited in Photoshop.

✔ **IPTC Information Pages:** You can enter information about the photographer and images per IPTC standards.

✔ **Adobe Stock Photos:** Provides information for images obtained through Adobe Stock Photos.

> ✔ **Origin:** Here you can enter additional information for images targeted to the news media.
>
> ✔ **Advanced:** Here you can view EXIF data about the image you're working with. The camera information includes zoom setting, shutter speed, aperture, white balance, and even the type of lens you used.

For the most part, the File Info and Metadata fields were built around IPTC standards, which cater to the international press community. (Hey, why not — they're one of the largest groups of professional photographers around the world!) Take advantage of the standards that IPTC has put forth and increase the manageability of your growing image library. You can visit the IPTC (International Press Telecommunications Council) site at www.iptc.org.

Applying Labels and Ratings

Organizing and searching a large number of digital photos in a detailed manner can be a daunting task. Thankfully, Bridge provides some simple methods of applying tags to images — which easily categorizes them for later viewing.

Make a habit of applying ratings or labels to your photos *when you first transfer the images to your computer.* View these new images with Bridge and apply your labels and ratings at the same time you apply any metadata information. You'll be thankful, in later months and years, that you took a little time to add this information. (Think of the savings on aspirin alone.)

Applying color labels

In previous versions of Photoshop, you could *flag* an image (toggle a special indicator on or off) to determine which images were keepers. Bridge now offers more advanced ways to organize and search images by applying color labels — which helps you develop a system of organizing images to reflect your priorities and choices with more options.

Figure 6-7 shows where to apply color labels to images in Bridge. For the example shown, I applied color labels to the images in the Bridge Content area (not hard — you just choose the Label menu and then select the color label for the image). Here I use green to mean "go" (that is, use the image and print it), red is a "no-go" (don't use the image), and yellow as a "maybe" (consider using this image later).

Applying color labels makes photos much easier to view and organize later. When you want to view only the images in a folder labeled with a particular color, you just click the Unfiltered button on the Bridge Option bar and then choose that color, as shown in Figure 6-8.

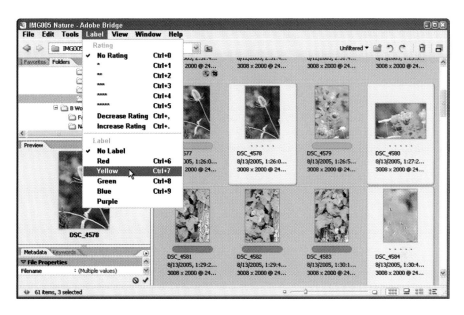

Figure 6-7: Applying color labels to images.

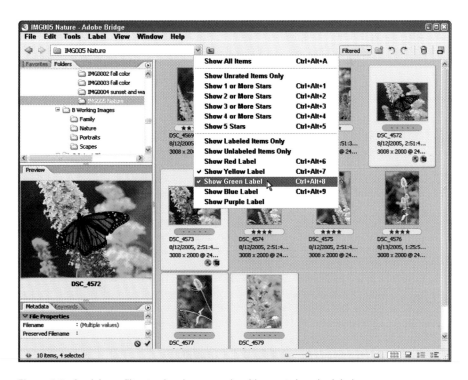

Figure 6-8: Applying a filter to view images only with a certain color label.

If you want, you can change the labels to descriptive names, such as "flowers, landscapes, keepers, possible, or print." Just choose Edit➪Preferences in Bridge, and choose the Labels category to change the default names.

Applying ratings to images

Another way to organize and view images is to apply a rating to your images. You can apply ratings to your images from one star to five stars, as shown in Figure 6-9. I apply high ratings — four or five stars — to images I intend to process, print, or post to the Web. Images that I rate at three stars or fewer may never get processed. (Feel free to come up with your own system of rating images.)

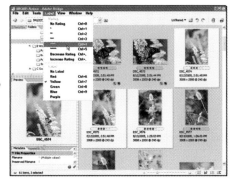

Figure 6-9: Applying ratings to selected images.

Two quick steps apply ratings to your images:

1. **Select images that you want to rate with the same rating.**

   Click the images while holding down the Ctrl key on a PC or the ⌘ key on a Mac.

2. **Choose Label➪Rating.**

   You can apply ratings from one star to five stars. You can also choose color labels.

Sorting and searching photos

Applying labels and ratings to your photos is a great method to sort and search for photos later. To sort photos in Bridge, choose View➪Sort. Select the sort method you want from the Sort menu. (I chose to sort by rating in Figure 6-10.)

You have various ways to sort images in a folder, using the sort methods available in the Sort menu — including by rating and by label.

Toggle your sorts by selecting and deselecting Ascending Order in the Sort menu. In Bridge, the default setting is Ascending; your highest-rated images appear at the bottom.

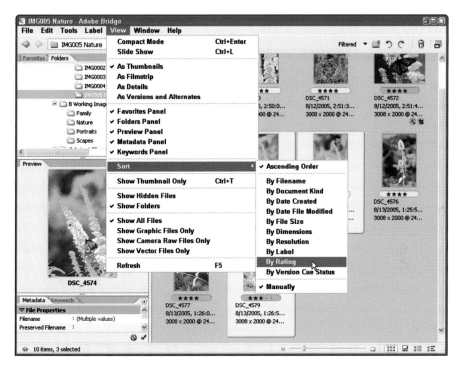

Figure 6-10: Sorting photos by rating.

Loading Photos to Camera Raw and Photoshop

Some digital photographers like to load their photos into Photoshop the old-fashioned way: by using the File⇨Open command in Photoshop. Many others, however, prefer the visual displays and search methods offered in Bridge. Bridge is so versatile, it can accommodate many personal preferences.

To load photos into Photoshop using Bridge, follow these steps:

1. **Use the Bridge Folders panel (or the Look In menu) to find the folder where the desired image files are stored.**

2. **View the images stored in the Content area of Bridge.**

   You can use the scrollbar to view the images that do not appear in the Content area.

3. Double-click the image you want to load in Photoshop or click the file, and then press Ctrl+O (⌘+O on a Mac).

The image loads into a Photoshop image window. If you haven't already started Photoshop, it starts automatically and displays the selected image, ready to edit.

There is no steadfast rule for how to browse and open images in Photoshop. It's totally up to personal preference. Play around with Bridge to find out the best way for you to browse and open images. Figure 6-11 shows another way of opening images in Bridge, which is to right-click the image thumbnail in Bridge and choose Open in Camera Raw.

Figure 6-11: Opening images in Bridge.

Part III
Working with Raw Images

The 5th Wave   By Rich Tennant

"I appreciate that your computer has 256 colors. I just don't think they all had to be used in one book report."

In this part . . .

When I first switched from film to shooting digital, I was amazed at the quality of the photos I was getting from those older 3- and 5-megapixel sensors. The JPEGs I produced are still staples in my portfolio today. When I graduated to more advanced digital cameras and started shooting photos in raw format, however, I felt that my photographic capabilities had suddenly shot through the roof!

I played and experimented with other raw converters when I started, but always used Camera Raw for my more serious work. Why bother mastering another software program when I could just use Camera Raw? After all, I was perfectly happy with the results I was getting from converting my raw images with Camera Raw.

I've reached the point where I can open a raw file in Camera Raw, make color and tonal adjustments, and then open the image in Photoshop to make any necessary edits and apply finishing touches. Often the color and tonal values I worked up in Camera Raw are right on — and those adjustments are a lot quicker to make than the same adjustments in Photoshop. After you get some practice with the steps in this part's chapters, I suspect you'll come to the same conclusion!

Understanding Exposure and Color

As you can probably tell by now, I'm a huge fan of Camera Raw and Photoshop. It rates right up there with football, big lenses, ice cream, and good science fiction on TV. (Live long and prosper!) Though you can do some amazing things with Camera Raw and Photoshop, the key to really getting the most out of your images is — first — to understand exposure, color, and tonality. After you get those down, the rest becomes easier, and a lot more fun!

The purpose of this chapter isn't to dazzle you with technical terms and the scientific background of image sensors, light, and color. Instead, I explain the different color adjustments and then get into what the tools are for adjusting tonality. Understanding both color and tonality sorts out what tasks need to be done when processing images in Camera Raw, and fine-tuning your images in Photoshop.

Getting to Know Color and Tonality

Camera Raw gives you control of a lot of important adjustments in your photos, but before you dive into your raw images, I explain what you need to look for and evaluate in your images before you start making adjustments to white balance, tint, exposure, shadows, brightness, contrast, and saturation. Collectively, those adjustments are referred to as *overall adjustments*. (Gotta love those fancy technical terms.)

It's important to understand each of these areas so you'll know what to do to an image to "make it look right" when you print it or prepare it for viewing. If you're into photos of people, you need to pay special attention to the *skin tones* of the people you're photographing. Whether your subjects are Asian, Caucasian, or even Martian, the last thing you want is to process a photo that makes your subjects' skin look too yellow or red (or too green or blue, depending on where their ancestors lived on this planet, or another). You want to make sure the "skin tone," the right amount of color in the skin, looks the way it's supposed to, as in the portrait in Figure 7-1.

Figure 7-1: It's important to properly evaluate skin tones for portraits.

Color is everything

Often you'll see the terms *color* and *tone* used in the same sentence to describe color — which isn't exactly accurate. *Color* adjustments refer to making changes to *a particular color in the entire image*. Changing white balance, adjusting tint, and increasing color saturation are examples of changing color in an image. (When you adjust *tone*, you're changing *the way those colors are distributed* across different parts of the image. See the next section, "Understanding tone," for more details.)

When you first open a raw image in Camera Raw, chances are you'll need to adjust color in the image. Your digital camera collects color information for each pixel, but doesn't process the image to adjust the color to any known standard. It's up to you to adjust the amount of color in your image. The controls you use in Camera Raw to change and adjust color include

- ✓ **White Balance:** White balance is first adjusted in your digital camera so you can properly set up your camera for the type of lighting conditions you're shooting in.

  The white balance setting in your digital camera (or the equivalent adjustment in Camera Raw) is actually a combination of *color temperature* and *tint.* In Camera Raw, you can actually set those two adjustments separately. Digital cameras today usually do a great job when you set them to do the white balance setting automatically; the camera adjusts both the color temperature and tint for the image. For instance, a room illuminated with fluorescent lighting gives a particular look to the color of the images shot there — and it's different from what you'd get in the same room illuminated with ambient lighting. Same goes for the great outdoors: Your digital camera automatically adjusts color temperature and tint differently for direct sunlight, shade, or cloudy conditions.

✔ **Temperature:** Temperature is the precise measurement of light using the Kelvin scale (that's *Kel*vin, not Kevin!). For instance, daylight is measured at 5500° and fluorescent light is measured at 3800°. An outdoor photo taken with a "fluorescent" color temperature of 3800° will have a blue cast to it, as shown in Figure 7-2. If your image appears blue in Camera Raw, you can adjust the color temperature to compensate for the blue cast.

Outdoor setting at 5500°   Flourescent setting at 3800°

Figure 7-2: An outdoor photo with different color temperature settings.

✔ **Tint:** Tint is another control you can use to tweak the look of a color in an image. The Camera Raw tint adjustment allows you to fine-tune white balance by increasing or decreasing the amount of green or magenta.

✔ **Saturation:** Saturation is simply the degree of intensity applied to a color in an image. Increasing or decreasing overall color (equal red, blue, and green channels) in an image is accomplished by using the Saturation slider in Camera Raw. In Photoshop, you can increase the Red, Green, or Blue (RGB) colors in the image individually, or by using the combined RGB adjustment.

In addition to the Saturation control in Camera Raw, the Calibration tab (shown in detail in Chapters 8 and 9) lets you fine-tune Red, Green, and Blue hues *and saturation* — as well as adjust for any color cast in the shadows.

Understanding tone

After you've adjusted the white balance, tint, and saturation of your image's colors in Camera Raw, you can make tonal adjustments to distribute those colors across different parts of the image. You're not changing any color: you're changing the *way it appears* in the light tone, dark tone, and *midtone* (in-between) areas of the image, as shown in Figure 7-3.

Figure 7-3: Light, dark, and midtone areas of an image.

Think of tone as not changing color within an image, but how you distribute color across it. When you adjust exposure, shadows, brightness, contrast, and curves in Camera Raw, you are making *tonal* changes to the image.

Tonal adjustments to your images are made by using these controls in Camera Raw and Photoshop:

- **Exposure:** Worth the price of Photoshop CS2 all by itself, the Camera Raw Exposure control allows you to increase or decrease the actual exposure of an image. Getting a good exposure with your digital camera is important, but it's nice to be able to increase or decrease the amount of exposure digitally. That capability helps prevent processing an image that's overexposed (too dark) or underexposed (too light). Check out the examples in Figure 7-4 to see what I mean.

| Underexposed | Overexposed | Just right |

Figure 7-4: Underexposed, overexposed, and just right!

A new feature in CS2 is the Exposure adjustment. It's a nice addition to Photoshop, similar to a feature used in Camera Raw for non-raw images such as JPEGs or TIFFs. The drawback to using the Photoshop Exposure adjustment is that it's considered destructive; you're potentially throwing away pixels.

If you're shooting raw, always adjust exposure using Camera Raw; reserve the Photoshop Exposure adjustment for other file formats.

- ✏ **Shadows:** Camera Raw gives us the ability to increase or decrease areas of the image that are *mapped* (assigned as black). Increasing Shadows in Camera Raw has a benefit of making the image appear as if it has more contrast. I recommend that you increase Shadows only until *clipping* (loss of detail) occurs. I explain more about the Shadows adjustment and clipping in Chapter 9.

- ✏ **Brightness:** In Photoshop, brightness is combined with the Brightness/Contrast adjustment. In Camera Raw, the Brightness adjustment is a standalone control.

- ✏ **Contrast:** The Contrast control allows you to increase or decrease contrast in the midtones of the image; you can make your light areas lighter and your dark areas darker. Another advantage to shooting raw is that you can adjust contrast in Camera Raw without throwing away any image data. Like the other color and tonal controls in Camera Raw, the Contrast control changes your images non-destructively.

As with the Shadows adjustment, be sure you monitor any clipping that may occur when you increase or decrease the contrast in an image.

Evaluating Color and Tonality

When you've got a good handle on what color and tonality means as applied to Camera Raw and Photoshop, the next skill to master is evaluating images. Thankfully, Camera Raw and Photoshop offer the photographer such tools as histograms (which I get to in Chapter 8), and clipping warnings to help you evaluate color and tonality. But don't forget the best judge of all — yourself!

Yes, it's true that Camera Raw and Photoshop enable you to make precise overall adjustments, but sometimes the dominant factor in adjusting color and tone must be the artistic taste of the photographer. Camera Raw and Photoshop are artistic tools, after all; the completed image should reflect your personal interpretation. Sometimes that means adding a touch more color, saturation, or contrast to an image to get a specific effect.

Personally, I tend to enhance shadows and color saturation a tad more than the norm in some of my nature and abstract images (such as the one shown in Figure 7-5). Hey, I like color! For my portraits, skin tones are far less forgiving; I tend to make my overall adjustments exactly as the portrait dictates — to match the photo I viewed through the lens of my digital camera. Skin tones need to be exact, or the portrait just won't look right.

Figure 7-5: Color and tonality can be a matter of the photographer's personal vision of the image.

Doing the evaluation

Before beginning any adjustments in Camera Raw or Photoshop, take these steps to evaluate your image:

1. **Open the image in Camera Raw.**

   To do that, find the thumbnail in Bridge of the image you want to evaluate, and click it. Then you can choose File⇨Open In Camera Raw or press Ctrl+R (⌘+R on a Mac).

2. **View the image in the Camera Raw window and evaluate white balance.**

   You'll get more proficient at judging white balance of an image with practice. Taking this step for every image you process will get you there quicker. Look for a portion of the image that is supposed to be white. Does that area have a blue or orange/yellow tint to it? If so, your white balance needs to be adjusted.

Color temperature will become more blue when decreased and more orange/yellow in cast when increased. If your image has a blue color cast, increase the color temperature in Camera Raw. If the image appears too yellow in cast, decrease the color temperature.

3. Evaluate the image for correct exposure.

Judging whether an image looks too dark or too light seems an easy way to judge exposure. For some photographs, I'm sure that's fine — but Camera Raw offers features that *really* let you fine-tune exposure. I show you those foolproof techniques in Chapter 9.

4. Evaluate shadows.

As explained earlier in this chapter, evaluating shadows is judging whether the midtones of the image should be lighter or darker. Camera Raw lets you adjust this to your personal taste, but it also shows you when your adjustment is causing clipping (loss of detail) in the shadow areas of your image.

5. Evaluate Brightness.

Though I often adjust exposure just up to where clipping is introduced, I may want to make an image lighter or darker, depending on what I want to convey. I use the Camera Raw Brightness control to increase or decrease brightness to my taste.

6. Evaluate Contrast.

For my scenic photos, whether they be cityscapes or landscapes, I tend to lean more toward higher contrast. For portraits, I'll only increase contrast if there is not enough contrast in the image, making the skin tones unrealistic.

7. Determine how much color you want to add or subtract to the image.

The last evaluation I make to an image is saturation. With raw images, often the way to reveal the color in the image as you had envisioned while taking the photo is to move the Saturation slider higher.

The breakfast-by-the-lake example

I have a great shooting arrangement with Bambi, one of my favorite models. I show up every Saturday morning at 7:30 a.m. at the park with my digital camera, tripod, and backpack, and hike over to the part of the lake where she has breakfast. On cue, she then hides behind some trees and I take photos of her. Strictly professional!

Figure 7-6 shows an original image of Bambi, and the same image adjusted for color and tonality in Camera Raw. I first evaluated the white balance of the image, and decided to increase the temperature slightly to add a little "warmth" (a little more orange and yellow). I then actually decreased exposure, not to correct the image, but to make it slightly darker. I decided to increase shadows a bit (remember, I like my dark areas to be a little darker than normal sometimes), and then increased the saturation to bring out some color.

Original   Evaluated and adjusted

Figure 7-6: Original image, and the same image after evaluating and making adjustments.

Except for an out-of-focus branch or two, I liked the way Bambi turned out! (Of course, I can always get rid of some of the branches covering her face with the nifty Healing Brush tool, which I further explain in Chapter 11.) I'm going to bring her a print next Saturday. (I hope she doesn't think I'm bringing her breakfast.)

It's easy to go bonkers with color and tonal adjustments in both Camera Raw and Photoshop. In Figure 7-5, for example, the background color is slightly exaggerated, but that's an effect I wanted for that particular photo. For other photos, I may not exaggerate saturation or contrast at all, it depends on how I want my image to be viewed. Be careful you don't make adjustments so extreme that your photos start to appear unrealistic — unless, of course, some of you Surrealists *want* them to be like that!

8

Getting Acquainted with Camera Raw

*I*f you shoot raw images (or are planning on doing so in the near future), you're going to find Camera Raw as your best friend. As a photographer, I've used Camera Raw exclusively to make my color and tonal adjustments since I switched to the raw format some time ago.

The more proficient you become at making adjustments in Camera Raw, the less you'll depend on Photoshop to make those corrections. You'll reach that level of "enlightenment" the moment you discover that after getting a raw image into Photoshop, you don't need to adjust any levels, curves, brightness, contrast, or saturation. All of your Camera Raw adjustments were right on . . . You have arrived!

Looking at Camera Raw

When you first load Camera Raw by opening a raw image, the first thing you'll notice is a large image preview (unobstructed by toolbars and palettes). Controls for adjusting images surround the image preview on the top, bottom, and right, as shown in Figure 8-1.

Figure 8-1: The Camera Raw tools and controls.

On top of the image preview is the Camera Raw Tool palette and Option bar. The Tool palette contains controls for zooming, moving, white balance, color sampling, cropping, straightening, and rotating. To the bottom of the image, you'll find workflow settings that let you set the color space to work in, image size, and bit depth. At the right of the image are the histogram, settings, Camera Raw menus, and Camera Raw control tabs.

Working with the Toolbar Controls

The Camera Raw toolbar, shown in Figure 8-2, consists of the basic tools needed to edit an image. Here's a rundown:

Zoom tool
White Balance tool
Crop tool   Rotate tool
Show shadow clippings
Show highlight clippings

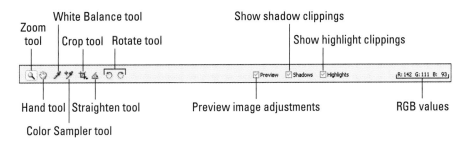

Hand tool | Straighten tool
Color Sampler tool
Preview image adjustments
RGB values

Figure 8-2: Tool palette and Option bar in Camera Raw.

▬ **Zoom tool (press Z):** Use this tool to enlarge your view of the image shown in the Image Preview.

▬ **Hand tool (press H):** If you zoom in to the image, you can move the image around by dragging it with the Hand tool. (Wouldn't it be nice to have one of these in real life when somebody nabs your parking spot?)

▬ **White Balance tool (press I):** Use this tool to select a neutral gray area of the image to use in improving the white balance.

▬ **Color Sampler tool (press S):** Use this one to select pixels whose RGB values you want displayed on-screen.

▬ **Crop tool (press C):** You can use this new tool to crop images in Camera Raw instead of waiting until the image is loaded into Photoshop.

▬ **Straighten tool (press A):** Cool tool alert! This is a great addition to Camera Raw — you can use it to straighten images without the hassle of straightening in Photoshop. Now making that horizon straight is easier than ever.

▬ **Rotate buttons (press L for left, R for right):** Rotate your image clockwise or counterclockwise with one click of the left or right Rotate buttons.

▬ **Preview check box:** Preview is a fun feature to use. If you want to compare what your image looks like with and without adjustments made in Camera Raw, you can toggle the image between those views by checking and unchecking the Preview check box.

▬ **Shadows check box:** I recommend this a few times in the next chapter, but I'll say it now: Make sure this check box is checked before you adjust images in Raw. When it's checked, Camera Raw shows you the *clipped* shadow areas of the image (pixels that contain no detail, due to under- or overexposure in that part of the image).

▬ **Highlights check box:** As with the Shadows check box, make sure this one is checked before you tweak an image in Raw; that way you can view clippings in the highlight areas of the image.

Reading the Histogram and RGB Values

The histogram and the RGB readout give you information about the color and exposure values of the image as it appears in the Camera Raw Image Preview. The RGB readout displays the Red, Green, and Blue color values when you point to a selection in the Image Preview with any of four tools (Zoom, Hand, White Balance, or Color Sampler). The histogram, as shown in Figure 8-3, shows the current exposure setting of the image.

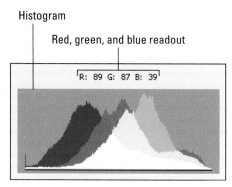

Histogram

Red, green, and blue readout

R: 89 G: 87 B: 39

Figure 8-3: The Camera Raw Histogram and RGB readout.

Reading the RGB values and viewing the histogram is cool, but what does it all mean to the photographer who's processing images in Camera Raw? In essence, they are both visual tools you can use to evaluate the adjustments you're making to the image.

The histogram shows you the current individual Red-, Green-, and Blue-channel histograms; you use it to evaluate exposure. White and colored spikes at either the left or right of the histogram indicate clipping. With that information, you can better judge where to adjust the tonal values of the image.

Image Settings

The Image Settings selection box (see Figure 8-4) lets you view different versions of the image as you make adjustments. Choosing Image Settings, for example, shows you the image as it was before you made adjustments. Choosing Camera Raw Defaults restores the default image settings in Camera Raw. And choosing Previous Conversion applies the Camera Raw settings from the *last* image you worked on in Camera Raw. The Custom selection shows how the image looks after applying the adjustments you've made.

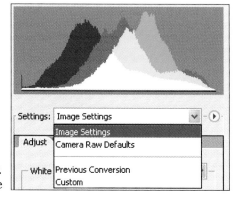

Settings: Image Settings

Image Settings
Adjust | Camera Raw Defaults
White | Previous Conversion
Custom

Figure 8-4: The Image Settings selection box in Camera Raw.

Camera Raw Menu

For some reason, they almost hid the Camera Raw menu! If you look hard enough, next to the Image Settings selection, there's that little triangle thingie button, that's the Camera Raw menu shown in Figure 8-5. The menu includes commands to load, save, or delete settings or subsets of settings.

It's an impressive list of alternatives for applying settings, including some really helpful timesaving commands to use on your raw images. I describe each Camera Raw menu setting in this list:

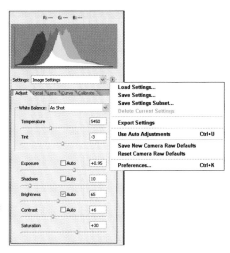

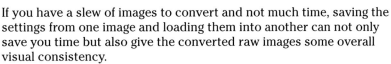

Figure 8-5: The Camera Raw menu.

✔ **Load Settings:** This command makes a lot more sense when you've reviewed the other menu options in this list. When you choose Load Settings, you can choose from saved Camera Raw settings you made in previous images.

If you have a slew of images to convert and not much time, saving the settings from one image and loading them into another can not only save you time but also give the converted raw images some overall visual consistency.

✔ **Save Settings:** This command saves the settings you've made to an image in Camera Raw with the intention of reusing those settings in other (similar) images. When you've finished making the Camera Raw adjustments, choose the Save Settings command and name the settings, or leave their default name (that of the image filename) in place.

✔ **Save Settings Subset:** If you don't want to save all of an image's settings, you can save subsets of the adjustments you make in Camera Raw. You choose those adjustments in the Subset window (see Figure 8-6) when you choose Save Settings Subset.

✔ **Export Settings:** This is an especially useful command when you're copying images to a CD or sending a batch of images via e-mail to an agency (or to others to work on your images), and you want to retain the adjustments you've made in Camera Raw. The Export Settings command lets you create a sidecar XMP file that can be copied with the image so it can be loaded with the image later. Export Settings will create sidecar files only if none exists, as in the case of the raw file being in DNG format.

Figure 8-6: Using Save Settings Subset to save selected adjustments.

✔ **Use Auto Adjustments:** With the improvements in CS2 including a new Camera Raw, one of the nice additions is Auto Adjustments. By default, Camera Raw applies auto adjustments to an image when it's first loaded. Auto adjustments works pretty well; sometimes I don't even have to do any tweaking at all!

I suggest leaving Use Auto Adjustments turned on, but if you want, you can turn Auto Adjustments off by pressing Ctrl+U (⌘+U on a Mac), or toggling it on or off in the Camera Raw menu.

✔ **Save New Camera Raw Defaults:** Camera Raw bases its default settings on the model of digital camera that's producing your raw images. For each different digital camera that Camera Raw supports, it uses a specific set of adjustments tailored for each. When you open a raw file produced by a Canon EOS 350D, for example (or a Nikon N70s, or any other digital camera supported), Camera Raw applies the corresponding adjustments. If you want to use your own set of defaults, just make whatever adjustments you want in your new default set, and then choose Save New Camera Raw Defaults from the Camera Raw menu.

✔ **Reset Camera Raw Defaults:** Although you can save new Camera Raw default settings for your specific model of digital camera, you can always switch back to the original defaults by choosing Reset Camera Raw Defaults from the Camera Raw menu.

✔ **Preferences:** Thankfully, there aren't a lot of settings to change in the Camera Raw Preferences window (shown in Figure 8-7), but some of the changes you can make in Preferences are very important.

Preferences lets you specify where to save Camera Raw adjustments (to a sidecar file or a database) and apply sharpening adjustments made in Camera Raw (to the raw image or for preview only), as well as tweak the Camera Raw cache and choose how sidecar files are stored. Here's the list:

Figure 8-7: The Camera Raw Preferences window.

- **Save Image Settings In:** In this selection, you can indicate whether you want to save Camera Raw settings for images in the Camera Raw database or sidecar (XMP) files. The default setting is XMP, which allows you to copy raw settings along with files.

  Camera Raw doesn't make any physical changes to your raw images, it saves any adjustments you make to sidecar files (which can later be copied with the raw images). If you change Save Image Settings In so your changes are saved to the Camera Raw database, you can still view your changes but you can't copy those changes to other computers, CDs, or DVDs later on.

- **Apply Sharpening To:** This is actually the only change to preferences I make. I make sure that I set this preference to apply sharpening to preview images only. If you set sharpening to preview images only, you can preview in Camera Raw what the image will look like sharpened, but not apply sharpening before opening the image in Photoshop.

  Sharpening images is a workflow step best saved for last. To maximize the quality of a final image, do your sharpening after you've done your editing and re-sizing in Photoshop. (I cover sharpening in Chapter 12.)

- **Camera Raw Cache:** *Cache* is a term used to describe storage space (in this case, storage on your hard drive) where image data for recently viewed and adjusted images is stored for fast retrieval. The default cache is 1GB — and one gigabyte is sufficient for most image processing needs — but if you work with hundreds of raw files at one time, you may want to increase the Camera Raw Cache setting.

- **DNG File Handling:** Settings for ignoring XMP sidecar files and updating image previews can be turned on in this section by clicking on the respective selection boxes. If you're working with DNG files, there really isn't any advantage to ignoring previous XMP sidecar files, so I'd leave that defaulted to not selected. I also leave the Update Embedded JPEG Previews option unchecked, as I usually don't have a need to update raw file JPEG preview images (after all, they are just previews!).

Camera Raw Workflow Settings

At the lower-left corner of the Camera Raw window is a set of Workflow options (see Figure 8-8). Unlike other settings that are image-specific, you can change or retain the Workflow settings for all the images you've worked on in Camera Raw. These settings include the color space you want your images to be converted to when they're opened in Photoshop, as well as the bit depth of the files, the image size, and the resolution in which to open the image. Here's the lineup:

Figure 8-8: Camera Raw Workflow options.

- ✔ **Space:** Choose one of four color spaces to use when converting the image: Adobe RGB (1998), Colormatch RGB, ProPhoto RGB, or SRGB. I always leave this setting at Adobe RGB (1998), as most of my work is prepared for printing or press. If your photographs are being prepared exclusively for the Web, you may want to choose the sRGB option.

- ✔ **Depth:** Raw images are typically set to 16-bits per channel, which gives you 128 times the tonal range of 8-bit images. That's a lot more information (hence more detail) to work with in Photoshop. Because most of your images will be further adjusted in Photoshop, I recommend leaving this set to 16-bits per channel.

- ✔ **Size:** Camera Raw will set the size to the default resolution of your digital camera. If you know you're going to be producing large prints or smaller images for your image, you can set the resolution higher or lower, and let Camera Raw do the resampling (which is quicker than resizing the image later in Photoshop). This feature can come in handy when you have to process multiple images in Camera Raw. For individual images, some photographers save resizing for later, as a step in their output-preparation workflow.

- ✔ **Resolution:** If you have determined the final resolution you want for your image, you can make that change in the Resolution setting. (I usually prepare my images for printing, so I set the resolution to 360 pixels per inch.)

Camera Raw Controls

The Camera Raw control panels, also known as *tabs* (see Figure 8-9), are where most of your work will happen when you process images. Color, tone, detail, lens, curve, and calibration adjustments are available in each tab.

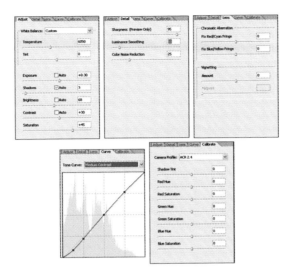

Figure 8-9: Camera Raw controls.

I show you the details of how to use them in Chapter 9; for now, here's a summary of what they do:

- **Adjust tab (Ctrl+Alt+1, ⌘+Option+1 on a Mac):** This tab contains all the controls that adjust color and tonal values in an image: White Balance, Temperature, Tint, Exposure, Shadows, Brightness, Contrast, and Saturation.

- **Detail tab (Ctrl+Alt+2, ⌘+Option+2 on a Mac):** This tab is home to the Sharpness, Luminance Smoothing, and Color Noise Reduction controls. Though I recommend that you use Camera Raw sharpening only for viewing images (save the real sharpening for later, in Photoshop), you can use this tab to reduce grayscale noise (with Luminance Smoothing) and turn down the color noise (with the Color Noise control) — a very welcome feature!

- **Lens tab (Ctrl+Alt+3, ⌘+Option+3 on a Mac):** The Lens Tab includes some advanced controls that let you make corrections to images that contain chromatic aberrations (also called *lens artifacts*) and *vignetting* (dark or light borders around an image).

Vignetting can actually become an artistic effect you can add to images, especially portraits. Sometimes I use the Vignetting control to actually *introduce* vignetting into an image.

✔ **Curve tab (Ctrl+Alt+4, ⌘+Option+4 on a Mac):** I find this control invaluable. The curve adjustment is a tool used to fine-tune the tonality of an image. You still need to make tonal adjustments in the Adjust tab, but the Curve tab is where you finish it off. Three preset curve adjustments are available: Linear (default), Medium Contrast, and Strong Contrast. You can also customize the curve by dragging different points on the graph.

Use the Curve tab to make your final brightness and contrast adjustments instead of using the Photoshop Brightness/Contrast control (which actually causes the image to lose detail in the form of valuable data).

✔ **Calibrate tab (Ctrl+Alt+5, ⌘+Option+5 on a Mac):** The controls in the Calibrate tab let you adjust the Camera Raw camera model (as recognized by the image you've loaded in Camera Raw) so you get the best shadow tint plus red, green, and blue hues and saturation.

Control Buttons

All these wonderful controls, preferences, and settings really won't help you unless you have a way of saving, opening, canceling (which you'll find you can do a lot of), and closing adjusted images — without having to open them in Photoshop. To the rescue come the Camera Raw control buttons, located to the lower right of the Camera Raw window, as shown in Figure 8-10.

Figure 8-10: Control buttons for Camera Raw.

Each control button has a specific function:

✔ **Save (Ctrl+Alt+S, ⌘+Option+S on a Mac):** This button saves the adjustments to the image while leaving the Camera Raw window open.

✔ **Open (Ctrl+O, ⌘+O on a Mac):** Use this one only when you want to open the image in Photoshop, because that's what it does — and then it closes the Camera Raw window.

✔ **Cancel (Esc):** Click this button when you want to exit from adjusting the opened image without saving any changes you've made.

✔ **Done (Enter):** This button saves the adjustments and returns you to Bridge without opening the converted image in Photoshop.

9

Processing Raw Images

*O*n to the raw workflow! In Chapter 8, I show you all the neat tools and controls Camera Raw has to offer. Here's where those tools go to work processing raw images. Developing and using a consistent workflow to process your raw images (while taking advantage of Bridge automation features) will help you become more efficient.

Camera Raw gives the photographer some serious tools for correcting color and tone. If you take the time to get some practice at using them properly, you'll find these corrections are actually easier to make in Camera Raw than in Photoshop. I've gotten to the point that many of the images I process in Camera Raw are pretty much ready for prime time when I open them in Photoshop. As you'll find, the better you get at making these adjustments in Camera Raw, the less you have to do later.

Using a Step-by-Step Raw Process

I've gone over workflows in Chapter 4, but here is where we really dive into the "raw" details of Camera Raw. As with all the processes I show you throughout this book, processing images in raw requires its own step-by-step progression of tasks:

1. **Evaluate your image.**

   Take a look at your image as opened in Camera Raw. Be sure to take advantage of the histogram, the shadows and highlights, and the clipping warnings.

2. **Correct the white balance.**

   White balance (the combination of temperature and tint) takes a little getting used to adjusting. The best way to become proficient is to experiment using the different white balance choices Camera Raw provides.

3. **Adjust exposure using the Exposure control.**

   It bears repeating: This control is extremely valuable. That's because it's hard to get dead-on exposures with your digital camera in some lighting conditions. The Exposure control lets you fine-tune the exposure of the image as you've envisioned it.

4. **Adjust shadows using the Shadows control.**

   Those dark areas of the image can use some tender loving adjustment once in a while — and the Shadows control helps you control clipping in those dark areas of an image.

5. **Adjust brightness using the Brightness control.**

   There are going to be images where you'll adjust the exposure exactly where you want it to minimize clipping in the highlights like the example shown in Figure 9-1. The Brightness control gives you the option of lightening up the image a bit without re-introducing those pesky "clips."

Figure 9-1: Clipped highlights show up in red.

About that technical term, "pesky clips" — it's a word I use to describe chunks of pixels that have no image definition, a condition known as *clipping*. ("Pesky" is a technical term for "colorful rude word we can't print here.")

6. **Adjust contrast using the Contrast control.**

   If the Camera Raw default contrast setting isn't "doing it" for you, use the Contrast control to increase or decrease the contrast in the image.

   In addition to the Contrast control, you can use the Curves control to increase or decrease contrast in an image.

7. **Adjust saturation using the Saturation control.**

   Increase the amount of color in your image using the Saturation control. As with other adjustments that apply color or tone in Camera Raw, increasing saturation helps bring out the color in your image.

8. **Apply the Curves adjustment.**

   Fine-tune the dark, light, and midtone areas of your image using the Curve control (located in the Curve tab).

9. **Reduce noise, using the Luminance Smoothing and Color Noise Reduction controls.**

   If your images were shot at a high ISO, a slower shutter speed, or both, you could wind up with a color-speckled effect called *noise*. The Detail tab contains two controls: Luminance Smoothing (which reduces gray-scale "grain") and the Color Noise Reduction control (which reduces those speckled artifacts found in some images).

10. **Correct lens aberrations and vignetting.**

    If you have noticeable lens shortcomings such as aberrations and vignetting, you can easily correct these by using the Aberrations and Vignetting controls in the Lens tab.

Incorporating DNG into your raw workflow

Adobe's new DNG format (described in Chapter 2) is an attempt to standardize a raw file format that stands a pretty decent chance of being compatible with computer software 10 or 15 years from now. Many photographers who shoot with cameras from multiple makers (hey, it happens!) want to use one standardized raw format for all their cameras — but also want some assurance that photo editors and raw converters will recognize their raw-format originals in the foreseeable future. DNG is the option that comes closest to filling the bill.

(continued)

(continued)

If you want to convert raw images to DNG format, the steps are simple:

1. **Open the DNG Converter from the shortcut on your desktop.**

2. **Select the folder that contains the original raw images you want to convert.**

3. **Select a folder destination to which you want to copy the converted DNG files.**

   You can also create a new folder by clicking the Make New Folder button.

4. **Click the Convert button.**

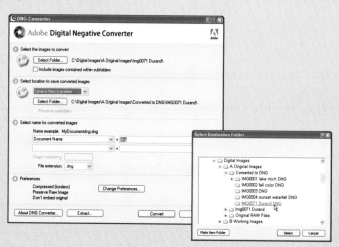

In my workflow, I always copy my original raw files first — to *two* quality DVD discs (one for on-site storage, one for off-site storage). These days I've also started converting my raw files to DNG, using Adobe's DNG converter. Those converted DNG files get backed up to separate DVDs as well (yes, two copies!). Incorporating DNG into your raw workflow would involve only three extra steps: converting your raw images to DNG, backing up the converted images to CD or DVD, and then opening these converted files in Camera Raw at the beginning of your raw workflow.

The jury is still out on whether DNG will become the favorite raw archiving format of the future, but just now it's the only option available that allows photographers and studios the ability to convert all disparate raw images to a common format for image archives.

Evaluating Images

The first step in processing raw images is to evaluate your image. Chances are, the first time you really view an image other than the thumbnails in Bridge is through the Camera Raw preview. When you first open an image in Camera Raw, Auto Adjustments are automatically applied. (That would explain why your raw images actually look pretty good!)

If you want to see what your image looks like *without* Auto Adjustments, press Ctrl+U (⌘+U on a Mac) to toggle Auto Adjustments on and off.

The image shown in Figure 9-2 represents an unprocessed image loaded in Camera Raw — with and without Auto Adjustments applied.

Figure 9-2: Raw image with (on left) and without Auto Adjustments.

For the most part, Auto Adjustments work pretty well to get me started for many of my images, and I view images with Auto Adjustments applied when evaluating for further adjustments. To evaluate images:

1. Open an image in Camera Raw.

2. Make sure Auto Adjustments are turned on.

You can either press Ctrl+U (⌘+U on a Mac) or click the Camera Raw menu and choose Use Auto Adjustments (see Figure 9-3).

Figure 9-3: Using Auto Adjustments.

3. Check the Preview, Shadows, and Highlights check boxes (which are located along the top of the window, above your image).

 To make sure your adjustments will be viewable later, make sure the Preview button shown in Figure 9-4 is checked. Also make sure the Shadows and Highlights check boxes are checked; you'll want to know if any clipping is present when you evaluate the image.

Figure 9-4: Checking the Preview, Shadows, and Highlights check boxes.

4. Evaluate white balance.

Look at the image and evaluate whether or not there is a blue or yellow cast to it. If so, you'll need to adjust the white balance of the image.

5. Evaluate exposure and shadows.

Check to see not only whether the image appears underexposed or overexposed, but also whether there's clipping in the shadow or highlight areas. This is where adjustments can get tricky. You'll want to use a combination of the Exposure and Brightness controls to adjust your image to gain the correct exposure and minimize clipping (as in the shadow area shown in Figure 9-5).

 When evaluating an image, enlarge the Image Preview so you can check more closely for clipping. Use the Zoom tool to enlarge the image from 100 to 200 percent, and then check the shadow and highlight areas.

Figure 9-5: Clipping in the shadow areas of an image.

6. **Evaluate brightness and contrast.**

   Almost all raw images will have a need to have the contrast increased. Auto Adjustments will make these adjustments to an optimum setting.

7. **Evaluate saturation.**

   Auto Adjustments don't affect saturation; when it comes to judging how much color you'd like to introduce into the image with the Saturation control, you're on your own. Often you can saturate to taste (so to speak), but be careful; oversaturation "blows out" parts of your image with too much color intensity. Pay special attention to the red and yellow areas; these colors are often the first to become oversaturated.

8. **Check for sharpness and noise.**

   When you're working with raw images, it's easy to overlook the controls that aren't in the other control tabs. Same goes for evaluating your image:

   a. Click the Details tab.

   b. Slide the Sharpness control slider all the way to the left.

   c. Enlarge the image in the Image Preview by clicking the Zoom tool, or by pressing Ctrl++ (that's the plus-sign key on your keyboard). You press ⌘++ on a Mac.

   d. View your image enlarged and check it for sharpness and image noise.

   I often view an image in Bridge, but until I open it in Camera Raw and zoom in, I won't know whether the image is sharp enough for me to even want to proceed!

Adjusting the Image with the Adjust Tab

Finally we're ready to edit some images in Camera Raw! I start by taking care of the major business first — making color and tonal corrections (including curves) to my image in the Adjust tab (Ctrl+Alt+1, or ⌘+Option+1 on a Mac).

When you first open an image in Camera Raw, the default tab shown is the Adjust tab shown in Figure 9-6. The Adjust tab is where you'll make all of your color and tonal adjustments that were described in Chapter 7, white balance (or color and tint), exposure, shadows, brightness, contrast, and saturation. I take you through each of these in order.

Figure 9-6: The Adjust tab with Auto Adjustments applied.

Adjusting white balance

White balance, temperature, and tint all relate to each other. White balance is actually a combination of color temperature and tint; in Camera Raw, you can set it quickly by choosing any of the predefined temperature-and-tint settings.

Setting the white balance can be accomplished in two ways, choosing one of the settings in the White Balance selection, or using the Temperature and Tint controls. If you choose one of the preset White Balance selections, you'll notice that doing so adjusts the temperature and tint for you, as shown in Figure 9-7.

Each White Balance selection will dynamically change the Temperature and Tint controls, displaying color temperature in degrees Kelvin.

On most digital cameras, you can set the white balance manually (and quickly) by choosing preset White Balance selections — but if you happen to choose one that doesn't produce an image with correct temperature and tint, now's your chance to make it right! The Camera Raw White Balance, Temperature, and Tint controls give the photographer the power to improve these values in images that didn't quite get photographed correctly.

As shot, temperature 4950°, tint -3

Auto, temperature 7500°, tint +1

Daylight, temperature 5500°, tint +10

Cloudy, temperature 6500°, tint +10

Shade, temperature 7500°, tint +10

Tungsten, temperature 2850°, tint 0

Fluorescent, temperature 3800°, tint +21

Flash, temperature 5500°, tint 0

Figure 9-7: The Adjust tab with Auto Adjustments applied.

Here's how to change the white balance of an image:

1. **Click the White Balance selection (see Figure 9-8).**

   Choose one of the predefined White Balance selections that best represent lighting conditions for the image when you photographed it.

Figure 9-8: Selecting from pre-defined White Balance selections.

2. **Fine-tune temperature.**

   If the White Balance setting still doesn't give you the adjustment needed
   to eliminate any blue or yellow cast, move the Temperature slider to the
   right to remove any blue cast or to the left to remove any yellow cast to
   the image.

3. **Fine-tune tint.**

   You probably won't need to adjust tint in many of your images, but if
   you see a visible green or magenta cast to your image, move the Tint
   slider to the right (to reduce green and increase magenta) or to the left
   (to reduce magenta).

Correcting indecent exposure

(Well, sometimes that happens when you shoot raw, right?) I think the Exposure
control in Camera Raw is worth the price of Photoshop itself! Okay, serious

photographers always strive to achieve the best exposures possible for their images, but difficult lighting conditions can sometimes throw a digital camera's exposure off by a few f-stops.

Figure 9-9 shows an example of difficult lighting conditions: backlighting. I was taking a photo of this troublemaker (he always gets into the bird feeders in the garden), but the sun was coming in behind the subject, resulting in underexposure. Backlit conditions are great for silhouettes, but not when you want to capture detail of the main subject, as in my case here, Rocky the squirrel. The Camera Raw Exposure control was the very thing I needed to expose the main subject of the image correctly.

Underexposed original image   Exposure corrected in
                                     Camera Raw

Figure 9-9: Rocky the "bird-feed-stealing-backlit-underexposed" squirrel.

To show you how to adjust exposure using the Camera Raw Exposure control, I'm switching topics from "pesky bird-feed-stealing squirrels of the Midwest" to "photos taken in London." The Camera Raw Exposure control lets you increase or decrease exposure of an image that's under- or overexposed. Unless you're already an old hand, evaluating the exposure you get from your digital camera can be tricky at first — but with some practice, you'll be comfortable in no time. Figure 9-10 shows the photo after the White Balance Daylight setting was selected (in the previous step), but with the Auto setting turned off in the Exposure setting so you can see the original exposure.

Figure 9-10: Image with the original exposure shown.

It's clear that the image is too dark — a common type of underexposure when a photo is taken in bright light and the digital camera meters its exposure from the bright sky. Fear not: The Camera Raw Exposure control can get that exposure to where you want it. Here's how:

1. **Click the Auto button.**

   Make sure Auto Exposure is turned on, and re-evaluate your image exposure with the Auto Exposure adjustment applied by Camera Raw. The Auto adjustment for Exposure will approach where you want the image to be corrected. For the image shown in Figure 9-11, the Auto adjustment adds +1.35 (about one-and-a-third f-stops) to the exposure of the image.

2. **Increase or decrease exposure to avoid clipping.**

   Moving the Exposure control slider to the right increases exposure; moving the slider to the left decreases exposure.

Figure 9-11: Camera Raw Auto set for the Exposure control.

REMEMBER

Make sure the Shadows and Highlights check boxes are checked so you can view any clipping that might occur as you adjust your images in Camera Raw. Clipping in the highlighted areas of the image will show as red; clipping in the shadow areas will show as blue. (Figure 9-12 shows an example of clipping in highlight areas of the sky, a result of overexposure.) When you start to see clipped areas in an image, you'll need to move the sliders back until no clipping occurs.

Figure 9-12: Clipped areas in an image where too much exposure is added.

TIP

You can also hold down the Alt key (Option on a Mac) while moving the slider to check for clipping. Holding down the Alt/Option key turns the image black and displays clipped pixels as they appear when you move the Exposure control slider. See Figure 9-13.

REMEMBER

Avoidance of clipping isn't the only goal of adjusting exposure. First you want to adjust till you get the best exposure for the image. You can minimize clipping with other controls (such as Shadows, Brightness, and the Contrast), but don't sacrifice the overall exposure of an image just to kill off a few clipped pixels.

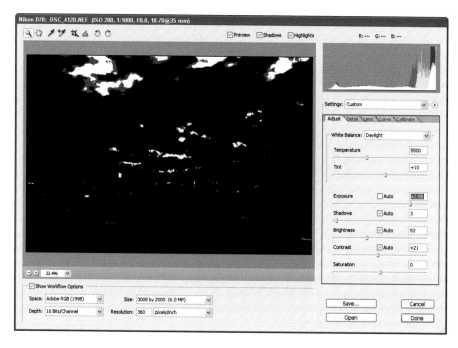

Figure 9-13: Checking exposure while pressing the Alt (Option) key.

Using the histogram

Histograms can be very useful when evaluating images, but are an often-overlooked or confusing tool used in Photoshop, Camera Raw, or even on your digital camera. The reason histograms are confusing and overlooked? Because nobody ever explains how to use them! When I first started using digital cameras, my owner manuals always showed how to *view* the histogram, but not how to *read* it. As an avid reader, I also haven't seen a lot written about reading histograms or using them to correct images either.

For the most part, a *histogram* is a chart that shows you the distribution of pixels from the dark areas (indicated on the left side) to the light (on the right side). While you're shooting photos out in the field, your digital camera shows you a histogram on its LCD to indicate the exposure of an image. When you're evaluating and adjusting images in Camera Raw, the histogram shows you how red, green, and blue pixels are distributed in the current image, using colored channels to represent red, green, and blue portions of the chart. You'll also see colors such as cyan, yellow, and magenta, too — but those are specific combinations of red, green, and blue.

Figure 9-14 shows three histograms: one without clipping, one with clipping in the image's shadow areas (black end of the histogram), and one with clipping in the highlight areas (white end of the histogram).

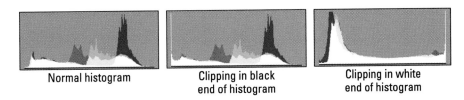

| Normal histogram | Clipping in black end of histogram | Clipping in white end of histogram |

Figure 9-14: Reading the Camera Raw histogram.

One really useful feature of the Camera Raw histogram is its indication of clipping. Spikes at the left end of the chart mean there is some clipping in the dark areas of the image; spikes at the right end indicate clipping in the light areas. You'll see the histogram change as you adjust color and tone.

Lurking in the shadows

With white balance and exposure adjusted, the next step is adjusting the image for the shadow tonal values. The Shadows control is located just under the Exposure control, which is a pretty clear hint about what to do next: Move the Shadows slider to the right (to darken the shadow areas of the image) or left (to lighten up the shadow areas).

Figure 9-15 shows the image with the shadow adjustment at a value of 9. That value may be a little too high; clipping will be highlighted in blue as it's introduced in the dark areas of the image. To reduce clipping, move the Shadows slider to the left until the blue highlight areas are minimized.

A couple of keyboard techniques come in handy here:

✔ Pressing Alt (Option key on the Mac) while dragging the Exposure slider shows you the areas of the image affected by clipping.

✔ Holding down the Alt key (Option key on the Mac) while clicking and dragging the Shadows slider will turn the Image Preview white — while showing the shadow areas of the image where clipping is occurring. Figure 9-16 shows the shadows clipping display.

Figure 9-15: Here blue highlighting shows clipping while adjusting shadows.

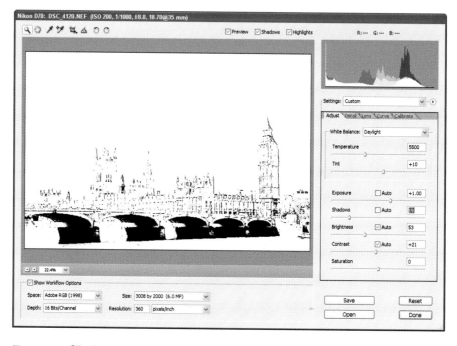

Figure 9-16: Clipping shown while adjusting Shadows.

The trick to adjusting Shadows is to attempt to achieve a "true black" in your image while minimizing any clipping in the shadow areas. Depending on the image and exposure, you may have only limited latitude for your adjustments. If you want an appearance of increased contrast in your image, you can always rely on the Contrast control or the Curves control to introduce more contrast. Use the Shadows slider to adjust the dark areas of your image to your preference, while minimizing clipping.

Adjusting brightness

The Brightness control can be mistaken for an exposure control; actually, all it adjusts is how bright the colors (in particular, the midtone values) are in your image. Moving the Brightness slider to the right lightens the midtones; moving it leftward darkens the midtone areas.

Figure 9-17 shows the Brightness adjusted to a value of 43. The Auto Adjustment for this image actually set the Brightness value at 53, but because I like my skies a little dark (especially blue skies!), I turned the Brightness slider down to the left to give me that darker sky without sacrificing too much highlight in the buildings.

Figure 9-17: Adjusting brightness.

Increasing and decreasing contrast

Located just below the Brightness control, the Contrast control increases the dark and light areas of your image when you move its slider to the right. Moving the slider to the left decreases contrast in the dark and light areas of the image.

I often use the Contrast and Brightness controls as tools to fine-tune the appearance of an image without affecting the overall exposure and shadows.

For the image shown in Figure 9-18, the Auto setting was set to 21, but I wanted to increase the contrast to darken the blue sky and lighten up the clouds a bit. A value of 31 gave me the effect I wanted without introducing clipping — and also without sacrificing detail in other areas of the image.

Figure 9-18: Adjusting contrast.

Adding color with the Saturation control

The Saturation control simply adds color to the image. That's possible because raw images don't actually contain visible color; instead they store color *information* (RGB values) for each pixel — which Camera Raw interpolates. The result may not match what you saw (or wanted to see) when you shot the image; when you view a raw image in Camera Raw, color almost always needs to be increased. You can do that by using the Saturation control to bring out the color values stored for every pixel in the image.

There isn't an Auto check box for the Saturation control; adding color is totally up to you. For most of my photos, a saturation setting of 20 to 30 usually gives me the amount of color I want in my photos. Experiment with the Saturation control to get closer to the results you want in your photos. Figure 9-19 shows the photo I've been working on with the Saturation control set to a value of 30.

Increasing saturation can affect the overall white balance of an image. When adjusting saturation, re-evaluate the color of the image and don't be afraid to tweak the white balance again using the Temperature control. After adding color to the image using the Saturation control, I went back to the Temperature slider and changed the setting from 5500 to 5350 to reduce the "warmth" in the image (which became exaggerated when I increased the saturation).

Figure 9-19: Increasing color saturation.

It's All in the Details

The controls in the Detail tab (Ctrl+Alt+2, ⌘+Option+2 on a Mac) contain a few little goodies that could easily be overlooked. Global adjustments include the Sharpness control, Luminance Smoothing, and the Color Noise Reduction control.

I find the Luminance Smoothing and Color Noise Reduction controls extremely valuable for cleaning up my images before getting them into Photoshop.

Figure 9-20 shows the Detail tab — and yes, a new raw image! To illustrate the controls in the Detail tab, I needed an image that needed a little help, so I decided to come back home from across the pond, back to the beloved Midwest. I chose this difficult image because it's hard to illustrate luminance and color noise in an image — this sunset was shot at a higher ISO of 400, so I was sure I could muster up some noise in the sky portions. (It's an Author's Prerogative.)

Figure 9-20: The Detail tab, ready to "improve" a sunset.

Sharpening things up

The Sharpness control lets you apply sharpening to the preview image, the converted image, or both. My recommendation is to apply sharpening *only* to the preview, just to check for the sharpness of the image. Actual sharpening should be applied to the actual image *only after* adjustments, edits, and sizing is made to the image in Photoshop.

The quality you get when you sharpen an image depends on its final size. If you sharpen an image *before* you resize it, you could do more damage than good, winding up with an extremely oversharpened appearance in the final output version. If you use the Sharpness control in Camera Raw, use it only temporarily — to add sharpness to *preview* images.

Here's how to set Camera Raw's Sharpness control to sharpen preview images only:

1. **Open Camera Raw Preferences.**

   Press Ctrl+K (⌘+K on a Mac) or click the Camera Raw Menu button and select Preferences.

2. **Set the Apply sharpening to selection to "preview only."**

   In the Camera Raw Preferences window (shown in Figure 9-21), choose Preview Images Only from the Apply Sharpening To drop-down list. When you make this selection, Camera Raw applies sharpening to preview images only.

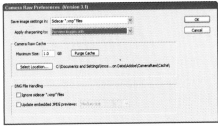

Figure 9-21: Applying sharpening to preview images only.

Getting smooth with Luminance Smoothing

I don't know about you, but I think the Luminance Smoothing control wins the Photoshop "Cool Name" award for adjustments. *Luminance* is an interesting word to begin with, but when you combine it with *smoothing,* you sound impressively technical and artistic to your friends. What it does is even better. Luminance smoothing reduces one of the two types of noise that can appear in an image: noise contained in the grayscale areas.

All digital camera sensors produce some sort of noise. It's not noise like someone yelling at you to take out the garbage, but *electrical noise:* graininess caused by an electrical field affecting the image sensor while it's collecting light. In most photos, you wouldn't even notice the noise, but for those taken at high ISO settings (400 to 1600) or long exposures, you can see the graininess when you zoom in on your image at 100 or 200 percent (as in the area shown in Figure 9-22). Visible noise. What a concept! And you won't even see noise in your viewfinder; it sneaks up on you later, like the boogie man.

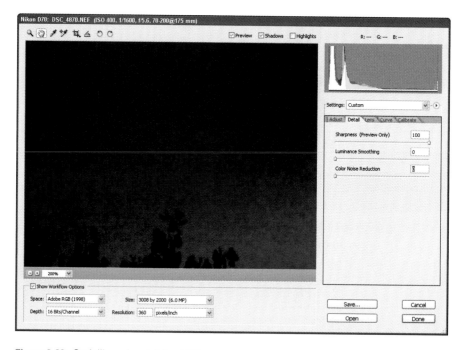

Figure 9-22: Grainlike noise visible at 200-percent zoom.

The Luminance Smoothing control reduces that grainy-looking noise lurking in the shadow parts of an image. Here's how to use it for that purpose:

1. **Zoom in 100 to 200 percent by using the Zoom tool or by pressing Ctrl+ (⌘+ on a Mac).**

2. **Use the Hand tool to move the Image Preview around until you can see a good sample of luminance noise that would usually be found in the dark areas of the image.**

3. **Move the Luminance Smoothing slider to the right to reduce luminance noise (as in Figure 9-23).**

   For this image, I moved the Luminance Smoothing slider rightward to a setting of 30, which reduced image noise to an acceptable level.

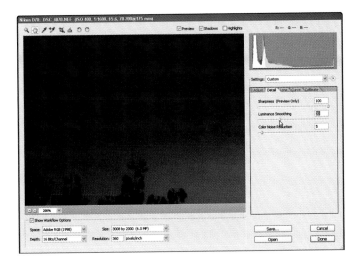

Figure 9-23: Reducing luminance noise.

Reducing color noise

Color noise visible in an image appears like little colored speckles in the shadow or sky areas of certain images.

If you're having a tough time figuring out the difference between color noise and luminance noise, experiment a little. Enlarge the image preview to 100 to 200 percent, and be sure to set both the Luminance Smoothing and Color Noise Reduction sliders to 0. Move the Luminance Smoothing slider to the right until you see the grainy-looking noise start to go away. If there is color noise in the image, you can still see it as those pesky *colored speckly thingies* (a seldom used technical term for *color noise*).

To reduce color noise, you don't have to move the slider to a value of 30 or 40; sometimes only slight adjustments to a value of 3 to 7 will do the trick.

Working with the Lens Tab

The Lens tab (press Ctrl+Alt+3 or ⌘+Option+3 on a Mac) gives the photographer the power to correct imperfections that can occur due to lens shortcomings. (Ack, wait! Don't go throwing away your digital camera or the lenses you bought for your digital SLR! The fact of the matter is that almost *all* lenses display chromatic aberrations or vignetting from time to time.)

As a rule, lens shortcomings appear when you adjust your zoom to either the extreme wide-angle or telephoto settings — or when the lens aperture is either wide open or closed down. Today's compact and prosumer model digital cameras come equipped with lenses of excellent quality, and they only keep getting better.

If you're going to be making large prints from your digital images or cropping to extremes, the controls in the Lens tab (shown in Figure 9-24) may come in handy. These are the controls for those ever-so-slight adjustments that make your images that much closer to perfect.

Figure 9-24: The Lens tab and its controls.

Those chromatic aberrations

Chromatic aberrations occur in areas where your lens can't focus red, green, and blue light along edges of the image to the necessary degree of precision. The Lens tab gives you two controls to counteract those aberrations: the Fix Red/Cyan Fringe slider and the Fix Blue/Yellow Fringe slider.

Here's how to use them to correct chromatic aberrations:

1. **Zoom in on your image to 100 to 200 percent.**

2. **Using the Hand tool, move around the image to determine whether color fringing exists.**

3. **If you detect red or cyan fringing on edges of the image (as illustrated in Figure 9-24), use the Fix Red/Cyan Fringe slider to minimize it.**

4. **If you detect blue or yellow fringing on edges of the image, use the Fix Blue/Yellow Fringe slider to minimize it.**

Reducing vignetting

Vignetting occurs when the outer edges of the image aren't properly exposed, often leaving a dark circular edge around an image. Vignetting will often occur when you shoot images with your lens set to a wide-open aperture setting. Using a lens hood can also affect an image where the lens actually captures the outer edges of the attachment.

The Vignetting Amount slider is an easy way to eliminate this condition. The photo shown in Figure 9-25 shows vignetting that occurred when this landscape was shot with a wide-angle lens.

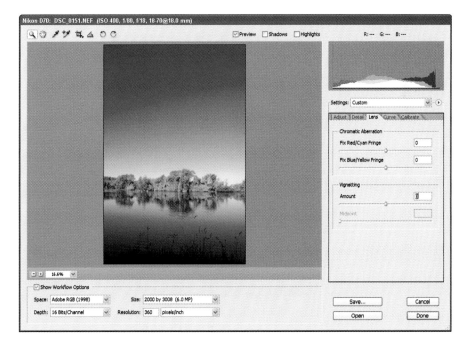

Figure 9-25: Image with some visible vignetting.

Using vignetting as a special effect

Though the Vignetting and Midpoint controls were designed to reduce vignetting effects, I'll often take them the opposite direction — and not just to be contrary. For years, portrait photographers have used vignetting as a portrait effect; here I can do that digitally: Adding a dark, graduated border around a portrait can have a pleasing effect on the total image, drawing attention to the area of the photo that is most important — the person you've photographed.

The Vignetting control in the Lens tab can be a quick, easy, no-fuss way to add this effect to your image.

Want to minimize the effect of vignetting on an image? Go for it:

1. **Move the Vignetting Amount slider to the right to reduce the darkened edges of the image.**

   Be careful not to overcompensate for vignetting so as to not affect any other tonal values of the image. Overcompensating (usually by moving the slider too far to the right) can produce light edges around the image!

   To reduce the lighter-edge vignetting effect, just back off your adjustment slightly by moving the slider to the left.

2. **Adjust the midpoint.**

   The Midpoint slider helps you adjust the area in which the vignetting effect is reduced. Move the slider to the left to shrink the area; move the slider to the right to increase the area of your adjustment. Figure 9-26 shows vignetting reduced by adding a Vignetting Amount value of 25 and a Midpoint value of 21.

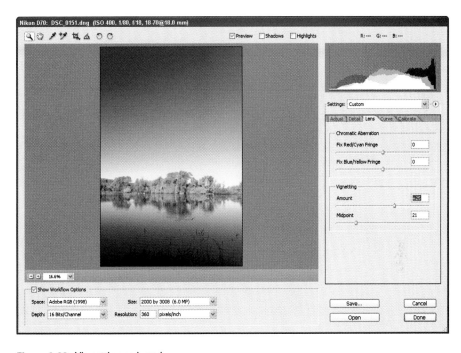

Figure 9-26: Vignetting reduced.

Love Them Curves

The Curve tab (Ctrl+Alt+4, ⌘+Option+4 on a Mac) provides an excellent addition for fine-tuning the distribution of tonality throughout an image. (I often use the Curve control to add a little extra contrast.)

The Curve chart resembles a histogram: The left of the chart represents the tonal distribution in the shadow areas of the image; the right of the chart represents the highlights areas. (See Figure 9-27.)

To adjust your images using the Curve control:

1. Select a Tone Curve setting.

I usually start out either selecting the Medium Contrast or the Strong Contrast setting, depending on how much contrast I want to add to an image. If I want to reduce contrast, I'll choose the Linear setting, which is a straight line in the curve that doesn't change the tonality of the image.

2. Fine-tune the curve.

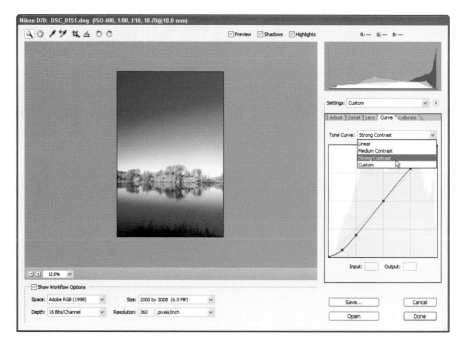

Figure 9-27: The Curve tab.

For fine-tuning the curve, either you can drag the existing curve points or add curve points on the curve by using the Ctrl+Click technique (⌘+Click a Mac). To fine-tune your adjustments, you can just drag a selected curve point. You can also move a curve point by clicking it and then clicking the up, down, right, or left arrow keys on the keyboard.

If you really want to get precise, you can enter numeric numbers for the selected curve points in the Input or Output fields.

Getting used to fine-tuning the tonal adjustments in the Curve tab can take a while. If you want to make some quick curve adjustments right away, you'll find that the Tone Curve pre-selected settings should do the trick for most of your photos. Experiment with the Curve tab before messing around with the curve too much. You'll find that subtle adjustments will give you the best results.

Caught Calibrating Again!

The Calibrate tab (Ctrl+Alt+5, ⌘+Option+5 on a Mac) wasn't meant for you to apply color correction to your images, but to fine-tune the camera profiles that are built into Camera Raw. When updates to Camera Raw are available (at http://adobe.com) for you to load onto your computer, typically those updates include profiles for new models of digital camera.

When Adobe adds a new digital camera model to Camera Raw, they program in specific color profiles for that particular model digital camera. The controls in the Calibrate tab (see Figure 9-28) are intended to be used to fine-tune the camera profile in Camera Raw with what your own digital camera is producing.

Most photographers wouldn't go through the hassle of calibrating their digital camera to the profiles available in Camera Raw, after all, the profiles provided work very well as they are set up now. Another reason, it's a real hassle to calibrate your digital camera!

To actually recalibrate the Camera Raw built-in profiles, you would have to purchase or download a calibration target image, take a photo of it in neutral daylight balanced lighting, then compare the image converted to ProPhoto RGB working space with the same image in Camera Raw. You would then have to match the colors of the text image with the photo in Camera Raw in order to adjust the colors in the Calibrate tab — with both windows visible on your computer monitor. If you understand all that, I think you'll appreciate why most of us just use the Camera Raw built-in profiles!

Although the Calibrate controls aren't meant for applying color corrections to photos, you can still use 'em to get some really cool color effects! The photo shown in Figure 9-29 (for example) was first adjusted normally, using the controls in the Adjust and Curve tab. Then I messed with it in the Calibrate tab and added some kinky colors.

Figure 9-28: The Calibrate tab.

Processed normally

Colors changed with Calibrate controls

Figure 9-29: Using the Calibrate controls to produce unnatural colors for special effects.

Part IV

Photoshop CS2 Image-Processing Workflows

The 5th Wave   By Rich Tennant

"I couldn't say anything — they were in here with that program we bought them that encourages artistic expression."

In this part . . .

*I*n those dark days before digital photographers could shoot in raw format and take advantage of the enlightened features of Camera Raw, we had to make all our color and tonal adjustments in Photoshop. (Uphill in the snow. Both ways.) Of course, just because you're now able to do *most* of your correction work in Camera Raw doesn't mean you're exempt from tweaking color and tone in Photoshop before you do your edits. But okay, things are better.

One reason to know how to make levels, curves, color balance, and saturation adjustments in Photoshop is to accommodate the changes you sometimes have to make in your color-management settings, or your targeted output media (say, a particular type of inkjet paper). This Photoshop adjustment know-how comes in especially handy when you want to adjust only certain parts of an image — and (hah!) that's something you can't do in Camera Raw. Yet, anyway.

In this part, you get a handle on making overall corrections and edits to your images — to finish what you started in Camera Raw. I also show you how to use adjustment layers and Layer Masks to make even finer adjustments and edits. Don't forget: Sometimes you still have some nagging "red eye," blemishes, and errant branches you need to edit in your photos. So hang on to your hat — it's time to shift Photoshop into high gear!

10

Adjusting Color and Tone in Photoshop

*A*djusting color and tone in Camera Raw might leave you with the feeling that most of your work on an image is done — and sometimes it is. What you're actually accomplishing in Camera Raw is applying *basic* adjustments to an image that wasn't processed in the digital camera, preparing it for Photoshop (where you can go wild with it). Chances are the photo still needs some minor color and tonal tweaks — which is what this chapter is all about.

Organizing those tweaks into an efficient routine is what I call the *overall-adjustments workflow:* a fine-tuning of the color and tonal corrections made in Camera Raw, tailored to get the photos ready for output that has a specific profile — say, a Web site or that photo-quality glossy paper you're loading into your inkjet printer.

Overall Adjustments as a Workflow

As with any other process explained in this book, this chapter explains the overall adjustment of an image's color and tones in Photoshop step by step — a workflow approach. Although that process is similar for both Photoshop and Camera Raw, making adjustments in Photoshop is more of a strictly linear process. In particular, watch for these differences when you adjust color and tone in Photoshop:

✔ **Make color settings and proof before you make color and tonal corrections:** Yep, here it comes again: color management. In Photoshop, you can work with images that have specific color spaces, such as Adobe RGB (1998), and you can proof your images as you work on them — simulating targeted output such as an image for the Web — or a printed image, on a specific paper, on your inkjet printer.

After making color and tonal adjustments in Camera Raw, you'll notice that the actual color and tones may change in appearance when you apply different color profiles or turn on proofing in Photoshop (check out the example shown in Figure 10-1). In Photoshop, you'll need to make further overall adjustments to match your intended output. (If the building looks familiar, it's where The Beatles recorded "Get Back" on the rooftop and the rest of *Let It Be* in the studio below. (Offhand, I think they passed the audition.)

Default color profile   Epson premium glossy
                               paper profile

Figure 10-1: Proofing images changes appearance.

✔ **Make color and tonal adjustments in layers:** In Camera Raw, you make color and tonal adjustments with the Adjust and Curve tabs. In Photoshop, you make these corrections in individual *adjustment layers* (which I explain in the "Just Layering Around" section, later in this chapter).

✓ **Consider more options:** In Camera Raw, you can adjust white balance, exposure, shadow, brightness, contrast, saturation, and curves. You have the same options in Photoshop (except for those great White Balance controls in Camera Raw), plus a few more I show you in this chapter.

Implementing color management first

Before diving into making overall corrections to your images, you'll need to make sure your color settings are made, and that you're proofing your image for the intended type of output. Working in the correct color space and proofing your images as you're making adjustments will ensure that what you're looking at on your computer monitor will be as close as possible to what you will print. (I cover color management in Chapter 3; here's where you put some of those color-management concepts into action.)

Selective color

The Selective Color adjustment (Image⇨ Adjustments⇨Selective Color) is supposed to be used for CMYK color processes, but you can still use it to adjust individual colors in a photo. Though it's not included in the typical overall-correction process, it's still useful for further tweaks when you want to enhance (or experiment with) your images.

I occasionally use Selective Color to adjust specific colors — enhance, lighten, darken, or change them, without affecting the other colors or tones in the image. I also use this adjustment to darken a blue sky when other methods might throw the sky color out of gamut.

Original image

With Selective Color

Here are the steps toward an overall-corrections workflow in a color-managed environment:

1. **Make sure the correct color profiles are applied.**

   Part of your color-management workflow, make sure that you'll be working in the correction color space. To check which color space you're working in, choose Edit⇨Assign Profile.

   Figure 10-2 shows the Assign Profile window with Working RGB: Adobe RGB (1998) chosen. This is a typical working space you'll be working in for most of your photos.

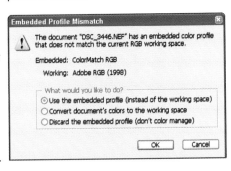

Figure 10-2: Making sure the correct color profile is chosen.

   If the color settings made in Camera Raw differ from those you specified in the Camera Raw Workflow settings to match the color space in Photoshop, you get a Color Settings Mismatch message like the one shown in Figure 10-3. At least the Embedded Profile Mismatch window lets you choose the profile embedded with the image (here, the Space setting chosen in Camera Raw) or the color space setting made in the Photoshop Color Settings.

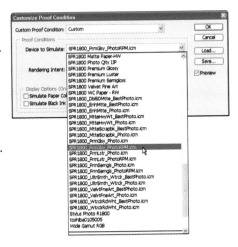

Figure 10-3: The Embedded Profile Mismatch window.

2. **Set up proofing and proof your colors.**

   If you're processing an image and know its final destination (such as a particular printer, paper, or the Web), make sure you set up and turn on proofing. Choose View⇨Proof Setup⇨Custom. Choose the target profile that matches your output destination from the Device to Simulate drop-down list (in the Customize Proof Condition window shown in Figure 10-4).

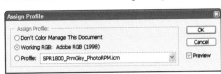

Figure 10-4: Selecting an output profile to simulate on your monitor.

TIP

If your color management is set up correctly, then choosing the correct color space and device to simulate on your monitor should give you an accurate view of the image as it will appear on your printer or the Web. Any adjustments you make from here should give you results that match what's finally printed or displayed on the Web.

3. Turn on Gamut Warning.

Pressing Shift+Ctrl+Y (Shift+⌘+Y on a Mac) turns on Gamut Warning, allowing you to preview areas of your image that are considered out of gamut for the device selected in the Customize Proof Condition window. Areas out of gamut will be highlighted in gray, as shown in the photo in Figure 10-5.

Figure 10-5: Gamut Warning shows the out-of-gamut areas in an image.

WARNING!

When areas of your image are *out of gamut*, it means they're beyond the range of colors that the selected output device can produce. Results may be disappointing because your printer driver translates any out-of-gamut areas as the closest color match it can produce. If you print an image with areas out of gamut, the colors may not match, or may appear too dark, or too light.

Developing an overall corrections workflow

As in Camera Raw, the most efficient approach is to do your global color and tonal corrections as a consistent, step-by-step workflow. After you get used to making any necessary corrections in a particular order every time, you can whip through those images, making corrections like a black-belt Photoshop master.

Now for a bird's-eye view of an overall-correction workflow. Note the various layers at which the procedures take place; there's more about them in the "Just Layering Around" section later in the chapter. Here's the sequence:

1. **Open a file from Camera Raw or Bridge.**

   (Okay, sometimes the obvious still has to be stated!) You can open PSD files directly from Bridge, or open raw files from Camera Raw directly into Photoshop. (Bridge handles the rest.)

2. **Save your image in PSD format.**

   After opening your image from Camera Raw into Photoshop, save your file in PSD (Photoshop) format — first into a working folder. (For more about file management, see Chapters 4 and 5.)

3. **Evaluate the image.**

   Instead of diving right in to make color and tonal changes in Photoshop, take a minute to look at the open image and plan the steps necessary to make corrections.

4. **Adjust Levels.**

   The Levels adjustment layer is where you adjust tonal ranges and color throughout an image's shadows, midtones, and highlights. Photographers find this level a useful tool for setting the white and black points of an image, adjusting color, and removing color cast.

5. **Adjust Curves.**

   As with the Curves control in Camera Raw, the Curves adjustment layer is where you fine-tune how tonal values are distributed across the tonal range of the image. This adjustment is a great way to increase or decrease contrast — without having to adjust brightness or contrast directly.

6. **Tweak Color Balance.**

   Adjusting color balance is another way you can fine-tune the color in an image. Unlike the generalized color adjustments made in Camera Raw, Photoshop Levels, and Photoshop Curves, the Color Balance adjustment layer lets you add and subtract red, green, and blue color while maintaining *luminosity* (tonal values) in an image. You'll use the Color Balance adjustment layer occasionally to fine-tune specific colors.

   If you've processed your image in Camera Raw — and used the Levels adjustment to remove any color cast — you may not need to use the Color Balance adjustment for many of your photos. Okay, that particular adjustment may not always add value to your workflow — but it gives you a great secret weapon if you ever need to fine-tune the colors in photos with finicky color balances.

   Figure 10-6 shows an image with too much magenta, and the same image corrected using the Color Balance adjustment.

Magenta cast   Corrected with Color Balance

Figure 10-6: Using the Color Balance adjustment to correct color in an image.

7. Adjust Brightness/Contrast.

When I first started using Photoshop, I used this adjustment a lot to increase contrast in dull photos and adjust overall brightness if needed. Over time, I've found the Brightness/Contrast adjustment to be highly destructive. It degrades the quality of your images — especially notice-able if you're making prints 5×7 or larger — so I recommend only sparing use of Brightness/Contrast in Photoshop.

If you need to adjust either brightness or contrast in your image, get in the habit of using Curves instead of the Brightness/Contrast adjustment. (Sneaky, sure, but it works.)

8. Adjust Hue/Saturation.

My favorite adjustment to make in Photoshop is increasing the color. I love adding color to my photos (no melted crayons!). Now that I use the Saturation control in my raw images when I convert them in Camera Raw, I rely a lot less on the Photoshop version of Saturation. When processing JPEGs from my image library (or from one of my compact digital cameras), I rely on the Camera Raw Hue/Saturation adjustment to get me closer to the colors I envisioned when I took the photo.

Just Layering Around

Making overall adjustments in Photoshop is different from making adjustments in Camera Raw. In Camera Raw, adjustments are made in linear increments, each adjustment is added to the metadata of the image, leaving the original file intact. In Photoshop, however, these adjustments are pictured and pre-sented in *layers* — you do each one as if it were on a transparent overlay stacked on top of the image. Each layer represents a separate adjustment to the original image, or background layer.

It's kind of like making a sandwich. You start off with a piece of bread — your original layer — and then you lay some bologna on top (another layer), a piece of cheese (another one), some mustard (ditto), and then finally another piece of bread, that's the final layer. Substitute specific adjustments for those layers, and you have the Photoshop approach to images. (I don't know about you, but I'm getting hungry!)

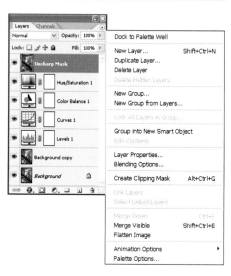

Think of each layer as a transparency that contains a specific addition. When you open an image file in Photoshop, the original image is used as a *background layer*. Add a layer to make an adjustment; that layer is placed on top of the background layer. Each new edit is contained in a new layer, stacked from the bottom on up. When the adjustments are done, the stack is complete — a composite image — maybe not edible, but a finished product.

Getting around the Layers palette

The Layers palette is the part of Photoshop that contains all the layers that make up an image. It's where you go to create and control all layers; you can create new ones, hide some, and work with them individually or in groups. Clicking the palette's menu button displays the Layers menu. Figure 10-7 shows the Layers palette and the Layers menu.

 By default, the Layers palette is visible when you start Photoshop. If you inadvertently close the Layers palette while you're working in Photoshop, you can always start it up again by choosing Windows➪ Layers or by pressing the F7 key.

Figure 10-7: The Layers palette with the Layers menu.

Here's a fast list of what you can do with the layers in Photoshop:

- **Understanding the background layer:** When you open an image file, Photoshop creates the bottommost Background layer. Because it's basic to the other layers, it doesn't allow you to make certain changes to it: You cannot delete it, re-order it, or change its opacity or blending mode.

  Before you edit your image, always make a duplicate of the Background layer. It's a best practice to avoid editing the Background layer altogether. Reserve that layer as the original to base all your edits on: It's your backup — your parachute in case anything goes wrong. Right-click (or ⌘+click on a Mac) the Background layer, and then choose Duplicate Layer from the menu.

- **Showing or hiding a layer's contents:** You toggle between Show and Hide by clicking the Eye icon (aye-aye, sir, that's what it looks like). If the Eye icon is visible, the contents of the layer are visible. If the Eye icon is not visible, the contents of the layer are hidden.

- **Creating new layers:** Click the Create a New Layer button (see Figure 10-8), and then choose the layer type in the flyout menu.

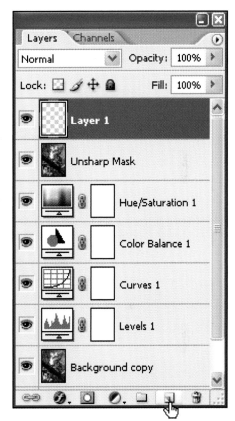

Figure 10-8: Creating a new layer.

- **Renaming layers:** Simply double-click the layer name and type the new name.

- **Changing layer order:** To change the order of your layers, click a layer and drag it to where you want it to appear in the stack.

  You can also create a new layer by dragging an existing layer to the New Layer button, which is located on the bottom of the Layers palette.

🖊 **Deleting layers:** Click the layer and drag it to the Trashcan icon at the bottom-right of the Layers palette. You can also right-click the layer and choose Delete Layer from the menu, as shown in Figure 10-9.

🖊 **Flattening layers:** When you *flatten* layers, you combine them all into one layer. When you flatten an image, you can make no further changes to any of the old layers. In effect, they disappear as layers, leaving only their effects in the flattened version of the image. Flattening layers is a normal step to do right before you print out an image or submit it for publishing. Three things to keep in mind here:

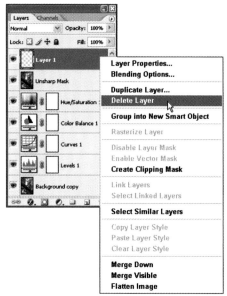

Figure 10-9: Deleting a layer using the Layers menu.

- If no layers are selected, the entire image is flattened into one layer that takes the top layer's name.

- If two or more layers are selected, only those layers are combined into one layer — again taking the top layer's name.

- To maintain your image edits, save your image *before* you flatten it — and be sure to give the flattened version of your image a different filename when you save it.

Creating adjustment and fill layers

Photoshop provides two sets of layers you can use to complete your image: adjustment layers and fill layers. Though they work the same (that is, as stacks of transparent overlays), each type of layer has its own purpose. This section shows you how to use — and make — both types.

Laying on the adjustments

Adjustment layers are reserved for specific adjustments, and only those. They allow you to change color or tonal values of an image and lay those changes over your original (background) image without affecting it; you can try out your changes till you get the ones you want. When you create an adjustment layer, changes made in that layer are viewable along with all the adjustments you made in the layers underneath it. You can use adjustment layers to enhance color balance, brightness, contrast, and saturation — and create new layers if you need them (more about that in a minute).

An adjustment layer affects all layers beneath it in the Layers palette. The advantage is that a change made to one adjustment layer doesn't have to affect the layers stacked beneath it. For example, if you want to change the brightness of an image, you make that change only once — in one layer — and it affects the overall image.

Filling in with fill layers

I've reviewed adjustment layers as the ones you create to make changes to levels, curves, color balance, hue, and saturation. The other group of layers, called *fill layers*, allow you to lay on solid colors, gradients, or patterns. As with an adjustment layer, a fill layer does not affect the layers underneath it.

Some fill layers also allow you to adjust them; here are the types of fill layers you can use in your image-editing workflow:

- **Solid color:** A solid color layer is considered a fill layer. Create a solid color layer to fill an image with a color. You can use it to create a colored background for an image.

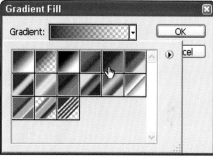

Figure 10-10: Choosing a gradient type.

- **Gradient fill layer:** You can use gradients to apply a color in a transition from light to dark. It's useful for creating a dark-edged vignette for some images or a transitioned color background. Figure 10-10 shows different types of gradients.

Gradients are used to create some cool special effects. You can (for example) experiment with how your images look by increasing or reducing the opacity of a fill layer.

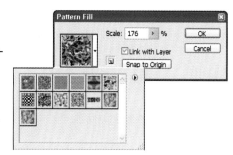

- **Pattern fill layer:** When you create this type of layer, it contains a pattern from the Pattern menu shown in Figure 10-11. Adjust the layer's opacity to strengthen or weaken the pattern effect.

Figure 10-11: Choosing a pattern fill.

Making Overall Adjustments

Overall adjustments (which are introduced in Chapter 4) to an image are just as amenable to becoming a workflow as the other processes in this book. Here's a look at the first five general steps of an overall-adjustment workflow:

1. **Double-check your color settings before you open any image for overall adjustment.**

2. **Open an image from Camera Raw in Photoshop.**

3. **Save the image to PSD format in your Working folder.**

4. **Proof for a specific output device.**

5. **Evaluate your image.**

   • Does the image look good straight out of Camera Raw?

   • Is it too dark, too light, too flat (lack of contrast and color saturation), or does it have a color cast?

Sometimes getting an image into Photoshop and then proofing the image for a specific device, printer, or paper will make it look different.

Evaluating images using Variations

One quick way to evaluate an image is to view the image using *Variations* — multiple thumbnails of an image that open different versions of the image, showing different color balance, contrast, and saturation. To view Variations, choose Image⇨Adjustments⇨ Variations. Figure 10-12 shows the different thumbnail choices offered.

The Variations command is available only for images in 8-bit-per-channel mode. Though you *can* choose thumbnails to make adjustments, I recommend using only the adjustment layers to apply actual adjustments. I use variations just for evaluation purposes.

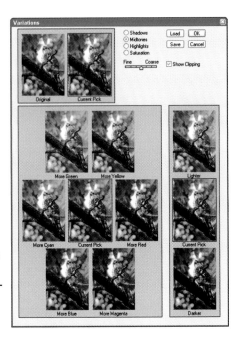

Figure 10-12: Using Variations to evaluate images.

Adjusting levels

In my overall-adjustment workflow, the first actual fix I make is adjusting levels — making exact corrections to the tonal values of an image by fine-tuning the colors in the highlights, midtones, and shadows.

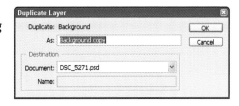

Figure 10-13: Duplicating the Background layer.

To adjust colors and tone using the Levels command, follow these steps:

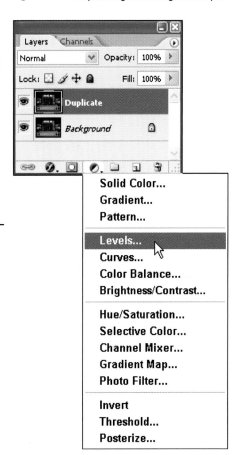

1. **Create a duplicate of the Background layer by choosing Layers⇨Duplicate, typing a new name into the As field (for example, Duplicate), and clicking OK.**

   The Duplicate Layer field appears for the purpose, as shown in Figure 10-13.

   Okay, this step really doesn't fit any particular niche in my overall-adjustments workflow — but it *is* a best practice. Always make a duplicate of the background layer *before* you create any new layers.

2. **Create a Levels adjustment layer by clicking the Create New Adjustment or Fill Layer button from the Layer palette (shown in Figure 10-14).**

   The Levels dialog box appears.

Figure 10-14: Creating a Levels adjustment layer.

3. **Make sure the Preview box is checked.**

   Keep the Channel selection RGB, as shown in Figure 10-15. You'll be correcting levels for the entire image — all three color channels (Red, Green, and Blue) at the same time.

   As you become more familiar with adjusting levels in Photoshop, experiment with changing the Channel selection to the Red, Green, or Blue channels and adjusting them individually. If you are a new user of Photoshop, keep the RGB Channel selected.

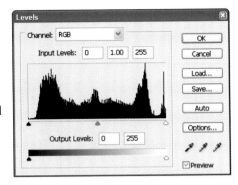

Figure 10-15: The Levels adjustment window provides controls to adjust color highlights, midtones, and shadows.

4. **View the histogram and slide the Shadows input slider to the right, till it gets to where the curve of the histogram begins (as shown in Figure 10-16).**

   With Preview selected, you can view the image changes as you move the slider.

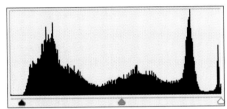

Figure 10-16: Moving the Levels Shadows and Highlights input sliders.

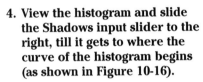

A histogram provides a snapshot of the tonal range of an image. The histogram shows how much detail is in the shadow area on the left, in the midtones in the middle, and in the highlights on the right.

Histogram data is different for every image. For many images, the histogram curve begins all the way to the left, where no Shadow input-slider adjustment is needed.

5. **Slide the Highlights input slider to the left, till it gets to where the highlights curve begins.**

   With Preview selected, you can view the image changes as you move the slider, as shown in Figure 10-17.

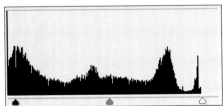

Figure 10-17: Adjusting shadows, midtones, and highlights can improve the tonality of the image.

6. **Move the Midtones input slider to the right slightly, checking the image for improved color saturation and contrast.**

Often you can improve the appearance of an image by using the Midtone slider to darken the midtones. If you do a lot of CMYK work for press, you may often need to nudge the Midtone slider to the left; this avoids images looking too dark and muddy. To be safe, always test print your images, then review them and readjust as necessary.

7. **Click OK to complete the Levels adjustment.**

If you are not satisfied with the effects of your Levels adjustment, you can reset the settings to the original values: Just press and hold the Alt key (Option key on the Mac) and click Cancel. You can then re-create a Levels adjustment layer and attempt to adjust levels again.

You can experiment with adjusting levels in any of the following ways — and view the results in your image:

- ✓ **Set the blackpoint of your image by clicking the Blackpoint Eyedropper and clicking a dark part of the image.** This provides a more accurate blackpoint as a baseline for adjusting levels in your image. (The *blackpoint* is an area in the image that represents a true black.)

- ✓ **Set the whitepoint of the image by clicking the Whitepoint Eyedropper and clicking a lighter part of the image.** Doing so provides a more accurate whitepoint as a baseline for adjusting levels in your image. (The *whitepoint* is a portion of the image that represents a true white.)

- ✓ **Try darkening shadow areas by moving the Shadows input slider to the right.**

- ✓ **Move the Midtones input slider to the left to adjust the darker midtones.** You can lighten midtones by moving the slider to the right.

- ✓ **Increase contrast and brighten up highlights by moving the Highlights input slider to the left.**

Figure 10-18 shows the results of adjusting these levels. Moving the Shadow input slider to the right darkened the shadow areas, moving the Midtones input slider to the right darkened the midtones, and moving the Highlights input slider to the left brightened the highlights.

Before   After

Figure 10-18: The image before, and then after, adjusting levels.

How 'bout them curves?

When you adjust the tonal range of an image using Levels, you make only three adjustments: shadows, midtones (gamma), and highlights. The Curves adjustment allows for up to 14 different points of adjustment throughout the tonal range.

I do mention this more than a few times in this book, but I like to adjust Curves instead of Brightness/ Contrast to increase contrast in my images. Works great, not destructive of data — what's not to like?

To adjust an image's tonality using the Curves adjustment layer, follow these steps:

1. **Create a Curves adjustment layer.**

   To do so, click the Create New Adjustment or Fill Layer button from the Layers palette and then choose Curves, as shown in Figure 10-19.

Figure 10-19: Creating a Curves adjustment layer.

2. Increase the number of grid lines to provide a more precise grid.

Press and hold the Alt key (the Option key on the Mac) while clicking inside the Curves grid to increase the number of grid lines, as shown in Figure 10-20.

3. Make tonal adjustments by clicking the curve line and dragging it to the desired grid point, or by clicking Auto.

Drag the curve upward and left to brighten, downward and right to darken. Experiment with creating adjustments for shadows, midtones, and highlights.

Figure 10-21 demonstrates how the Auto curves feature can improve color in shadows, midtones, and highlights.

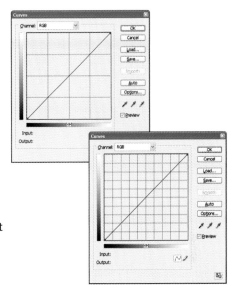

Figure 10-20: Using the Curves adjustment window.

Before

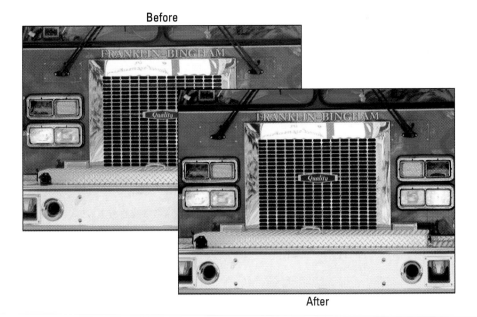

After

Figure 10-21: Using the Curves adjustment layer to improve this underexposed image.

Adding color with the Hue/Saturation adjustment layer

The next step in the overall-adjustment workflow is to add some visual "pop" to your image, adding color saturation to increase vibrancy and eye appeal.

With any overall adjustment, sometimes *less is more;* you may need to make only a slight correction. When adjusting color saturation, for example, sometimes all you have to do is budge the slider to the right until you see the colors pop up a little. "Easy does it" is the rule if you don't make your images appear unrealistic.

To create a Hue/Saturation layer, follow these steps:

1. **Click the Create New Adjustment or Fill Layer button from the Layers palette, and then choose Hue/Saturation, as shown in Figure 10-22.**

    The Hue/Saturation dialog box appears.

2. **Make sure Preview is selected.**

    You want to be sure you see these changes before you apply them.

3. **Increase image saturation by moving the Saturation slider slightly to the right, as shown in Figure 10-23.**

    As a rule of thumb, increase the saturation until you see the colors start to pop.

   Be careful not to add too much color saturation; it can make certain colors in the image *blow out* — that is, lose detail as they're overpowered by the color. If some areas look blown out, back off your adjustment slightly until you're pleased with the result.

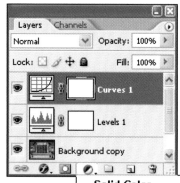

Figure 10-22: Creating a Hue/Saturation layer.

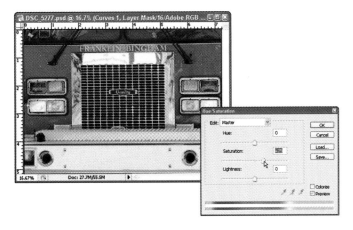

Figure 10-23: Increasing saturation in the Master channel.

You can use the Hue/Saturation adjustment layer to adjust individual color hues or saturation amounts. This is an advanced method of color-correcting your images. Experiment with changing the hue and/or saturation of each color to see the result. You may find that adjusting the Master (the default setting) alone can work just fine for your photos.

4. Check Gamut Warning by choosing View⇨Gamut Warning.

For the photo of the fire engine, I actually had to *decrease* some saturation in the Red channel to bring the image more within the gamut of my selected output (but then I punched up some other colors).

5. Click OK to save your settings.

Figure 10-24 shows the original fire-engine image, with Levels and Curves added, and then with Hue/Saturation adjusted. The photo now appears slightly more vibrant — but not overprocessed — and that's what you're shooting for.

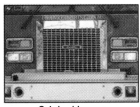

Original image   Levels and Curves adjustments   Hue/Saturation adjusted

Figure 10-24: The fire engine looks a little more vibrant with a bit of overall adjustment.

11

Editing Images

*A*fter you convert an image from raw to Photoshop and make overall corrections to color and tone, you're about half done with the image. With many photos, you still have to *edit* — make improvements that are unique to the image, such as removing "red eye," fixing dust spots (digital SLRs can get 'em from dirty image sensors), or erasing those power lines you didn't see when you were shooting outdoors.

There are other traditional photographic tricks us old-school darkroom wizards used to do, such as dodging and burning. The editing phase is also the time that you can let your artistic intentions run wild, using an array of Photoshop special effects — in particular, *filters*, which I cover in more detail in Chapter 14. This is always one of my favorite subjects to talk about, so let's get into some Photoshop editing!

Using an Image-Editing Workflow

Typically an effective image-editing workflow is put together much like the overall-correction workflow I describe in Chapter 10. Here, too, I encourage you to make your image edits in a step-by-step sequence of best practices. Unlike the procedure for overall color and tonal corrections, however, you do have the freedom to mix up the order of your edits a bit. But I still like consistency, so I take these edits in individual steps:

1. **Plan your edits.**

   After you complete overall corrections, evaluate your image to determine what type of edits if any are needed. Common types of edits to plan for include these:

   a. *Dodging and burning.*

   Dodging is a technique you use to lighten a certain area of an image; burning darkens a certain area of an image. Whether you're working on landscape, still life, portraits, or photos of your pets, evaluate your images to see if areas need to be dodged (like when you want your dogs eye's to be more bright), or burned (like when you need to darken areas of a landscape).

   Dodging and burning areas of an image can rescue out-of-gamut parts of an image and bring them back into a printable range. (For more about out-of-gamut colors, see Chapter 10.)

   b. *Removing spots.*

   Dust spots on digital images aren't really possible for images taken with compact digital cameras because the lens is built into the camera. But when you're shooting with digital SLRs, dust spots can happen when particles find their way onto your image sensor. It's happened to me, and is fairly common for digital SLR shooters.

   On a recent trip to England, I had the opportunity to stop off at this one interesting spot to take photos of some big stones sticking out of the ground. I slapped a circular polarizer on my lens to get some darker blue skies and to reduce the glare off the stones. To my later dismay, I discovered (while zooming in on those photos in Photoshop) spots in the sky caused by water spots on my circular polarizer. I called up the trusty Healing Brush tool and used it to remove those spots, as shown in Figure 11-1.

   c. *Retouching.*

   Nature is not always kind. Time and again, the people whose portraits I take want to make sure I get rid of the wrinkles, pimples, and blemishes we all seem to have. No problem: When editing images in Photoshop, you can soften skin using the Blur tool or one of the blur filters. You can use the Dodge tool or Paintbrush to help whiten teeth and eyes. (If you get good at retouching portraits, you can save your friends and clients some money: They won't have to go to a plastic surgeon for a facelift or the dentist to get teeth whitened — provided they never venture out.)

Spots

Original image

Spots removed

Figure 11-1: Removing spots with the Healing Brush tool.

If you're shooting portraits, retouching in Photoshop is an important phase of your work. Plan your edits carefully.

  d. *Sharpening.*

To make a general statement, all digital images need some sharpening. Sharpening should be the last step you take before printing a photo or posting it to the Web. I show you more about sharpening in the next chapter, but I'm mentioning it here because sharpening is considered an image edit.

Figure 11-2 shows a zoomed portion of the photo of those stones in the ground before — and after — sharpening with the Unsharp Mask filter. (I didn't see any Druid sacrifices there that day, but I did have to sacrifice my lunch hour so I could take the time to shoot some photos.)

Not sharpened   Sharpened with Unsharp Mask

Figure 11-2: Applying the Unsharp Mask for sharpening photos.

2. Create separate layers for each edit.

After you evaluate an image, and then decide (say) to dodge it, then burn it, and then make the cigarette butts disappear from its floor, do each of those edits in its own layer. That way you can delete layers whose edits just didn't do the job, without affecting other image-editing layers.

Here's the fast way to create an editing layer:

a. Create a new layer.

Press Ctrl+Shift+Alt+E or ⌘+Shift+Option+E on a Mac to merge a copy of all visible layers into a new target layer. (Run out of fingers yet?)

By combining all the previous layers into the new layer, you're essentially merging all the adjustment layers and other edits you've made so far. Press Ctrl+Shift+Alt+E (⌘+Shift+Option+E on a Mac) to combine the previous layers into your new editing layer.

b. Give the layer a proper name.

For example, if you're creating a new layer to use the Healing Brush to remove spots on your image, give the layer a descriptive name (such as "Healing Brush Edits"). After you create the layer, double-click the layer name in the Layers palette, and type in a new name like the example shown in Figure 11-3.

WARNING!

If you use the Merge Visible command (Layers➪Merge Visible), you wind up *flattening* all the visible layers into one layer. That's not a good idea if you want to preserve all your changes in separate layers. Instead of using the Merge Visible command, press Shift+Ctrl+Alt+E (Shift+⌘+Option+E on a Mac) to retain all the previous layers but to merge those layers into the one you just created. *Now* you're ready to make an edit!

TIP

After you've created your first editing layer and combined all the visible layers into that layer, you can simply duplicate the new layer for whatever new edit you want to perform next.

3. **Edit your image.**

Now that you have a fresh newly "merged" layer to work on, go ahead and remove a blemish, whiten some teeth, and dodge or burn parts of the image to see how those features work.

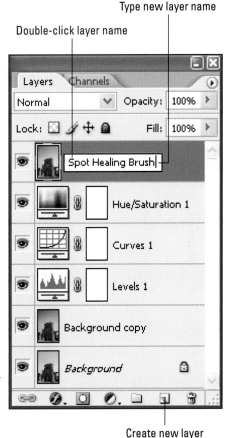

Figure 11-3: Typing a new layer name.

REMEMBER

Keep each edit to its own layer.
If you start by removing a blemish and then decide you want to dodge or burn some other part of the image, create a new layer first (by choosing Layer➪Duplicate Layer).

Getting to Know Your Tools

When working with images and making edits in Photoshop, many of the graphic tools you'll be using are accessed from the Photoshop Toolbox. The Toolbox, shown in Figure 11-4, includes more than 60 tools to manipulate and edit your photos.

Just as an artist carries an assortment of pencils, brushes, erasers, and a few other tools in an art-supply box, you have the same arsenal at your disposal. The Toolbox includes all the drawing and painting tools the artist can't do without — plus a few others that a *digital* artist can't do without (such as the Red Eye Removal tool, the Healing Brush, and the Magic Wand tool).

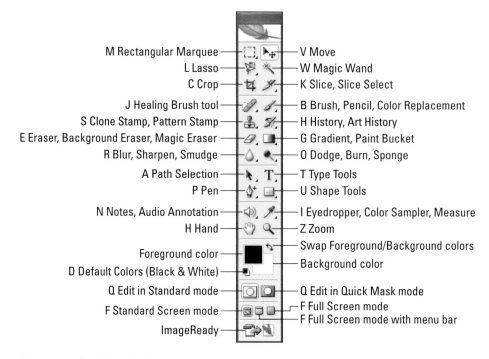

M Rectangular Marquee — V Move
L Lasso — W Magic Wand
C Crop — K Slice, Slice Select
J Healing Brush tool — B Brush, Pencil, Color Replacement
S Clone Stamp, Pattern Stamp — H History, Art History
E Eraser, Background Eraser, Magic Eraser — G Gradient, Paint Bucket
R Blur, Sharpen, Smudge — O Dodge, Burn, Sponge
A Path Selection — T Type Tools
P Pen — U Shape Tools
N Notes, Audio Annotation — I Eyedropper, Color Sampler, Measure
H Hand — Z Zoom
Foreground color — Swap Foreground/Background colors
D Default Colors (Black & White) — Background color
Q Edit in Standard mode — Q Edit in Quick Mask mode
F Standard Screen mode — F Full Screen mode
— F Full Screen mode with menu bar
ImageReady

Figure 11-4: The Photoshop Toolbox.

Using the Marquee tool

Use the Marquee tool to draw rectangles, ellipses, horizontal columns, or vertical columns in an image. Right-clicking the Marquee tool icon in the Toolbox brings up the flyout menu, which includes other Marquee tools (see Figure 11-5).

Figure 11-5: The Marquee tools give you four ways to draw marquees.

Using the Marquee tool is a quick way to make edits to the selection, or even to crop part of an image:

1. **Select the Marquee tool.**

2. **Draw a marquee around the image portion you want to crop.**

3. **Make edits to the selection.**

   If you simply want to crop the selection, choose Image⇨Crop to crop the image to your selection.

The Lasso tool

The Lasso tool is essential for making selections within parts of an image — and editing just those areas you've selected. The Lasso tool flyout menu, shown in Figure 11-6, offers three tools for creating selections: the Lasso tool, the Polygonal Lasso tool, and the Magnetic Lasso tool. (See the "Lasso this!" section, later in this chapter, for more about the Polygonal Lasso and Magnetic Lasso tools.)

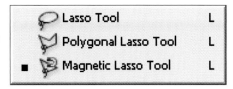

Figure 11-6: The Lasso tool's flyout menu.

The Lasso tool is commonly used to make selections in an image that can be easily traced; it's like drawing an outline on tracing paper placed over a picture. Select the Lasso tool, and then — while holding down the left mouse button — trace over the part of the image you want to select.

Snip-snipping with the Crop tool

The Crop tool is as simple as an artist's mat knife: You draw a boundary around the parts of your image in which you want to crop, as shown in Figure 11-7. You can specify the width and height of your crop as well as the resolution you want to make the cropped image.

Complete crop

Crop tool Option bar   Cancel crop

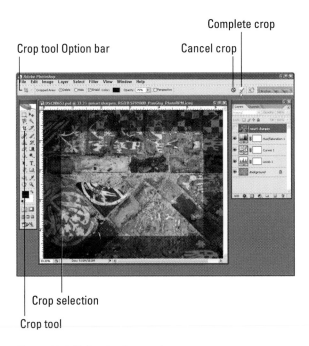

Crop selection

Crop tool

Figure 11-7: Using the Crop tool.

Editing with the Healing Brush

Some of the coolest editing tools that Photoshop offers are the Healing Brush tools. The flyout menu shown in Figure 11-8 includes four Healing Brush tools that enable you to correct minor details. Imagine eliminating pimples, hair, and dust from all the places you don't want them. (Digitally, at least.)

Figure 11-8: Healing Brush tools.

✔ **Spot Healing Brush tool:** New in CS2, this tool is easier to use than the Healing Brush tool. Just select the Spot Healing Brush and start painting areas to retouch. Because the tool samples surrounding pixels for you, you don't have to worry about making a selection.

✔ **Healing Brush tool:** With this tool, you can sample a selection of pixels, and then paint those selected pixels onto other areas. Using this tool is a great way to retouch areas of your images.

✔ **Patch tool:** This works similar to how the Healing Brush tool works. The difference is, with the Patch tool, you're actually making a selection of an area to use for painting in the selected pixels.

✔ **Red Eye tool:** Also new in CS2, this handy little tool provides a quick way to remove that ghoulish "red eye" from your cherished photos.

Cloning around with the Clone Stamp tool

The Clone Stamp tool is the equivalent of a rubber stamp (you know — press a stamp on an ink pad and then on paper), only it's digital: You sample part of an image (color, texture, whatever) and apply that sample elsewhere in the image. All Brush tips work with the Clone

Figure 11-9: The Clone and Pattern Stamp tools.

Stamp tool, so it's a great retouching alternative. One of its special versions, the Pattern Stamp tool, re-creates patterns from the cloned selection and applies to another part of the image. Figure 11-9 shows the Clone Stamp tool's flyout menu.

Removing pixels with the Eraser tool

The Eraser tool is the digital equivalent of those pink erasers at the ends of pencils. You can erase pixels as you move the cursor over them, changing them in ways specified in the Eraser mode you choose on the Option bar.

Use the Background Eraser tool to remove the effects of overall image adjustments (see Chapter 10) made to only certain areas or layers of the image. To erase all similar pixels within a layer, use the Magic Eraser tool. Among the tools shown in Figure 11-10 are the Background Eraser and Magic Eraser.

Figure 11-10: The Eraser, Background Eraser, and Magic Eraser tools.

Sharpen or blur with the Blur tool

The Blur tool can be a quick way to edit a too-sharp edge by blurring a portion of your photo, in much the same way you'd use the Sharpen tool to add crispness. If you are editing a portrait and want to get a blurred effect, you can make an overall adjustment to the photo using the Gaussian Blur filter — but then use the Sharpen tool selectively to sharpen hair and eyes. Figure 11-11 shows the Blur tool's flyout menu.

Figure 11-11: The Blur, Sharpen, and Smudge tools.

The Smudge tool warps and pushes pixels in the direction you are dragging the tool, giving you a morphing or *smudge* effect. Like the Liquefy filter, the Smudge tool enables you to hide flaws or achieve some really cool special effects.

Drawing shapes with the Pen tool

The Pen tool actually does a wee bit more than a pen you use to write love letters, shopping lists, and checks. The Pen tool in Photoshop creates lines, curves, and shapes (also called vector paths) for a variety of editing and drawing purposes. The Pen tool flyout menu (shown in Figure 11-12) shows its different options — including the Freeform Pen tool and a variety of anchor-point Pen tools.

Figure 11-12: The Pen tools.

Load up an image and experiment with the Pen and Freeform Pen tools. The Pen tools offer a valuable way to create special effects when you want to make complex selections.

Making selections with the Magic Wand tool

One of the most valuable editing tools in the Toolbox is the Magic Wand. You can use it to make selections — one of the most widely used processes in editing images — for example, to select similarly colored areas in your photo. You can specify the color range and tolerance for a selected area by using the Option bar to set them.

Selections are used to select contiguous and discontiguous areas of an image so you can make edits specifically to that area selected. For instance, if you want to select only the clouds in an image of sky, use the Magic Wand tool to select only the white areas (the clouds, which are discontiguous) and not the blue (the sky). I often use the Magic Wand tool to select portions of the backgrounds in my portraits so I can lighten, darken, or even blur those areas to get the effect I want. Another way I use selections is to isolate — and fix — areas of my image that are out of gamut. I want the whole image to match the gamut range of my selected printer and paper combination, but I don't want to change the entire image — just the areas that are out of gamut.

Figure 11-13: Using the Magic Wand to select similarly colored areas of an image.

Figure 11-13 shows the Magic Wand tool used to select a section of an image that is overexposed relative to the rest of the image. I selected that portion so I could adjust its brightness to match the rest of the image.

Painting with the Brush tool

The Brush, Pencil, and Color Replacement tools are commonly used to paint changes on your photos. Figure 11-14 shows the Brush tool and its flyout menu.

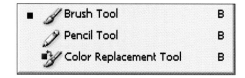

Figure 11-14: The Brush, Pencil, and Color Replacement tools.

Numerous brush sizes, tips, and modes are available on the Option bar, as shown in Figure 11-15. They're useful with many Photoshop image-editing techniques.

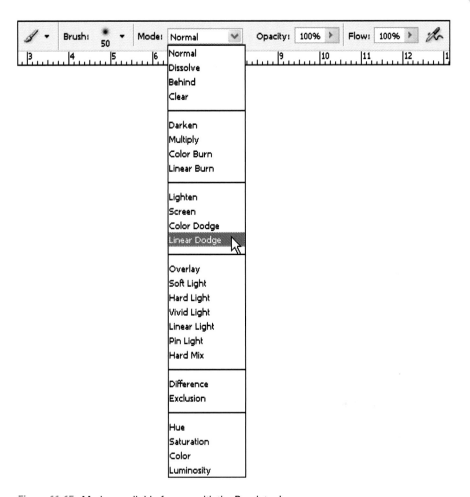

Figure 11-15: Modes available for use with the Brush tools.

Dodging and burning using Dodge and Burn tools

One of the most common edits that discerning digital photographers make in Photoshop is *dodging and burning.* Back in the day when photographers like me developed photos using enlargers and chemicals, I had a few tricks up my sleeve to touch up my work. Dodging and burning allowed me to darken or lighten certain areas of a print to my liking by either reducing or increasing exposure to certain parts of the print. Photoshop lets old-timers like me do those same things with the Dodge and Burn tools shown in Figure 11-16.

Figure 11-16: The Dodge, Burn, and Sponge tools.

The Sponge tool is useful when you want to make slight color-saturation adjustments to an area. For example, you can decrease the color saturation of a certain area where the red may be too bright or "blown out," giving an unnatural look to the photo. The Sponge tool can also come in handy to help bring out-of-gamut areas of your image back into a color range that your printer can handle.

Writing text with the Type tools

Used most often by graphic designers who combine both text and images in their everyday work, the Horizontal and Vertical Text tools, shown in Figure 11-17, are methods to insert text into an image. Add text to your photos in just three steps:

Figure 11-17: Type tools let you add text to an image.

1. **Click the Horizontal Type tool in the Toolbox.**

2. **Choose the font you want to use.**

   New in CS2 is the ability to view WYSIWYG (what-you-see-is-what-you-get) samples of each font by clicking the Font menu located on the Option bar, as shown in 11-18.

Figure 11-18: Choosing a font and font size on the Option bar.

3. **Click your image and type the text.**

For my photography Web site, `http://kevinmoss photography.com`, I always type a description, name, or location for each photo on my site. I use the Text tool to easily add the text to my image canvas. After you type some text, you can move it around with the Move tool and place it exactly where you want it, as shown in Figure 11-19.

Shaping things up with the Shape tools

For situations when you want to draw simple shapes (or insert predefined shapes into your photos or canvas), the Photoshop Toolbox offers Shape tools to do just that. Figure 11-20 shows all the Shape tools available in the Rectangle tool flyout menu.

Suppose I want to insert a copyright symbol next to my text for the Orchid art poster example I used in the previous section. The process for adding this symbol is as follows:

1. **Right-click (single-click on the Mac) the Rectangle tool and choose the Custom Shape tool.**

2. **Choose the copyright symbol from the Option bar Shape selection menu shown in Figure 11-21.**

3. **Drag the Custom Shape tool over the part of your image where you want to insert the symbol, as shown in Figure 11-22.**

Figure 11-19: Type and move your text to the desired location on your canvas.

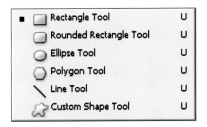

Figure 11-20: Shape tools available in the Photoshop Toolbox.

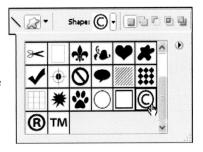

Figure 11-21: Selecting a shape to insert onto the canvas.

Wells, England © 2005, Kevin L. Moss

© 2005, Kevin L. Moss

Figure 11-22: Adding a copyright symbol to the canvas.

Zooming in and out

The Zoom tool provides one of many ways to enlarge or shrink your view of the details in an image: Click the Zoom tool, place your cursor over your image, and click. You can also right-click (Option+click on a Mac) with your mouse and choose Zoom Out to reverse your zoom, as shown in Figure 11-23.

Other methods for zooming in and out of an image include using the Navigator palette or pressing Ctrl+/-. On a Mac, the preferred method for zooming in is to press Spacebar+⌘+Click; to zoom out, press Spacebar+⌘+Option+Click.

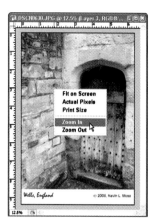

Figure 11-23: Right-click in the image to view the Zoom tool's options.

Using tool presets

One timesaving feature of Photoshop is that you can set up tools the way you like them. You work with these every day, so it's nice to have some of them set up with your own customized settings and shortcuts. When you save settings for commonly used tools in Photoshop, you create *tool presets*.

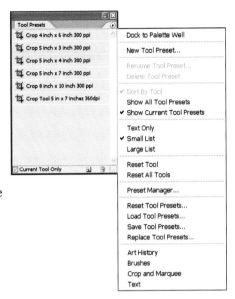

I prepare a lot of photos for print and for the Web. One set of presets I use on a regular basis is my crop settings — for both my Web site and for printing. I create crop presets including 11×14 inches at 360dpi for prints and 4×5 inches at 72dpi for the Web. Then I save these crop settings as presets so I don't have to go in and manually specify a crop setting every time I want to crop an image.

Other common presets to consider are for Brush sizes, frequently used fonts, and font sizes. As you become more familiar with Photoshop and really nail down your everyday image-editing workflow, try setting up your common tools using the Tool Presets palette shown in Figure 11-24.

Figure 11-24: The Tool Presets palette and flyout menu.

The Tool Presets palette offers some useful features for creating presets:

- You can drag the Tool Presets palette from the Palette well to your image window.

- If you need to view all presets instead of the presets for the tool selected, uncheck the Current Tool Only check box. Re-check Current Tool Only to view only the presets for the selected tool.

- You can organize presets by tool type, delete presets, or change the way presets are displayed. To do so, use the Preset Manager located in the Tool Presets flyout menu.

To set up a tool preset, follow these steps:

1. **Click the tool in the Toolbox that you want to create a preset for.**

   In Figure 11-25, I'm selecting the Crop tool.

Figure 11-25: Select the Crop tool.

2. Make the settings to the tool that you want to preset.

For the Crop tool preset, I created a crop size of 19×13 inches at 360dpi in the Crop tool options on the Option bar, as shown in Figure 11-26.

Figure 11-26: Making a preset for Crop settings.

3. Click the Tool Presets palette in the Palette well, and click to save the tool settings made in Step 2 as shown in Figure 11-27.

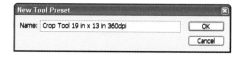

Figure 11-27: Naming and saving the preset.

You can also access the tool presets by clicking the tool button on the far-left of the Option bar or by choosing Window➪Tool.

4. Type a name for the tool that you're saving.

Photoshop creates a default name for your preset that you can customize to your liking.

As you can see, there are a number of ways to open the Tool Presets palette and create tool presets that can save you editing time.

Making Selections

If you're editing photos that look just fine for the most part, often you want to change only certain parts of them. Photoshop offers a variety of tools to make *selections* — defined, editable areas within an image. When you make a selection in Photoshop, you can then edit only that part of the image, without changing the rest. Getting familiar with these capabilities — especially the editing of selections — is necessary if you want to edit your individual images with consistent quality. To keep that quality, the larger goal is to set up an image-editing workflow for your photos.

Selecting only certain parts of your images — and editing only those selected parts with tools covered in this chapter — gives you great creative control. You can replace a dull background with a vibrant color, darken a bright sky, brighten a dark sky, and selectively sharpen or blur a part of your image to get the desired effects.

Making selections with the Magic Wand tool

The Magic Wand tool is probably the most popular selection tool used to make the most common selections in photos. I often use the Magic Wand to select areas of an image that are similar in color if I want to make color or tonal changes to only the selected areas.

The typical process for making — and then adjusting — a selection looks like this:

1. **Create a new layer by choosing Layer⇨Duplicate Layer.**

2. **Select part of the image you want to modify using the Magic Wand tool.**

   I use the Magic Wand tool to select backgrounds in images that I want to change. I can lighten or darken the background, replace the background with parts from another image, or blur the background. Whichever adjustment I want to use, I have to separate the subject from the background before I make my edits.

   The Magic Wand tool works best when the area you're selecting is one color (or close to one color) and has distinct boundaries from the remaining area.

   The Magic Wand tool works just as well as a way to select the subject of an image instead of the background. Select the background and then choose Select⇨Inverse to swap the selections for the rest of the image.

   The amount of feathering determines how sharp or smooth the edges of the selection are. For the image in Figure 11-28, I applied a Feather radius of 2 pixels by choosing Select⇨Feather (Ctrl+Alt+D or ⌘+Option+D on the Mac) and then typing **2** in the Feather Radius field in the Feather Selection window.

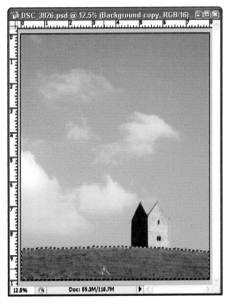

3. **Apply corrections to the image.**

   For the landscape in Figure 11-28, I adjusted the color and tone of the grass without adjusting color and tone for the rest of the image. The image was shot with direct sunlight, which "washed out" some of the color of the grass area. I chose Image⇨Adjustments⇨ Hue/Saturation and then turned

Figure 11-28: Making selective adjustments.

up the saturation of the Yellow and Green channels to get the effect I wanted — without affecting the sky or the old building.

Putting a twist on the whole concept of selecting just one part of the image, I then wanted to adjust the color of the sky. So I chose Select➪Inverse (Shift+Ctrl+I, Shift+⌘+I on a Mac) to reverse the selection from where it was to the rest of the image. I then chose Image➪Adjustments➪Hue/Saturation and tweaked the Blue channel to get the sky the way I wanted it. Figure 11-29 shows the finished product.

Figure 11-29: Selective adjustment of selected areas can change an image dramatically.

Using rulers and grids

Photoshop offers the capability to precisely position elements of your images. Rulers, grids, and guides are used to map out your photos, allowing you to make edits in a measured environment. The combination of these precision tools with the Snap-To feature lets you navigate precisely with your mouse or tablet's stylus.

You can apply rulers to your image window, providing measurements along the left and top of your image window. Applying grids to an image adds horizontal and vertical lines in your image window to better help you navigate. Guides provide horizontal and vertical lines to your specification in the image window. Hold down the Alt (Windows)/Option (Mac) key as you're dragging a guide to switch the guide's orientation 90 degrees.

I use rulers to help me make precision crops to images when the Crop tool just doesn't cut it (no pun intended). To bring up rulers in your image window, choose View➪Rulers or press Ctrl+R (⌘+R on the Mac). You can change the actual units of measure on the ruler from inches to centimeters (or other units) by right-clicking the ruler (⌘+clicking the Mac); see the image on the left here for an example.

Using grids in your image window allows you to make more precise edits to your image. *Grids* are nonprinting lines you can add to your image by choosing View➪Show➪Grid. The image on the right shows an image window with grids turned on.

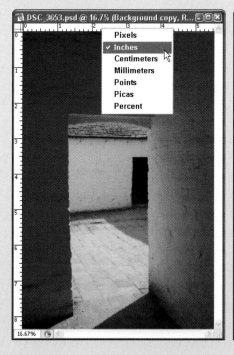

Lasso this!

Seeing the Magic Wand tool at work might make you wonder what other selection tools Photoshop has in its bag of tricks. The three lasso tools are used to create finer selections in your image:

- ✔ **Lasso tool:** Used for free-form drawing of selections, such as the one shown in the upper-left image of Figure 11-30. I chose this selection so I could edit out the selected yucky spot on the peach without affecting the rest of the image. (I like my fruit to be perfect — no worms!)

- ✔ **Magnetic Lasso tool:** Best used to trace more complex shapes. The *selection marquee* (the dotted line surrounding your selection) snaps to the selection like metal to a magnet when you use this tool. If you want to select (for example) the entire orange, the Magnetic Lasso tool (shown in the upper-right image of Figure 11-30) does a more accurate selection than the other Lasso tools.

- ✔ **Polygonal Lasso tool:** Used for drawing straight edges of a selection, the Polygonal Lasso tool is great for making selections like the one shown in the bottom image in Figure 11-30, where the areas to select are shapes that have straight lines (such as boxes, rectangles, triangles, or windows).

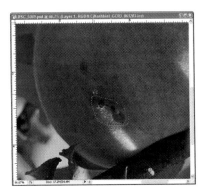 

Figure 11-30: Selecting an area of an image you want to edit separately from the rest of the image.

You can always get rid of a selection if you want to start over by choosing Select⇨Deselect or by clicking Ctrl+D (⌘+D on the Mac) to deselect your selection.

Selection options

When you make selections with any tools, options are available to make your selections more precise. Figure 11-31 shows the Select menu, which provides functionality to help you work with selections.

The most commonly used options in the Select menu include these:

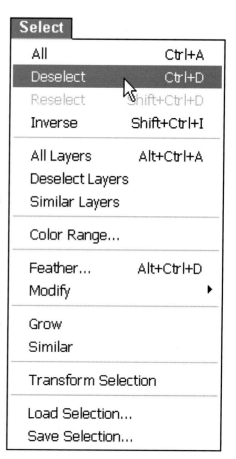

Figure 11-31: The Select menu provides additional commands to use when making selections.

- **All:** Use this command to select the entire image. You can also use the shortcut Ctrl+A (⌘+A on the Mac).

- **Deselect:** Choose Deselect to remove the selection outline you have made. When making selections you often have to deselect in order to start over to make the correct selections. You can also use the keyboard shortcut Ctrl+D (⌘+D on the Mac).

- **Inverse:** Sometimes you want to select an area that's tricky, complex, or otherwise just tough to select. If you're lucky, the rest of the image may be easier to select; if that's the case, select the easier area — and then choose Select⇨Inverse. The Inverse command reverses your selection, selecting the previously unselected portion of your image.

- **Feather:** Choose this command, and then indicate the number of pixels. A feather of two or three pixels provides a smooth, realistic edge for your selections in many photos. Experiment with setting the feature to different numbers of pixels until you find the right setting for your photo. To feather a selection, choose Select⇨Feather or press Ctrl+Alt+D (⌘+Option+D on the Mac).

🖊 **Grow:** When you choose the Grow command, you can increase the contiguous areas of your selection to include areas that are similar in color. To grow a selection, choose Select➪Grow.

🖊 **Similar:** The Similar command increases your selection to all like colors of the current selection, regardless of their place in the image. To expand a noncontiguous selection with similar colors, choose Select➪Similar.

Before you can use the Select commands, you must have actual selections made in your image. And it bears repeating: *Make sure you duplicate the background layer before making selections.* Selections can be cumbersome, but with practice, you can become more proficient.

Editing Techniques

Many photos have imperfections that you would rather do without — and here it's no fault of the photographer: Unnoticed (or immovable) power lines, oddities of contrast, dust specks, and even flies can find their way into images. When you view the photos later on a computer, you may want to change the imperfections that bug you (pun intended). Or some details stick out when vagueness would be more forgiving. (I don't know about you, but I've found that digital cameras can capture a lot better resolution than my own eyes can!) When you're taking photos of people, keep in mind that some folks don't *want* the sharpness today's digital cameras can deliver. After all, who wants to see all the pores or wrinkles on someone's face?

Worm holes in a peach? You can fix that. Pimples on a teenager? You can fix that, too (on-screen anyway). Power lines running across your horizon? You have an editing trick for that too!

Getting the red (eye) out

One of the most common complaints I hear about photos of people is the "red eye" effect: Bright red dots in the center of the subjects' eyes detract from the rest of the image.

The digital cure for those devilish eyes is now literally one click away: the new Photoshop Red Eye tool. Here's how to use it:

1. **After opening your image, duplicate the background layer by choosing Layer➪Duplicate Layer or pressing Ctrl+J (⌘+J on the Mac).**

Your loved ones will thank you for fixing this problem. Unfortunately for me, I had to pick a family photo that *had* the red-eye problem so I could demonstrate it here; it's not easy to get a loved one to agree to that. (Can't think why. Oh well. Disclaimer: The photo in Figure 11-33 has been cropped to hide the identity of the test red-eye subject.)

2. **Zoom in on the subject's eyes by pressing Ctrl+ (on a Mac, Spacebar+⌘+click) a few times until the eyes are large enough to edit.**

3. **Click the Red Eye tool in the Toolbox, as shown in Figure 11-32.**

4. **Drag a box around the red portion of the eye to remove the red, as shown in Figure 11-33.**

If all the red is not removed, drag the marquee over the eye again and let go of the mouse button. Repeat the process for both eyes. Figure 11-34 shows the effects of using the Red Eye tool.

Figure 11-32: Choosing the Red Eye tool from the Photoshop Toolbox.

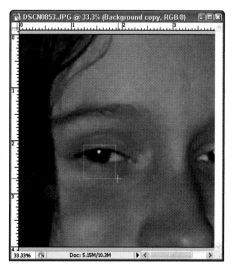

Figure 11-33: Removing "red eye" with the Red Eye tool.

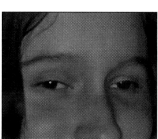

Before After

Figure 11-34: The original image and as corrected with the Red Eye tool.

Removing spots

You may think that with today's digital cameras, dust spots are a thing of the past. That's not necessarily so. Digital SLRs use interchangeable lenses; when you change these lenses, dust can sneak into the camera and onto the image sensor — and you have *digital* dust spots. Fortunately, the Spot Healing Brush tool offers a digital remedy.

Finding a photograph to use as an example of how the Spot Healing Brush tool eliminates blemishes was hard to do; not many models would approve of a page or two about their imperfections! But a landscape can't argue — so I use one here to show you how to fix dust spots with the Spot Healing Brush tool.

Might as well get right to it: Figure 11-35 shows a photo that contains a dust spot that has to be removed.

Here's how to remove a portion of the image, such as a blemish or a dust spot:

1. **Create a new layer to use for editing: Press Shift+Ctrl+Alt+E (⌘+Shift+Option+E on a Mac) to create a new target layer with all of your previously visible layers combined.**

   If you've taken this step before to do another edit, just duplicate the previous layer by pressing Ctrl+J (⌘+J on a Mac), or select the layer to duplicate and Choose Layer⇨Duplicate Layer.

2. **If needed, zoom in on the portion of the image that includes the blemish, dust spot (as in the example shown), or unwanted pixels.**

   To zoom in, you can use the Zoom tool or just press Ctrl+ (on a Mac, press Spacebar+⌘+click to zoom in).

3. **From the Photoshop Toolbox, right-click the Healing Brush tool and choose the Spot Healing Brush tool (see Figure 11-36).**

4. **Adjust the size of your brush so it's just a little larger than the spot you want to remove.**

   Enlarge the brush size by pressing the right-bracket key (]) or reduce the brush size by pressing the left-bracket key ([).

5. **Drag the brush over the dust spot while holding down your mouse button, and then let go of the mouse button.**

   Figure 11-37 shows the image before and after I removed the spot from it.

Figure 11-35: Dust on a digital SLR sensor can show up in photos.

TIP

The Healing Brush tool works the same way as the Spot Healing Brush, with one exception: Using the Healing Brush tool, you can pick the sample of pixels it uses to replace what's in the area you paint. To select an area to clone pixels *from*, press Alt+click (Option+click on a Mac) that area.

Figure 11-36: Selecting the Spot Healing Brush tool.

Figure 11-37: Removing a dust spot with the Spot Healing Brush tool.

Dodging and burning to make your images pop

Going back to the old days of printing in a darkroom, one of the *only* tricks I had up my sleeve to edit prints was to dodge and burn. *Dodging* was the process of blocking light from certain portions of the photographic paper as it was being exposed, reducing light to that part of the image. The result was a lightening of the area.

Burning was a technique used to *add* light to certain areas of the image that I wanted to be *darker* than the rest of the image. If I wanted part of the background darker, I burnt it. If I wanted a petal of a flower lighter, I dodged it.

It wasn't an exact science, and I couldn't see the results of my efforts until the print came out of the chemical process, washed and dried. Worse yet, I had to dodge or burn each print *individually* to have the same effect across all prints. Multiple copies of the same print meant multiple dodges and multiple burns — a long, hard process. With Photoshop, you can edit your images, dodge and burn each image once, and print as many as you want.

Here's a hands-on look at dodging and burning your images:

1. **Create a new layer to edit your image.**

   Create the new target layer with the other visible layers combined by pressing Ctrl+Shift+Alt+E (⌘+Shift+Option+E on the Mac).

2. **Evaluate the image.**

   Look at the photo to evaluate which areas you want to darken and which you want to lighten. (If you haven't noticed yet, one of my favorite subjects to photograph is stuff found in backyards — such as butterflies and birds. They're great models, don't complain, and they like to fly around and pose for photos.)

3. **If necessary, zoom in on the portions of the image you want to darken or lighten with the Zoom tool. Then click (first) the Zoom tool in the Photoshop Toolbox and (next) the image.**

   Press Ctrl+ to zoom in on your images. Press Ctrl– to zoom back out. On the Mac, zoom in by pressing Spacebar+⌘+Click; zoom out by pressing Spacebar+⌘+Option+Click.

4. **Click and hold the mouse button over the Dodge tool or press Shift+O a few times to get to the tool you want to use.**

   Use the Dodge tool to lighten areas or use the Burn tool to darken areas.

5. **Make your brush larger by pressing the] key to enlarge the brush or the [key to reduce the size of the brush.**

You can also choose a softer brush by choosing the Brush Preset Picker on the Option bar. Using a softer-edged brush can reduce the harsh edges that can appear with burning or dodging.

6. **Choose the Burn tool to make the light areas you want to darken.**

7. **From the Option bar, experiment with different Brush and Exposure settings.**

I usually accept the defaults and make sure my Exposure setting is around 35 percent. You can dodge and burn Highlights, Midtones, and Shadows by making those individual selections in the Option bar, as shown in Figure 11-38.

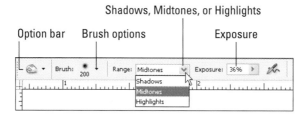

Figure 11-38: Adjusting the Brush and Exposure settings.

8. **Choose the Dodge tool to make the dark areas of the image brighter.**

Figure 11-39 shows the original image, and then how burning and dodging (in that order) can help make your image more correct in high-contrast areas.

Before   After

Figure 11-39: Comparing the images, before — and after — burning and dodging.

Using Layer Masks

One of the more advanced features of Photoshop separates the casual user from the serious user: *Layer Masks*. These specialized layers let you hide or expose specific parts of a layer by painting the portions you want to hide — or emphasize or expose — with the Paintbrush tool.

You have many ways to accomplish the same task in Photoshop. Using Layer Masks is just one of many techniques you can use to hide portions of images and replace with other effects, layers, or adjustments. Some pretty slick uses of Layer Masks include these:

- **Creating a layer in a portrait to blur or soften the subject's skin (a portrait-editing technique).** With most portraits, the subjects don't want to see their wrinkles, pores, or blemishes! Many photographers use techniques such as a Gaussian blur to blur the flaws, but then paint in the sharpened portions of the portrait (such as hair and eyes) that they do not want blurred.

- **Creating a Layer Mask to selectively paint in the effects of an overall adjustment, blur, or sharpening.** Using Layer Masks is a common technique for retouching photographs selectively.

- **Selectively darkening a background.** Darken the entire image using the Hue/Saturation Lightness slider to the level where the background is darkened to your liking. (Don't worry! You can create a Layer Mask and then paint back in the areas that you don't want darkened.)

- **Replacing the background of an image by masking a selection from an image.**

The following steps give you a detailed taste of the Layer Mask's power, showing you how to use one to hide the sharp portions of a blurred image and then selectively "paint back in" the parts of the image you want to remain sharp. You can apply many such effects and filters, and then use Layer Masks to selectively paint in the effects. I call this process the "Bad Tie Day" effect.

1. **Make a duplicate of the image's background layer by choosing Layer⇨Duplicate Layer or pressing Ctrl+J (⌘+J on the Mac).**

   Provide descriptive names to your layers when you create them. You can change the layer name by clicking the layer name in the Layers palette and typing in the new text.

2. **Blur the image by choosing Filters⇨Blur⇨Gaussian Blur.**

   Try a blur setting from one to four, as shown in Figure 11-40.

3. Create a Layer Mask by choosing Layer⇨Layer Mask.

Choose the Reveal All option in the flyout menu to fill the layer with white, allowing the effects of the layer adjustment to show through. Choosing the Hide All option in the flyout menu paints the layer with black to hide the effects of the Gaussian Blur layer adjustment. For this example, I've chosen Reveal All.

The Reveal All option lets the effects of the Gaussian Blur continue to show in the image, as shown in Figure 11-41. Choose this option to paint the areas to hide the Gaussian Blur effect. Choosing the Hide All option hides the Gaussian Blur effect, allowing you to use a Paintbrush tool to paint in the areas of the image where you want the Gaussian Blur effect.

4. Click the Paintbrush tool in the Photoshop Toolbox.

Press D to set the foreground color to white and the background color to black. The D key always changes these back to the Photoshop default colors (hence the *D*): white for foreground and black for background. Press X to reverse these colors.

Using black as the foreground color in the Reveal All mode paints away the Layer Mask; using white as the foreground color paints the Layer Mask back in.

5. Lower the opacity to around 70 percent in the Opacity field on the Paintbrush Option bar.

Lowering the opacity reduces the "strength" of your painting, resulting in a more realistic transition between the masked and the painted areas of the layer.

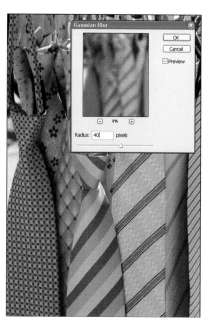

Figure 11-40: Applying a Gaussian Blur to the bad ties.

Figure 11-41: Painting in the sharper portions that are hidden under the Layer Mask.

6. Paint in the areas of the image you want to sharpen.

Yes, it's a bit more work, but here's why it works:

- Painting areas of the image hides the Gaussian Blur and reveals the sharper image behind the Gaussian Blur mask, leaving the unpainted areas still blurred.

- Painting reveals the sharper details of the chosen "bad" tie but leaves a softened look for the rest of the ties (which is probably a good thing; these were hanging on a clearance rack for a reason!), as shown in the image's final form in Figure 11-42.

Figure 11-42: Softened photo, after painting in the sharp areas hidden by the Layer Mask.

To selectively sharpen an image, use the same approach used to blur the image: Create a layer and merge the previous layers. Sharpen the entire image, and create a Layer Mask to hide the sharpening. Paint the areas you want to sharpen, and that's it!

Preparing Photos for Output

*O*ne of the biggest challenges a photographer faces is producing *output*. It's not that it's difficult (or that we're lazy), but we do spend a lot of time shooting, messing around with images in Photoshop, and cruising the Web for photo sites when we have some spare time. It just seems many photographers don't *print* enough of their work to show off those stunning images!

Have you ever gone through and viewed images you've taken a few years ago, and wonder why you never processed them or printed them for your portfolio? (See, I *know* you've done that before!) This chapter shows you the process and techniques needed to produce beautiful prints and images for the Web. The ultimate destination for all our work is the final image — and I have one more set of steps to show you that will get you there: the *output workflow*. Hopefully, you'll realize that by incorporating this final workflow into your overall process, for *every* image, you'll have many more photos to hang on your wall, do a show, or post to your photo Web site.

Using an Output Workflow

Turning those pretty on-screen pictures into scintillating Web images — or into actual hard copy you can hold in your hands or hang on a wall — is another whole kettle of fish. This section shows you how to put the fish in the kettle in the right order, in an output workflow that looks like this:

1. **Organize your output photos.**

   When you edit images in Photoshop, keep those versions of your image files in a folder named to indicate that you've edited those images. When you prep your photos for output, set up folders to save separate versions of the images in folders for prints, Web, or press.

2. **Make sure color management is implemented.**

   From making color settings (Edit↪Color Settings) to proofing (View↪ Proof Setup), two best practices will help you ensure effective color management:

   • Edit your images in the correct color space.

   • Proof your images while editing, using the correct *output* profile in the Customize Proof Condition window shown in Figure 12-1.

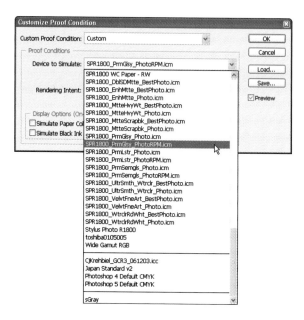

Figure 12-1: The Customize Proof Condition window.

3. Properly resize your images.

Use the Crop tool or the Image Size command to resize your images to match your output needs. Make sure you specify the correct output resolution, such as 72ppi for Web images or 300ppi for prints. Resize your images using the Bicubic resampling method (for enlarging photos) or the Bicubic Smoother resampling method (for reducing the size of photos).

4. Sharpen your photos.

Almost all digital photos look better when you sharpen them in Photoshop. To sharpen photos, use the Unsharp Mask or the new Smart Sharpen filters available in the Filter menu. For best results in most photos, first increase the amount to a setting between 100 and 300, set the Radius to around 1.3 or 1.4, and then slide the Threshold slider to about 5 to 7 to reduce sharpening artifacts.

These settings are typical, but the Amount, Radius, and Threshold settings might be different for your photos.

5. Save the image in an output folder.

Don't forget a little thing called *image management* (which I cover in Chapter 4): Before printing, save your image using the File⇨Save As command; save the modified output file to a folder you've designated for your output files.

6. Print.

Printing isn't like typing your resignation letter to your boss in Word (*after* you won the lottery, right?) and then clicking the Print button. In Photoshop, there are a number of printing options that have to be set up correctly to ensure that your prints come out of the printer just the way they look on your computer monitor. I don't want to throw a curve ball here, but there are two methods for printing. (Don't worry, I show you both of them later in this chapter.)

A Little Color-Management Reminder

Confusing as color management can be, when it comes to printing with accurate colors, you need to be thoroughly familiar with *spaces*:

✓ **Working space:** This term refers to the color area Photoshop uses to work with colors. Images are edited in Photoshop using the working space color settings, and *then* converted to the printer space during printing. Figure 12-2 shows the Photoshop Color Settings window, where your working space is applied in Photoshop.

✓ **Printer space:** This term refers to the settings that tell Photoshop the printer, paper, and level of quality you're printing to. To make great prints, Photoshop needs to know the printer and paper you're using so it can convert your photo's data correctly by using the printer driver (loaded when you first set up your printer). All that happens when you use the File⇨Print With Preview command.

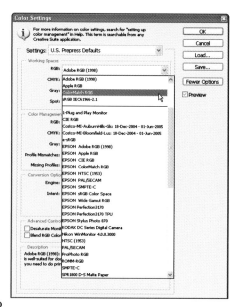

Figure 12-2: Photoshop color settings.

For photographers, there are only two working spaces to consider using: Adobe RGB (1998) and ColorMatch RGB. Deciding which color space to use in Photoshop depends on the type of printer you have. In my case, ColorMatch RGB best matches the colors my inkjet photo printers can produce. Choosing either working space produces excellent results.

To set your Photoshop color space, follow these steps:

1. **Choose Edit⇨Color Settings.**

   The Color Settings window (refer to Figure 12-2) is where you set up your working space for editing photos.

2. **Choose U.S. Prepress Defaults in the Settings field.**

   This selection provides the best options for photographers.

3. **Choose Adobe RGB (1998) or ColorMatch RGB in the Working Spaces RGB field.**

   You get great results using either choice for photos. ColorMatch RGB may provide more accurate color for use with some inkjet printers. Experiment with using both Adobe RGB (1998) and ColorMatch RGB to see what results are best for the printer you are using.

4. Choose Preserve Embedded Profile in the Color Management Policies RGB field.

When you open a file that has an embedded working space other than that specified in the Working Spaces RGB field, Photoshop either converts those files to the specified working space or preserves the embedded profile.

I keep the default Preserve Embedded Profiles. That way, I'll be notified of any mismatches (see Figure 12-3) when I open the file, and have the opportunity to convert the file to my working space at that time. By leaving the Profile Mismatches Ask When Opening option selected, Photoshop prompts me to either leave the image in its embedded working space or convert the image to the working space I've specified in the Color Settings window.

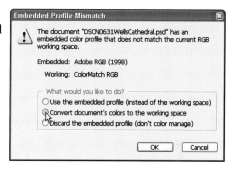

Figure 12-3: The Embedded Profile Mismatch window.

5. Set Conversion Options.

Make sure to choose Adobe (ACE) (Adobe Colorimetric Engine) in the Engine field, and Relative Colorimetric in the Intent field. Adobe (ACE) is the engine used to convert colors; Relative Colorimetric is the best choice for rendering intent for photographers.

6. Select Use Black Point Compensation.

This is the default setting. Black point compensation ensures that your black points are set in the shadow areas of your photos. Selecting Black Point Compensation is best for photos. If you don't have this checked, your images will appear muddy.

7. Click OK to save.

Sizing Images

Sooner or later, as you work with your photos, you have to resize them. I always save this step until *after* I've made my overall color corrections and image edits. Depending on the type of output you have planned for your photos, you have to determine two factors:

✔ **Image size:** The image size includes the dimensions you specify for width and height. Do you want an 8×10, a 5×7, or a 4×6 photo? If your photo's destined for the Web, you want something smaller. 4×6 may be the biggest size you'll want to display images at on the Web, and smaller sizes are preferred.

✔ **Print resolution for your photo:** If you are preparing the image for printing, set the resolution to 300 or 360 pixels per inch (ppi). If you are targeting the file for the Web, you'll want to set the resolution to 72ppi. Anything more would be a waste of resolution (and of the time it takes to transmit the file to the printer). Choose a resolution of 72ppi for your Web images.

Resolution of sorts

Before resizing images, you want to understand *pixels* and *resolution* so you can make the correct decisions in Photoshop when you resize your photos. The first step is getting familiar with some basic terms:

✔ **Pixels:** Pixels are those little square dots illustrated in Figure 12-4 that make up an image. Each pixel is uniform in size and contains one color. If you're shooting with, say, an 8-megapixel camera, each image captured can contain 8 *million* pixels. That's a potential. You always have the option to capture images at smaller resolutions (say, at 3.2 megapixels or lower). In any case, that's *a lot* of pixels.

✔ **Image resolution:** This is the setting used to size an image for output. For example, images to be viewed on-screen or on the Web should be set to a resolution of 72ppi (pixels per inch, sometimes referred to as *dots per inch* or *dpi*). Images targeted for printing should be set to around 300ppi.

Image resolution is relative. Different digital cameras produce different-size images, but it's the number of pixels per inch that actually determines resolution: More pixels per inch means better image quality when you print large photos. My 7-megapixel compact digital camera (for example) captures images at 300ppi where the image dimensions are 10.24 × 7.68 inches. My older 5-megapixel compact digital camera captures images at 72ppi — but the dimensions are 35.5 × 26.6 inches.

If you change the resolution of the image you get from a 5-megapixel compact digital camera from 72ppi to 300ppi, the dimensions then shrink to 8.5 × 6.4 inches. You really haven't changed the actual size of the image; you've just shrunk the image on-screen to achieve a desired output resolution that matches your printer's optimum printing conditions. If you had a 35-inch-wide printer, you could change the ppi setting back to 72 to achieve that image-output size, but the image quality at that huge print size would be crummy.

Figure 12-4: Most digital camera's produce square pixels.

- ✔ **File size:** For digital images, the best way to describe the size of a file is by the number of pixels it contains. The 7-megapixel file my compact digital camera produces is 3,072 × 2,304 pixels. Multiply those two pixel dimensions together and you have 7,077,888 pixels — 7 _megapixels_.

- ✔ **Image dimension:** Image dimension is the actual physical size of an image when it's printed or sized for display. Image dimension should not be confused with resolution or file size.

Understanding interpolation

Interpolation is the process of increasing the resolution of an image (or a section of an image) when cropping to increase the number of pixels per inch. A

6-megapixel digital camera should be able to produce 8×10 prints without a problem, even if you have to do some cropping.

If you print large prints — say, 11×14, or 13×19 — your digital camera can produce more resolution without interpolation, and that's a better result. Larger prints require a larger amount of image information, however; for larger prints, the more megapixels, the better. Though you can get acceptable large prints from 5-megapixel cameras (or even some photos shot with a 3- or 4-megapixel camera), you're usually limited to prints no larger than 8×10 inches.

If you do a lot of cropping, and still maintain image sizes of 5×7 or 8×10, the image quality may noticeably decrease at that print size — unless you tell Photoshop to interpolate by indicating a higher resolution in the Crop tool's Option bar when you crop.

I'll often crop out small portions of a photograph — it's sort of like creating a photo from a photo — but indicating a higher resolution in the Option bar may degrade the quality somewhat, depending on how much of the image you're eliminating in your crop. Images from 7- or 8-megapixel cameras can still provide enough resolution to produce high-quality large prints even if you do some extreme cropping — as I've done in the example shown in Figure 12-5.

Original as 360ppi

Extreme crop at 360ppi

Figure 12-5: Extreme cropping at the same ppi setting.

A great Photoshop plug-in to use to further interpolate images is Genuine Fractals. You can enlarge an image up to 700 percent without image degradation, a perfect solution for extreme cropping or when you want to enlarge your digital images to poster-size prints. For more information on Genuine Fractals, visit its Web site at www.ononesoftware.com.

When you choose a resample method, Photoshop actually assigns an *interpolation method* — which assigns color values to the new pixels that are created when you enlarge an image. Photoshop bases those color values on a sample of neighboring pixels (hence the term *sampling*). The resampling method you choose helps preserve the quality of the image when you size an image larger than its *native* (original) resolution.

Here's your range of resampling choices:

- ✔ **Nearest Neighbor:** Used for basic illustrations when quality isn't an issue. Not recommended for photos.

- ✔ **Bilinear:** Another method not recommended for use with photos, but still useful for some illustrations.

- ✔ **Bicubic:** The preferred method of resampling photos. This method uses the values of surrounding pixels to interpolate. Leave Bicubic as your default resampling method because it provides the highest quality interpolation method in Photoshop.

- ✔ **Bicubic Smoother:** This method (similar to the bicubic resampling method) *increases* the size of an image — with smoother results than with other resampling methods. May be good for some images and portraits.

- ✔ **Bicubic Sharper:** This resampling method is used for *reducing* the size of an image while enhancing sharpness.

   Note: Because sharpening is a step that should come *after* resizing, the Bicubic Sharper option really isn't needed.

Resizing using the Crop tool

One easy way to size your images is by using the Crop tool to specify the exact width, height, and output resolution of an image. Figure 12-6 shows the Crop tool used to crop and size an image.

To use the Crop tool, follow these steps:

1. **Open an image.**

2. **Click the Crop tool in the Photoshop Toolbox.**

3. Type the width in the Width field in the Option bar.

This measurement is how wide you want your output image to be when it prints out or appears on the Web. Here I've chosen a width of 7 inches.

Crop tool   Set width   Set height   Set resolution (ppi)

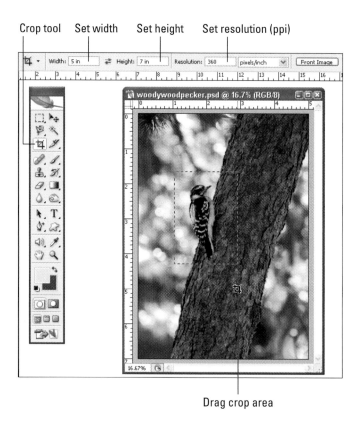

Drag crop area

Figure 12-6: Cropping with the Crop tool.

4. Type the height in the Height field.

I've chosen a height of 5 inches.

5. Type the resolution you want for your file.

If you're preparing an image for printing, enter 300ppi to 360ppi in the Resolution field. If file is destined for the Web, enter 72ppi. I've chosen a resolution of 360ppi for the purpose of printing. To avoid getting the dreaded jaggies, don't increase the resolution greater than what the image is already set to.

6. **Click and drag the area in your image that you want to crop.**

   Release the mouse button. When you do, the crop area you selected remains bright; the area you want to eliminate darkens. Additionally, you can hold down the Spacebar while dragging the Crop tool, and the selection area moves without changing dimensions.

7. **Resize or move the crop area to the position you like best.**

   Click the crop area and, while holding down the mouse button, move the highlighted crop area around until you position the crop where you want it.

   Click any of the corners of the crop box and drag the corner up or down to resize the crop area. Click just outside any corner to rotate the crop area.

8. **Click the check mark icon in the Option bar to complete the crop.**

   Alternatively, you can just double-click inside the selected area to complete the crop.

   The image is sized exactly as selected at 5×7 at 360ppi.

Resize using Image Size

Instead of using the Crop tool to size images, you can use the Image Size command to change the size of images that don't need cropping.

To change the size of an image using the Image Size command, follow these steps:

1. **Choose Image⇨Image Size or press Ctrl+Alt+I (⌘+Option+I on the Mac).**

   Figure 12-7 shows the Image Size window.

2. **Deselect the Resample Image option.**

3. **Type in the width of the image.**

   If you are printing an 8×10, type 8 in the Width field if the image is in Portrait orientation or 10 if the image is in Landscape orientation.

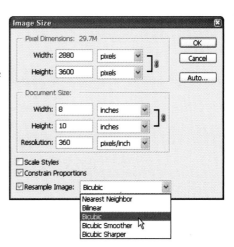

Figure 12-7: The Image Size window.

If you type the width first, then the height and resolution automatically change to accommodate the new width. The Image Size adjustment automatically changes the height and resolution as long as the Resample Image check box is not selected.

4. Select the Resample Image option.

Selecting this option now locks the width and height so those dimensions don't change when you enter the resolution you want.

5. Type in the resolution for the photo.

Leave the default resampling method, Bicubic, which is the best setting for photographs.

6. Click OK to close the window and save your changes.

Sharpen Up!

The final step in an output-preparation workflow is to *sharpen* your photos — that is, enhance the edges and increase contrast. Almost all images produced by digital cameras need some sharpening before you print them or save them for use on the Web. But don't start returning your digital cameras for refunds; they do indeed take sharp pictures. But after you've adjusted, edited, and resized your digital images, they'll need to be sharpened enough to give them back some crispness. Different photos need different amounts of sharpening applied; there is no standard amount that works for all images.

Sharpening is the *last* step in running an image through Photoshop, so if you need to get rid of visual noise, run your image through noise reduction *before* you sharpen. Other tips for sharpening include these:

- **Sharpening does not help photos that are out of focus or blurred.** Sharpening only benefits photos that were properly focused in the camera when you shot them.

- **Only sharpen images after an image has been sized for final output.** If you sharpen images before you resize, you'll get undesirable sharpening artifacts in your image, like the dreaded jaggies.

- **Create a separate layer for sharpening the image.** If you resize the image later, you can always delete the original sharpening layer. Create a layer by pressing Ctrl+Shift+Alt+E (⌘+Shift+Option+E on a Mac). The new target layer will be created with the visible layers merged together.

- **Sharpen images using the Unsharp Mask or Smart Sharpen filters located in the Filter⇨Sharpen menu.** The Smart Sharpen filter offers enhanced sharpening capabilities not found in the Unsharp Mask filter — including finer-tuned control over shadows and highlights.

By now you may wonder why Adobe gave the best sharpening tool for photos a nonsensical name like *Un*sharp Mask. Tradition, I guess; Unsharp Mask is a term left over from the old sharpening processes used in the darkroom. I'm not sure why Adobe didn't just change the name to Photo Sharpening, or to USE THIS FILTER TO MAKE YOUR PHOTOS SHARP. For now, just remember that Unsharp Mask is a good and easy-to-use tool for sharpening your images.

You can selectively sharpen specific portions of your image by using the Layer Mask techniques I explain in Chapter 11.

Here's how to sharpen a photo using the Unsharp Mask filter:

1. **Open the image that you want to sharpen.**

   Figure 12-8 shows an image before sharpening.

   Before you sharpen an image, make sure that you have *already* resized the image for final output. Sharpening an image before resizing it decreases its quality.

Figure 12-8: Original image before sharpening.

2. **Zoom in on the image to get a better look at what happens when you sharpen.**

3. **Choose Filter⇨Sharpen⇨Unsharp Mask.**

   The Unsharp Mask filter window appears.

4. **Click a part of the image that contains straight lines or contrast.**

   Doing so helps you judge the amount of sharpening to apply. It's easier to see the effects of using too much sharpening when you view zoomed sections that include straight lines or noticeable contrast between areas.

5. **Move the Amount slider to the right, as shown in Figure 12-9.**

   How much to set depends on the image. Increasing the amount actually increases contrast along edges, giving you the *appearance* of a sharpening effect. For portraits, settings around 100 to 150 may be sufficient; for landscapes, 200 to 300 may produce the results you want.

6. **Move the Radius slider to the right.**

   The Radius is simply the amount of edge pixels that are affected by the Amount. Move the slider to the range of 1.3 pixels to 1.5 pixels; boosting it beyond 1.5 can mean poor results. View the image in the Unsharp Mask window and the Image window to judge what you get.

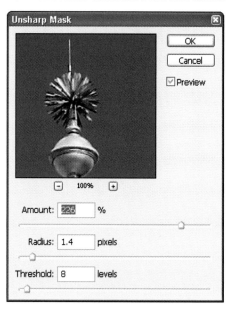

Figure 12-9: The Unsharp Mask filter window.

You can also type the value you want into the Radius field instead of using the slider. Sometimes it's not worth the hassle trying to use the slider for precise adjustments like the Radius setting. I just type in the value of 1.4 or 1.5, and retype it in the field if I need to readjust.

7. **Move the Threshold slider to the right until the zoomed preview shows a reduction of sharpening artifacts.**

Sharpening increases the unwanted artifacts that appear as noise in your image. Moving the Threshold slider to the right (so the setting is somewhere between 4 and 7) reduces those artifacts in your image after you set the Amount and Radius; increasing the Threshold reduces some sharpening. Judge the amount of Threshold you use; as with other things in life, Sharpen and Threshold have a give-and-take relationship.

Figure 12-10 shows the image at 100 percent zoom before and after the Unsharp Mask filter was applied.

Before sharpening   After sharpening

Figure 12-10: Zoomed view before and after applying the Unsharp Mask filter.

The Smart Sharpen filter

Photographers have always used the Unsharp Mask for sharpening photos in Photoshop. New in CS2 is the Smart Sharpen filter, which will change the way we sharpen our photos. The Smart Sharpen filter seems to be like the Unsharp Mask filter on steroids, and not only that, it has a much better name!

Smart Sharpen offers the photographer more sharpening control than what's offered in the Unsharp Mask filter by adding the capability of controlling the amount of sharpening that's applied to both the shadow and highlight areas of an image. As a bonus, you can save the algorithms you've set up for use with other images.

Printing, the Final Stop

All the work you've done organizing, converting, adjusting, editing, and preparing images for output is intended for one thing, the final print. Wouldn't it be nice if all you have to do in this final step is to choose File⇨Print and click OK? Well, sure, that would be nice, but . . . nope. You still have a few more steps to take before you send your image to the printer (see Figure 12-11).

Figure 12-11: Printing away.

Your *printer driver* — the printer-setup software you load on your computer when you install a new printer — gives you many options for controlling how it prints your photos. When you print from Photoshop, you'll be viewing these printer driver windows to customize the way you want to print. Not only that, there are two methods for printing: You can let Photoshop determine color conversions, or you can let your printer driver determine color conversions. Both methods have their advantages and disadvantages. I review those in a little bit.

Choosing papers

If you are printing using a photo-quality printer, you have a slew of paper choices. There is no right or wrong paper to use; follow your personal taste. Personally, I lean toward papers that have a longer display life (also called *longer image permanence,* though of course "permanence" is relative here).

When choosing papers, keep these ideas in mind:

- **Choose photo-quality papers manufactured for your printer model.** There are a lot of papers on the market, but choosing papers that were intended for your model of printer works best.

- **If available, choose papers where individual profiles for that specific paper type are available.** For some printers and papers, you can install files on your computer that tell your printer driver and Photoshop how to handle colors. These files are called ICC or ICM files, also referred to as paper profiles. Check your printer manufacturer's Web site for the latest printer drivers and paper profiles to load on your computer.

✔ **Make sure the paper type is compatible with your printer.** There are two different types of inkjet printers: those that use dye-based inks, and those that use pigment-based inks. For best results, make sure the paper you choose is compatible with your printer and the type of ink it uses. Dye-sublimation printers (printers that use thermal printing technology) work only with papers made for those types of printers.

A popular method for printing is to send your image files over the Web to companies such as Kodak or (for that matter) Costco. If you want to use these printing services, make sure you can download printer profiles from their Web sites. I recently went on vacation, and took about 300 snapshots with my compact digital camera. Instead of waiting weeks to print them all on my inkjet at a higher cost, I transmitted them to my local Costco — *after* I'd downloaded the ICC paper profile from the Costco Web site for the paper I wanted them to use, made my adjustments in Photoshop, and proofed those photos with my Costco profiles. The extra work paid off; the 4×6 prints I picked up were very accurate.

Letting Photoshop do the printing

I mentioned at the beginning of this section that there are two workflows you can use for printing. Here's the first (and preferred) choice: Letting Photoshop handle color management. (The second choice is letting the printer handle color management; more about that shortly.)

To set up Photoshop to handle the color management for your images during the printing process, follow these steps:

1. **Open the file you want to print.**

   If the Embedded Profile Mismatch window (refer to Figure 12-3) appears, select the working space that you set up in the Color Settings window.

2. **Indicate the print orientation.**

   After you choose File➪Page Setup, choose Portrait or Landscape orientation to match your image. Figure 12-12 shows the Page Setup window.

3. **Choose File➪Print with Preview or press Ctrl+Alt+P (⌘+Option+P on a Mac).**

   The Print window appears, showing a preview of your image.

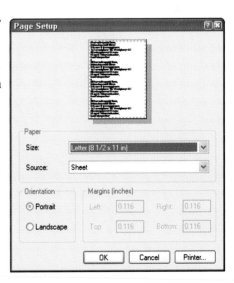

Figure 12-12: Selecting Portrait or Landscape in the Page Setup window.

4. Click Show More Options to view all the settings shown in Figure 12-13.

Click to proceed

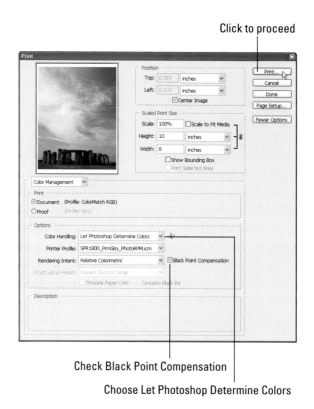

Check Black Point Compensation

Choose Let Photoshop Determine Colors

Figure 12-13: The Print With Preview window.

5. Choose Color Management from the drop-down list below the print preview.

6. Select the Document option in the Print area to indicate the image's color space.

The color space should be listed as Adobe RGB (1998) or ColorMatch RGB, depending on what you chose in the Color Settings window.

7. Choose Let Photoshop Determine Colors in the Options Color Handling field.

8. **Choose Relative Colorimetric in the Rendering Intent field.**

   Make sure the Black Point Compensation option is selected. This setting ensures that the Black Point Compensation is correctly set in the image's shadow areas.

9. **Click Print.**

   The Print window shown in Figure 12-14 appears.

Click to view Printer Driver window

Select printer

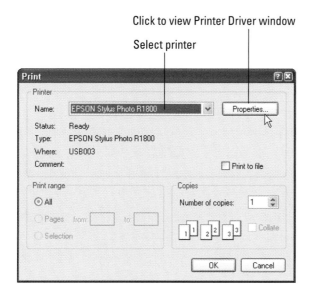

Figure 12-14: The Print window.

10. **Choose the correct printer from the Print window Name drop-down list.**

11. **Click Properties in the Print window.**

    The Printer Driver window appears, as shown in Figure 12-15.

     A *driver* is software you load onto your computer when you install a new device; it tells the computer how to find and control the new hardware. The Printer Driver window is different for different printers; the one shown in Figure 12-15 is for the Epson R1800 printer.

Choose print quality

Choose paper

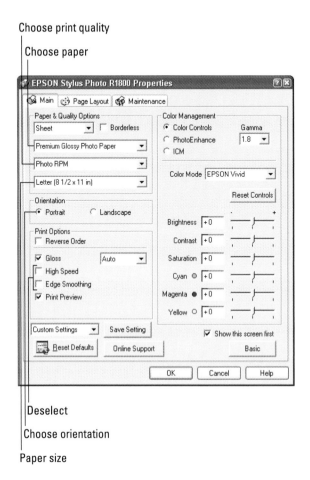

Deselect

Choose orientation

Paper size

Figure 12-15: A typical Printer Driver window.

12. **In the Printer Driver window, select the appropriate paper feed type in the Paper & Quality Options area.**

Usually the default setting is fine for this selection.

13. **Select the paper type.**

This selection is important because how the printer prints depends on the type of paper you have loaded.

If the paper you're using is not listed in the Paper & Quality Options area of the printer driver window, try downloading the latest printer driver from the printer manufacturer's Web site.

14. **Select the quality you want to print your photo with**.

   I usually use the highest quality setting, Best Photo.

15. **Select the paper size.**

   Make sure you select the paper size you have loaded in the printer.

16. **For better print quality, make sure High Speed and Edge Smoothing are *not* selected in the Print Options area.**

17. **Select ICM in the Color Management area.**

   Figure 12-16 shows how the Printer Driver window changes when you select ICM.

Click to turn off printer color management

Click to select ICM

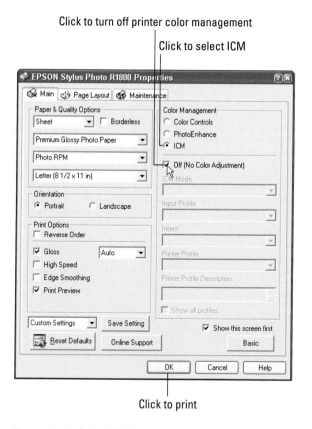

Click to print

Figure 12-16: Select ICM in the Printer Driver window.

18. Select Off (No Color Adjustment) in the ICC/ICM Profile section.

This turns off the printer's color management and lets Photoshop convert the colors.

Selecting the Off (No Color Adjustment) option is important. Doing so prevents color management from being applied twice to the photo. If that were to happen, it would make your photo too dark and too red.

19. Click OK to complete your work and send the image to the printer.

Admire your printed photo!

If you selected the Print Preview option in the Print Options area of the Printer Driver window, the Print Preview window (shown in Figure 12-17) is what you see next. The Print Preview window gives you a quick peek at the photo before you send it to the printer. Click OK in the Printer Driver window to send the image to the printer.

Figure 12-17: The Print Preview window.

Typically, prints need 24 hours to dry after coming out of the printer. Lay the prints on a flat surface and let them dry overnight. If you have to, you can stack multiple prints with photographic tissue paper in between them.

Don't count on the Print Preview to give you an accurate representation of how your print will look coming out on the printer. Color, tone, brightness, and contrast may not appear correctly in the preview. Use Print Preview as a "sanity check" to make sure you selected the right orientation, size, and so on.

Letting your printer do the printing

If letting Photoshop handle the color management doesn't work out for you, you can choose a second workflow — letting your printer handle the color duties.

As mentioned in the previous section, letting Photoshop handle the printing is the preferred method. Let the printer manage color *only* if your printer's paper profiles or driver produce unacceptable results when you try to print from Photoshop.

TIP

This method is also best used to print when printer profiles aren't available, or when you don't know what type of paper you're using. You may also get good results from this method if the paper profiles provided for your printer don't print with accurate color when you're printing from within Photoshop. That problem usually stems from an inaccuracy in your printer driver, paper profile (ICC profile), or color-management settings.

To set up your image for printing while letting the printer handle color management, follow these steps:

1. **Open the file you want to print.**

   If the Embedded Profile Mismatch window (refer to Figure 12-3) appears, select the working space that you set up in the Color Settings window.

2. **Indicate the print orientation.**

   Choose File➪Page Setup and select Portrait or Landscape orientation, depending on your image.

3. **Choose File➪Print with Preview or press Ctrl+Alt+P (⌘+Option+P on a Mac).**

   The Print window appears, showing a preview of your image.

4. **Click Show More Options to view all the settings shown in Figure 12-18.**

5. **Choose Color Management from the drop-down list below the print preview.**

6. **Select the Document option in the Print area to indicate the image's color space.**

   The color space should be listed as Adobe RGB (1998) or ColorMatch RGB, depending on what you chose in the Color Settings window.

7. **Choose Let Printer Determine Colors in the Options Color Handling field.**

TIP

   With this choice, you are telling Photoshop to let the printer convert the image color information to what works for the printer, not Photoshop.

Choose Let Photoshop Determine Colors

Figure 12-18: The Print window, with a preview of your image.

8. **Choose Relative Colorimetric as your Rendering Intent selection.**

9. **Click Print.**

    The Print window (shown in Figure 12-19) appears.

Click to view Printer Driver window

Select printer

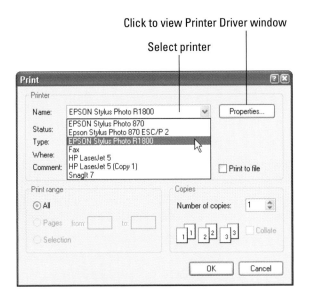

Figure 12-19: The Print window.

10. **Choose the correct printer from the Print window's Printer Name drop-down list**.

    If you've installed your printer driver on your computer, your printer model should appear in this list.

11. **Click Properties.**

    The Printer Driver window appears, as shown in Figure 12-20.

The printer-driver software is loaded into your computer when you install your printer. Different manufacturers have their own versions of these utilities. Here I demonstrate using the Epson R1800 printer driver (see Figure 12-20). The Printer Driver window may differ from printer to printer, but the concepts remain the same.

Choose print quality

Choose paper   Select 2.2 Gamma

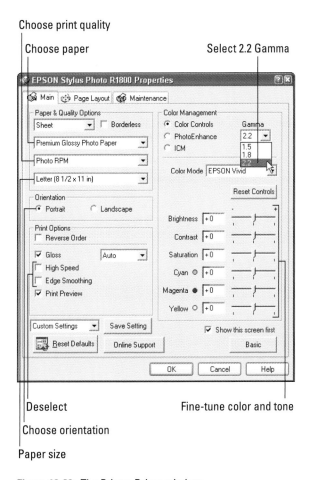

Deselect   Fine-tune color and tone

Choose orientation

Paper size

Figure 12-20: The Printer Driver window.

12. **In the Printer Driver window, select the appropriate paper feed type in the Paper & Quality Options area.**

   Normally you can select the default setting and get fine results.

13. **Select the paper type.**

   This selection is important because how the printer prints depends on the type of paper you have loaded.

14. **Select the quality you want to print your photo with.**

   I usually use the highest quality setting, Best Photo.

15. **Select the paper size.**

    Make sure you select the paper size you have loaded in the printer.

16. **For better print quality, make sure High Speed and Edge Smoothing are *not* selected in the Print Options area.**

17. **Select the Color Controls option in the Color Management area.**

    This turns *on* the printer's color management and lets the printer convert colors.

18. **For the first print, leave the image adjustments set to their defaults.**

    You can readjust color or brightness later to fine-tune your prints if you need to.

19. **Click OK to complete your work and send the image to the printer.**

    Admire your printed photo!

Understanding Image Permanence

Remember all those photos taken when you were a kid? I bet a lot of them are turning orange and fading — even if you're in your twenties. Color photographs typically don't last all that long — depending how they're stored, you've got maybe five or ten years before they begin to fade. That doesn't seem long for photos intended to be treasured for many years. They *looked* like they'd last forever when you took them, but . . .

Image permanence is actually the lifespan of a photographic print before it starts to deteriorate. After that, photos start to lose their color definition: They begin to fade and change colors.

The question for you is how important image permanence is in your digital-photography work. If a print fades after 10 years, you can just print another one! (I have to admit, that argument does have merit, but I can't help thinking that if I'm busy printing today, the last thing I'll want to do is print my photos all over again in a few years. Life is short — for everything, it seems.)

When it comes to longer-lasting prints, inkjet printers have come a long way in the past 10 years or so. The first photo-quality inkjet printers produced prints with an image permanence rated at about 30 or 40 years, if you used the right paper. That length of time is pretty good, often surpassing the permanence of prints received from the corner drugstore.

As a digital artist, I want my prints to last 100 to 200 years without any noticeable deterioration. Fine art prints should last as long as technically possible.

A few recent desktop inkjet printers offer papers and inks that have an image-permanence rating of 100 to 200 years, depending on the paper you use.

To make prints that last for the next several lifetimes, keep these guidelines in mind:

- **Choose a printer that produces good photo-quality images and offers paper and ink options rated to last at least 100 years.** Do your homework by researching printer models from the top photo printer manufacturers. Photo-quality printers should be able to produce photos at least at 1440dpi (dpi ratings are applied by the manufacturer). Some printer models can produce images at 2880dpi. I suggest visiting http:// epson.com, http://hp.com and http://canon.com for information on their latest models of photo-quality printers. All provide excellent choices. For further information, check out the printing forum at http://dpreview.com.

- **Only use ink cartridges and paper intended for your particular brand of printer.** Be very careful about using third-party inks in your printers. The printer wasn't designed with third-party inks in mind. Manufacturers, by the way, make their money off selling supplies, not hardware. They have a monopoly on the supply market for their printers, but I still recommend sticking with your manufacturer's brand of inks.

- **Use papers manufactured for your printer model.** Your printer wasn't engineered to work with most third-party papers. Image permanence ratings are sometimes non-existent for these papers. You'll get best results using the printer manufacturer's brand.

- **Adhere to the manufacturer's suggested storage and display standards for your photographs.** Typically, photographic paper/ink combinations are rated with the assumption in mind that the photographs are stored in archival conditions.

Archival is a term used mostly by museum curators, librarians, and classic book dealers to mean *long-lasting and harmless to what you're storing.* In the photographic area, archival means specific handling of photographs and media using papers, mounting boards, gloves, and special glass that encourage preservation. A whole industry is out there for archival supplies.

To preserve the life and quality of your prints, consider using the following for storing and displaying your prints:

- **Archival matte and backing boards:** Whether you cut your own mattes or have a professional framer do the work, make sure you're using 100-percent acid-free materials. Adhesives, tapes, and photo corners also need to be acid-free.

- **Archival photo storage boxes:** Store unframed and photos in archival boxes. Any light and air pollutants such as dust or pollen can quickly degrade the permanence of photos. Make sure you store your prints in boxes specifically sold as archival quality.

- **Display mounted photographs in frames and behind UV-protected glass (or Plexiglas):** UV-protected glass filters out harmful ultraviolet light, which can degrade the color of an image over time.

Part V
The Part of Tens

The 5th Wave By Rich Tennant

"My God! I've gained 9 pixels!"

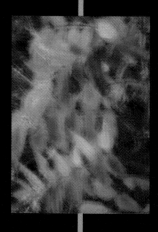

In this part . . .

*I*f the earth hadn't been created in seven days, it could easily have taken ten. Maybe that's why there are exactly 10 working days in a one-month period (for me, anyway!), it takes 10 steps to get from my desk to the refrigerator, and it's about a 10-mile round-trip from my house to the zoo, where they have accommodations for 10 monkeys. (I like monkeys.) I have about 10 dollars in my wallet. I can eat 10 Hostess cupcakes in one sitting. I must have included 10 photos of squirrels in this book because there must be 10 nests of the darn things around my house. Do you see a pattern here? Ten! Yes, the number 10, five plus five, eleven minus one — the theme of this part!

The Part of Tens is my personal favorite part of writing these books. I can get a little more creative with these chapters, and assemble them as sets of 10-cool-things-about-Photoshop. In Chapter 13, I show you 10 ways to improve and share your photographs, such as converting color images to black and white, creating photo Web sites directly from Photoshop, and stitching together panoramas. Very cool stuff, and easy to do!

THE BUTTERFLY SERIES

KEVIN MOSS PHOTOGRAPHY

I also show how to add special effects that turn ordinary photos (maybe some you wouldn't bother using) into works of art. I even impress myself sometimes when messing around with a "blah" image (or an artistic photo) produces something beautiful — or downright weird. But the main point is to open your mind to the possibilities, be creative, and (most of all) have fun with your images. I sure do!

13

Ten Ways to Improve Your Photos and Show Off Your Work

As a "traditional" photographer, I put a lot of work over the years into using proper shooting techniques — and into producing prints using the regular chemical methods. Straight shots, straight prints. Since making the transition to digital, I've incorporated more and more effects into my work, as well as displaying photos in new media such as the Web.

Photoshop offers photographers almost endless possibilities to improve photos — and to process them creatively. To add further zest and originality to your work, you can get third-party add-ons (also called *plug-ins*) that give you even more ways to jazz up your work. Hey, if living life to its fullest means an anything-goes attitude, adapt that strategy to your photography. You'll produce photos you've never dreamed of.

I still do a lot of traditional photography, but whenever I get a chance, I push Photoshop to its limits to see what I can do. In this chapter, I show you some tricks I use to enhance my photos.

Creating Black and White from Color

For traditional fine art photo collectors, purists, so-called "fine art photographers," and the artsy-fartsy crowd in general, the only photographic "art form" is supposed to be the old silver-halide-produced black-and-white (B&W) photographs. Personally, I've never believed that for a second. I like color — and I'm of the opinion that art is what you make of it. Whatever happened to personal taste? The most important question to ask yourself is, why limit yourself to either black and white *or* color? Do both! Hey, its like I always say — "whatever blows your hair back!"

As with a lot of the cool things you can do in Photoshop, converting a color digital image to a B&W image can be done in a number of ways. I show you a few that I use. The first is a "quickie" method. The second technique uses the Channel Mixer. The third method (my favorite) uses the Hue/Saturation adjustment layer to convert color photos to black and white. One method isn't really better than the other; I suggest you try all to see which you like best.

Quickie B&W from color

Sometimes less *is* more; I find that quick methods sometimes work best. For instance, here's a quickie method that takes the complexity out of B&W conversions, using one simple command to convert your color image to black and white. Here are the steps to that quick conversion:

1. **Open a photo in Photoshop that you want to convert to black and white.**

   Make sure you've made your tonal and color corrections *before* proceeding. Though you're converting your image to black and white, you still may want a color version as well. I cover those corrections in Chapter 10.

2. **Create a new layer to use to make your B&W conversion:**

   a. Create a new layer by pressing Shift+Ctrl+Alt+E (Shift+⌘+Option+E on a Mac).

   b. Name this new layer **selections**.

3. **Choose Image⇨Adjustments⇨Desaturate, or press Shift+Ctrl+U (Shift+⌘+U on a Mac).**

   This procedure to convert your image to B&W is about as easy as they come. The Desaturate command simply converts the entire image to black and white.

Using the Channel Mixer to convert to B&W

Using the Channel Mixer, you can *desaturate* (that is, remove color) your entire image, and then fine-tune the Red, Green, and Blue channels to obtain more control over the tones of the image you are converting. It bears repeating: Photoshop always gives you many ways to obtain similar results — and using the Channel Mixer is another way to convert color images to B&W (while obtaining a slightly different result). To use the Channel Mixer to make your conversion, follow these steps:

1. **Open a photo in Photoshop that you want to convert to B&W.**

   Figure 13-1 shows a shot I've chosen to convert. The photo has some color, but I thought it would look more interesting in black and white.

   Process the photo as you would any other, making the color and tonal adjustments I cover in Chapter 10.

Figure 13-1: The original color photo.

2. **Create a Channel Mixer adjustment layer.**

   From the Layers palette, click the Create New Fill button (or the Adjustment Layer button) and choose Channel Mixer. You can use the Channel Mixer to convert your image quickly from color to B&W, and then make minor adjustments.

3. Click the Monochrome check box.

Clicking the Monochrome check box immediately converts your image to black and white. Figure 13-2 shows the Monochrome check box.

4. Make moderate adjustments to the Red, Green, and Blue channels in the Channel Mixer dialog box.

You don't need to move the Red, Green, or Blue sliders much. Most of the time, you'll want to adjust the Red channel slightly to get the B&W effect you want.

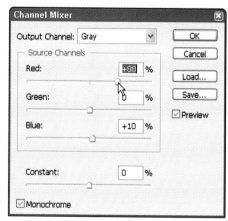

Figure 13-2: Creating a Channel Mixer adjustment layer.

Experiment by moving each slider — Red, Green, and Blue — and you'll probably find that only slight (or even no) adjustment does the trick. Figure 13-3 shows the image converted using the Channel Mixer.

Figure 13-3: Converted image to B&W using the Channel Mixer.

To increase or decrease contrast in the image after you convert it to black and white, create a Curves adjustment layer that you can use to increase or decrease the contrast in your image to your liking.

Desaturating color using Hue/Saturation

Another way to convert color images to B&W involves Hue/Saturation adjustment. I like to use this method to desaturate yellows, greens, blues, cyans, and magentas in a color image. Then I use the Red Saturation control to add a little *selenium-toned* (you know those black-and-white photos with that brownish toning to them) look to my B&W converted photo. Here's the drill:

1. **Open a photo you want to convert to B&W.**

   As in the first method, make sure you've made your tonal and color corrections before proceeding. (I cover those corrections in Chapter 10.)

2. **Create a Hue/Saturation adjustment layer.**

   Figure 13-4 shows creating a Hue/Saturation adjustment layer by clicking the Create a New Fill or Adjustment Layer button and then choosing Hue/Saturation from the resulting menu.

3. **Desaturate colors, starting with yellow:**

   a. Click the Edit menu, and select Yellows (Ctrl+2 [Windows] or ⌘+2 [Mac]).

   b. In the Saturation control, move the Saturation slider all the way to the left to a setting of –100 to remove the yellow color.

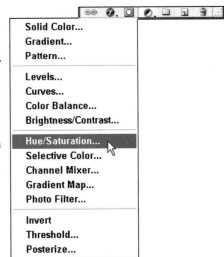

Figure 13-4: Creating a Hue/Saturation adjustment layer.

   c. Repeat this step for each of the other colors: greens, cyans, blues, and magentas. (You adjust the reds in the next step.)

4. **Desaturate the Red channel.**

   Move the slider all the way to the left to a setting of –100. Move the slider back to the left slightly until you obtain a toned effect. A setting of –70 to –40 usually gives me the toned effect I like in some of my B&W conversions. The photo, when converted to B&W as shown in Figure 13-5, is slightly toned with a Red-channel Saturation setting of –40.

Color image   Converted to B&W using Hue/Saturation

Figure 13-5: Converted image using the Hue/Saturation adjustment to add tone.

Selective Color

You may have seen photos and film of B&W scenes where only a portion of the frame is in color. In Photoshop, that's a fairly easy effect to accomplish. I've added a few of these photos to my portfolio, and it adds a nice surprise for someone viewing my work on the Web or in a collection of prints.

My technique is simple — it's almost the same as the previous technique that converts color to B&W, except I save a selection in which color will remain. The process that achieves this selective color follows:

1. **Open a photo you want to convert to B&W while retaining an object with color.**

   As in the first method, make sure you've made your tonal and color corrections (see Chapter 10) *before* proceeding.

2. **Create a new layer you can use to make selections:**

   a. Create a new layer by pressing Shift+Ctrl+Alt+E (Shift+⌘+Option+E on a Mac).

   b. Name this new layer **selections**.

3. **Select a part of the image to remain in color.**

   Using the selection techniques covered in Chapter 11, select an area of the image where you want color to remain. Figure 13-6 shows a zoomed portion of my image with an area selected; here I'm using the Magic Wand tool to select areas I want to retain their colors.

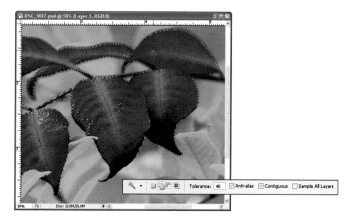

Figure 13-6: Making selections using the Magic Wand tool.

As you use the Magic Wand, experiment with different Tolerance settings. (You can find the Tolerance setting in the Option bar shown in Figure 13-6.) For like colors, I'd use a lower setting (such as 20), but for colors like those of the leaves in my example, I have to select a broader range of colors — so here I change the Tolerance setting to 40. This higher setting allows me to select more of the image with each click of the Magic Wand.

4. **Duplicate the layer.**

   Right-click (Ctrl+click on a Mac) on the active layer and choose Duplicate layer. Name the new layer **Convert to B&W**.

5. **Inverse the selection.**

   Because I want to keep the color in the selected leaves, I choose Select⇨ Inverse, or Shift+Ctrl+I (Shift+⌘+I on a Mac), which *inverses* the selection so the rest of the image (and not the leaves) gets converted to B&W.

6. **Desaturate color.**

   Choose Image⇨Adjustments⇨Hue/Saturation, or press Ctrl+U (⌘+U on a Mac). As in the B&W conversion technique covered in the "Desaturating color using Hue/Saturation" section (earlier in this chapter), you desaturate reds, greens, and blues by clicking the yellows, greens, blues, cyans, and magentas, and moving the Saturation slider for each color all the way to the left to desaturate it.

Slide those reds only as far to the left as it takes to give you the slightly toned effect. If you don't want a toned effect in your image, you can slide the reds all the way to the left to a setting of –100.

7. Adjust contrast by using the Curves adjustment.

I often find that my B&W conversions need a touch of contrast added. Use the Curves adjustment to add or reduce contrast in the B&W areas of the image to your personal taste.

Figure 13-7 shows the original color image, compared to the same image converted to B&W with selective colors remaining.

Converted to B&W with selective color

Color image

Figure 13-7: Original color image and the converted image with selective color.

Creating a Cool Blurring Effect

Often I'll shoot a series of photos of a subject, and use the best one as my final working image. Other photos in the series may be good, but I've already picked the best one. When I'm bored, and there's nothing on TV like football, *The Three Stooges,* any show with monkeys in it, or *The Simpsons,* I'll fire up the computer, start Bridge, and cruise for photos to have fun with.

One technique I like to use on these "lost treasures" is a *selective blur* effect. I'll apply a blur to the image, create a layer mask, then selectively paint in the parts of the image I want blurred.

Here's the procedure that creates the blurring effect:

REMEMBER

1. **Open a photo you want to convert and apply the blur effects to.**

   Make sure you've made your tonal and color corrections (discussed in Chapter 10) *before* proceeding.

2. **Create a new layer to use to apply the blur by pressing Shift+Ctrl+Alt+E (Shift+⌘+ Option+E on a Mac) and then name the layer gaussian blur, as in the Layers palette shown in Figure 13-8.**

3. **Choose the Gaussian Blur filter by choosing Filter⇨Blur⇨ Gaussian Blur.**

   The Gaussian Blur filter window appears, as shown in Figure 13-9. This is the filter you use to apply the blur to the entire

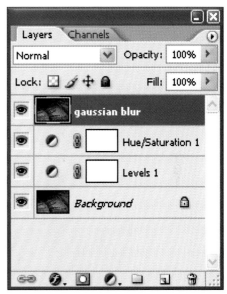

Figure 13-8: Layers palette with a new layer created for editing.

image. Don't worry — the next few steps show you how to bring back the sharp parts of the image you want to retain.

Figure 13-9: The Gaussian Blur window.

4. Blur the image.

Move the Radius slider to the left until the image and the preview displays the amount of blur you want. For this example, I'm settling for a Radius value of 21.5.

5. Create a Layer Mask.

Create a Layer Mask by clicking the Create Layer Mask button located at the bottom of the Layer palette (shown in Figure 13-8).

You can also create a Layer Mask by choosing Layer⇨Layer Mask⇨ Reveal All (or Hide All). The Reveal All option will create the mask, revealing the blur you applied in Step 4; the Hide All selection will hide the blur effect you've added.

6. Paint in the blur (see Figure 13-10).

In this step, click the Paintbrush tool in the Toolbox to paint in the effect of *revealing* the sharp areas of your image that you've decided to reveal. The rest of the image will remain blurred.

Figure 13-10: Painting the sharp areas back into the image.

If your Paintbrush tool isn't revealing any sharp areas, click the Switch Foreground and Background Colors button on the Toolbox, or type X. Doing so changes the foreground color to black in this case, revealing the blurred areas of the image.

Figure 13-11 shows the original image, next to the image with selective blurring applied.

Original image

Selective blurring

Figure 13-11: Comparing the original with the selectively blurred image.

Creating Abstracts with Extreme Cropping

In the course of writing books on digital photography and discussing techniques (some of which are pretty abstract themselves) with other photographers, I've come to the conclusion that none of us can come up with a good definition for what a photographic *abstract* is. To me, an abstract is a representation of an object — possibly distorted — that doesn't represent what exactly an object actually is. (Ack. See what I mean?) It's a visual description that doesn't make sense. Fortunately, that's the point: Abstracts aren't *supposed* to make sense!

I often like to shoot subjects that don't quite look like anything you'll normally see in the everyday world. If you view a photo and can't quite tell what you're looking at (as in

Figure 13-12: Abstract of lights.

Figure 13-12), then I guess that's an abstract. (Okay, it's holiday lights shot at night with a slow shutter speed while moving the camera. That's how it was done, but what *is* it? Good question. Take an aspirin.)

One technique I like to use involves some extreme cropping of macro (extreme close-up) shots. If you haven't noticed by now, I shoot photos of flowers whenever I can. Often I take macro shots of flowers, crop small areas of the flower in Photoshop, and zoom in even more, till you can't tell what you're looking at. Because the original was a macro shot, there's detail that the human eye can't see without aid. The final images you can get with this technique can be fun, unusual, and often provide interesting subject matter for (yes) artsy conversations.

Using this technique involves cropping. Cropping even small areas of an image means you're throwing away a lot of pixels. If the photo you want to crop was shot with a 5-megapixel compact digital camera, you may wind up with an image that doesn't have enough resolution for large prints. You can try interpolating the image (using the Image⇨Image Size command), but interpolation will get you only so far. For this technique, make sure (if possible) that you start out with images shot at the highest resolution your digital camera will offer.

My technique is pretty simple:

1. **Choose a close-up photo.**

   Many digital cameras have a *macro mode* that gets you within an inch of your subject (or closer), filling the frame with an extreme close-up like the photo in Figure 13-13.

2. **Make overall color and tonal corrections to the image.**

   Make sure you've finished adjusting white balance, shadows, exposure, levels, curves, and hue/saturation *before* cropping your image. (For more about these adjustments, see Chapters 10 and 11.)

3. **Crop a portion of the image as you desire.**

   Using the Crop tool, crop the portion of the image you want, as in the example shown in Figure 13-14. Be sure to specify width, height, resolution, and dimension settings on the Option bar.

   Figure 13-15 shows the final abstract image.

Figure 13-13: Original macro image.

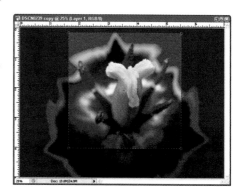

Figure 13-14: Cropping, using the Crop tool.

Figure 13-15: Final abstract.

Stitching Panoramas

As a photographer who shoots landscapes often, I've grown quite fond of the Photoshop Photomerge feature: You use it to stitch together some chosen images that were shot in a panoramic sequence to create (well, yeah) a panorama. I've used it often, and can't resist showing off great results like the panoramic of the London riverfront in Figure 13-16.

Figure 13-16: Panorama stitched with Photomerge.

Shooting panoramas

I'd be remiss in my duties if I showed you only how to stitch together panoramas without first mentioning how to *shoot* them! For best results, take 3 or 4 photos of a scene, all with the same exposure and white-balance setting. All you need is a really cool panoramic scene to shoot, and a couple of basic techniques.

Speaking of basics, here are some tips for shooting panoramic scenes:

- **Select a scene that's either wide or tall**. Hey, nobody ever said panoramic images *had* to be horizontal! You can also shoot tall scenes from top to bottom to stitch together later. (Too bad nobody builds giant moon rockets anymore.)

- **Mount your digital camera to a sturdy tripod.** I always recommend shooting as many of your photos on a tripod as humanly possible. A tripod helps you achieve the sharpest possible photos, especially when you're shooting in low-light conditions and your shutter speed is less than $\frac{1}{125}$ of a second. Look through your viewfinder or LCD and pan the scene from left to right (or top to bottom) to make sure your camera is level. If you see that your panning is a little off, adjust your tripod head to level your camera as best as you can.

- **Meter the main part of the scene**. I recommend using manual shutter-speed, aperture, and white-balance settings. Look at your LCD or viewfinder to see how your digital camera is metering the scene. Switch to manual mode, and then set your shutter speed and aperture to match your digital camera's first meter reading of the scene. The idea is to ensure that the exposure is the same for every photo sequence you shoot. Additionally, set your white balance manually to match the conditions you're shooting in, such as daylight, overcast, or shade.

- **Take a series of photos.** If you're shooting a horizontally oriented scene, start on the left, and take the first shot. Pan your camera to the right until you've overlapped the previous shot by $\frac{1}{3}$. Take the second shot. Pan to the right again until you've overlapped the previous shot by $\frac{1}{3}$, and take the photo. If your panorama requires a fourth frame, repeat the process, overlapping the previous frame by $\frac{1}{3}$.

- **Review your photos.** Using your digital camera's LCD, review your photos to make sure you achieved the results you intended. Check to make sure your images are sharp and properly metered. If you need to, take another series of panoramic shots using different zoom settings on your lens. Keep shooting different aspects of the scene to make sure that you captured the panoramic frames you know will make a great continuous scene. Figure 13-17 shows three separate frames I shot to use for my panorama, overlapping each by $\frac{1}{3}$ of a frame.

Figure 13-17: Three photos taken in overlapping sequence.

Using Photomerge

Now that you have a number of images taken in sequence that you can use to stitch together into a panorama, it's time to use Bridge and Photomerge. Photomerge is a Photoshop utility that's accessible from both Bridge and the Photoshop File⇨Automate menu. I find it easiest to use Bridge to choose my images first:

1. **Open Bridge and select the folder to choose your images from.**

2. **Process the images using Camera Raw.**

   Assuming that the images you want for your panorama are still in raw format, you'll need to process each of the 3 or 4 images you'll be using.

   To ensure all of the images you'll be using for your panorama share the same Camera Raw adjustments:

a. Process the first image in the sequence in Camera Raw.

Make necessary raw adjustments to White Balance, Exposure, Shadows, Brightness, Contrast, Saturation, and Curves.

b. Copy raw settings.

You'll want to apply the settings made to the first image to the remaining 2 or 3 images in your sequence. This will ensure that adjustments are the same for each image in your panorama, which is important because you want all the images to have the same color and tone throughout.

To copy raw settings, right-click (Ctrl+click on a Mac) on the image thumbnail in bridge, and choose Copy Camera Raw Settings as shown in Figure 13-18.

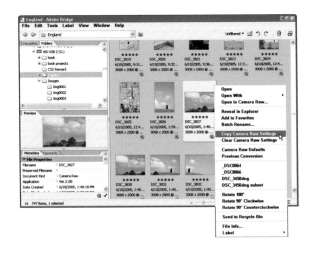

Figure 13-18: Copy Camera Raw Settings.

c. Paste raw settings to the remaining images.

Select the remaining images in your sequence into which you want to paste the Camera Raw settings: Click their thumbnails while holding down the Alt key (Option key on a Mac); then right-click (Ctrl+click on a Mac) and choose Paste Camera Raw Settings from the flyout menu.

3. Select images in Bridge to Photomerge.

Select each photo intended for your panorama in Bridge by holding the Alt key (Option key on the Mac) while clicking each image.

4. **Choose Tools⇨Photoshop⇨Photomerge (see Figure 13-19).**

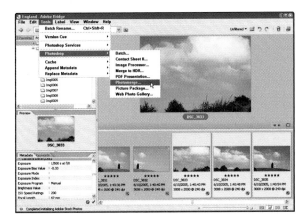

Figure 13-19: Choosing Photomerge from the Tools menu.

Photomerge attempts to assemble the images as one. For some panoramas, Photomerge can't quite figure out the entire panorama on its own, so you'll have to drag the images into the Photomerge window yourself (and line them up in the proper position there) to complete your panorama.

Figure 13-20 shows the Photomerge window with the panoramic image stitched together.

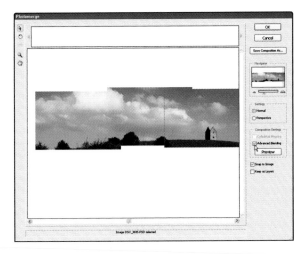

Figure 13-20: The Photomerge window.

5. Click the Advanced Blending check box.

After checking the Advanced Blending check box, click the Preview button. Advanced blending gives you a better preview of how well Photomerge combined your images. You may have to use the Select Image tool to move individual images around so they overlap properly.

Use the Zoom tool to magnify the different overlapping areas of your image so you can check the overlap for each part of the panorama.

6. Click OK to load the panorama into Photoshop.

7. Crop the image.

When you get the image into Photoshop, crop the image to ensure the borders of the image don't contain any white space. Figure 13-21 shows the final cropped image.

Figure 13-21: Final panorama.

8. Complete final color, tonal corrections, and edits.

As with any image, go through your overall corrections and editing workflows to finish the image and get it ready for output. Start by using the Levels, Curves, and the Hue/Saturation adjustment levels to fine-tune color and tone. Make any needed edits such as dodging and burning, covered in Chapter 11.

Creating a Thin Black Line

A nice touch I like to add — especially to photos printed in magazines and books or displayed on the Web — is a thin black line around the image. It's an efficient way to separate the image from the rest of the page and add a classy look. To create a thin black line, follow these steps:

1. Open a photo that's been corrected and edited.

2. Create a new layer.

The Stroke command will not start using the background layer unless you make a selection by choosing Select➪All, but I would rather perform this step in a separate layer; duplicate the background layer (by choosing Layer➪Duplicate Layer) to give the command something to work on.

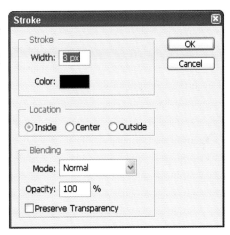

Figure 13-22: The Stroke command.

3. **Choose Edit➪Stroke (see Figure 13-22).**

   Enter a width of 3 or 4 pixels. Choose black in the Color field, and then click Inside as your setting for Location.

4. **Click OK.**

   The image shows a 3-pixel-wide black border like the one in Figure 13-23.

Figure 13-23: Image with a thin black line.

Creating a Photo Web Site

Sure, I've used a lot of tools such as FrontPage to create my own photo Web site (shown in Figure 13-24). But I've also used the Photoshop Web Photo

Gallery to create photo Web sites to display images to clients — and I'm amazed how good a job the Web Photo Gallery does. It's a built-in Web-site generator within Photoshop — and a quick way to show off your photos on the Web or create custom sites for clients.

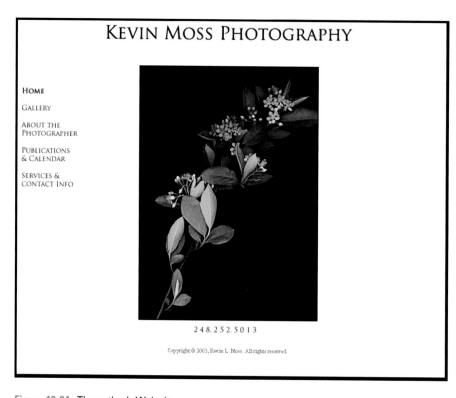

KEVIN MOSS PHOTOGRAPHY

HOME

GALLERY

ABOUT THE
PHOTOGRAPHER

PUBLICATIONS
& CALENDAR

SERVICES &
CONTACT INFO

248.252.5013

Copyright © 2005, Kevin L. Moss. All rights reserved.

Figure 13-24: The author's Web site.

Web Photo Gallery is part of Photoshop, but it's also accessible through Bridge, where its easier to browse for images you want to include in your Web site. Here's how to create a Web site using Web Photo Gallery:

1. Select images in Bridge to include in your Web site.

If you followed the image-management workflow described in Chapter 4, you have a group of images in an Output folder, awaiting their shot at the Web. As a best practice, process your images in Photoshop, and then convert each image in a format that's Web-friendly. Images shown on the Web should be processed in the RGB working space and saved in the JPEG format at 72dpi. Figure 13-25, for example, shows images in an output folder I created for Web images selected in Bridge.

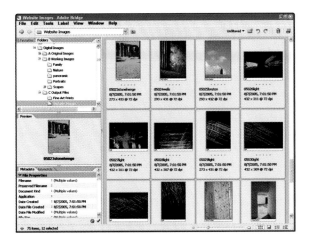

Figure 13-25: Selecting images in Bridge for your Web site.

2. **Start Web Photo Gallery.**

   Choose Tools⇨Photoshop⇨Web Photo Gallery.

3. **Browse styles by clicking the Styles selection box (shown in Figure 13-26).**

   Web Photo Gallery offers a variety of templates you can use for your photo Web site. When you browse the styles by selecting them one at a time, you can view the style in the preview area located on the right side of the Web Photo Gallery window.

4. **Select source images and destination.**

   In the Source Images section of the Web Photo Gallery window, make sure Selected Images from Bridge is chosen in the Use field. Click the Destination button and choose a folder to store your Web site files in.

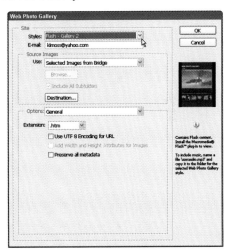

Figure 13-26: The Web Photo Gallery window.

5. Click the Options selection box and choose Banner.

Fill in the Site Name, Photographer, Contact Info, and Date fields. Web Photo Gallery uses this information as a header on your Web site.

If you want to change the color scheme of the style you've chosen, click the Options selection box and choose Custom Colors to change the foreground and background colors of your Web site. Figure 13-27 shows you a sample Web site I created using Web Photo Gallery.

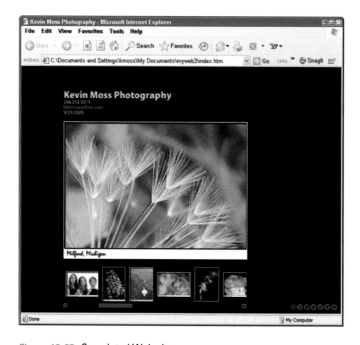

Figure 13-27: Completed Web site.

Uploading your site to a Web provider makes it available to the world. Free Web providers are readily available on the Internet, or your Internet service provider may already offer Web hosting. Many Internet providers such as Comcast offer subscribers free Web space. If you want to get fancier and set up a Web site with your own URL, try services such as Yahoo Small Business or Geocities; both offer low-cost solutions. However you go about it, no excuses — get your images up there on the Web now!

Creating a Fine Art Poster

Do you ever walk into someone's office, place of business, or home and see those beautiful photographic posters framed and hanging on the wall? Do you see the works of Ansel Adams or other famous photographers, in the form of fine art posters, and ask yourself, *Why can't I do that?* Well, you can — using Photoshop!

1. **Choose a photo that you'd be proud to hang in a large poster frame.**

   Make sure that the image has enough resolution to print clearly at a size of about 11×14 inches. If you shoot with a 6-megapixel digital SLR (or an 8-megapixel compact digital camera), you may have the resolution in your photo needed to achieve good detail at that size — about 300 pixels/inch. I've chosen the photo in Figure 13-28 for the poster.

2. **Add a thin black line around the image.**

   Create a new layer and choose Edit➪Stroke. Add a 3-pixel black line on the inside of the image.

3. **Choose Select➪All.**

   Selecting the entire image will let you copy it easily to the new poster canvas you create in Step 4.

4. **Create a new document in Photoshop.**

   Choose File➪New. In the New Document window shown in Figure 13-29, make these settings:

Figure 13-28: Photo chosen to use for a poster.

Figure 13-29: New document window.

   a. Set the Width to 20 Inches.

   b. Set the Height to 24 Inches.

   c. Set the Resolution to the same resolution as your chosen photograph.

   A value of 300 pixels/inch should be sufficient for most printers.

5. Make the chosen Photo window active by clicking the photo.

6. Choose Edit⇨Copy to copy the photo into memory.

7. Make the new document active by clicking the new document window.

This will make the 20×24-inch poster active. Choose Edit⇨Paste to paste your photo into the new document.

8. Click the Move tool and drag the photo to where you want to place it in the poster.

Figure 13-30 shows how I placed the photo in the poster so I have more space on the bottom. That's so I can fit my text into that spot.

9. Using the Type tool, add text to your poster.

Choose your favorite font, click the area of the poster where you want your text to appear, and then type in your text. Make sure the font is large enough to read well and look good on the poster.

Figure 13-31 shows the finished poster.

Figure 13-30: Dragging the photo into position.

Most of us don't have large-format printers in our offices or homes that can print high-quality 20×24-inch posters; send that job out to a printing service bureau. Be sure to use a reputable service that can offer ICC profiles you can proof your colors against while you're tweaking your poster in Photoshop; otherwise, you won't be satisfied with the results. Look for a local photo lab that has experience in printing digital files at large-format sizes.

THE BUTTERFLY SERIES

KEVIN MOSS PHOTOGRAPHY

Figure 13-31: Finished fine art poster.

Creating Slideshows

Want to share your photos with loved ones, friends, or clients? It's easy: Create a PDF slideshow. The PDF Presentation utility is available in both Bridge and Photoshop, but I prefer to choose my images in Bridge first, and start PDF Presentation from there. To create a PDF Presentation, follow these steps:

1. **Choose the photos for your slideshow using Bridge (see Figure 13-32).**

Figure 13-32: Choosing images in Bridge.

Your photos will be viewed on a computer monitor, so all you need here is a resolution of 72ppi; anything more would be a waste. If you have created Web images for all the photos you've processed, use those. (They *are* stored in your Web output folder, right? If not, you may want to review the image-management workflow in Chapter 4.)

2. **Choose Tools⇨Photoshop⇨ PDF Presentation.**

The PDF Presentation window appears, as shown in Figure 13-33. The chosen images are listed in the Source Files area.

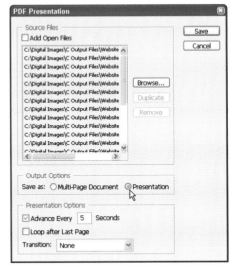

Figure 13-33: PDF Presentation window.

3. Select the Presentation radio button in the Output Options section.

You can also choose options that set how many seconds you want your slides to appear before moving on to the next slide, and what kind of transition you want to make from one slide to another. There are some really cool transitions to choose from!

4. Save the presentation.

In the Save window shown in Figure 13-34, choose a place to save the PDF Presentation on your computer. Choose an existing folder (or create a new folder), click the Open button, and then click the Save button.

5. Choose settings in the Save Adobe PDF window.

The Save Adobe PDF window appears. Click the Adobe PDF Preset selection box and choose Smallest File Size (shown in Figure 13-35) if the presentation is to be viewed on a computer. You may want to choose larger sizes if your presentation is to be printed out at high quality.

6. Click the Save PDF button.

Your new PDF Presentation is ready for viewing in the Adobe PDF window, as shown in Figure 13-36.

Your presentation should start automatically after you've saved it to the designated location. You can always restart your presentation by double-clicking its file icon.

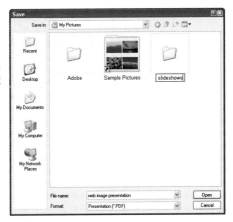

Figure 13-34: The Save window.

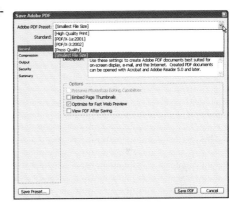

Figure 13-35: The Save Adobe PDF window.

Figure 13-36: Viewing a presentation in Adobe Reader.

Mount and Frame Your Photos

The last and most important section of this chapter deals with the final showing of your photos. As a photographer, I love to show off my photos, but (as a rule) only in their final form. The Web is a great place to show off your images, but nothing beats viewing a photograph that's mounted, framed, and displayed at eye level, hanging on the wall. To me, a mounted and framed photograph is the ultimate reward for all the work that goes into digital photography.

Here's a gallery of tips for mounting and framing photographs:

- **Plan for doubling the image size to determine your frame size.** If you're printing 8×10-inch prints, your frame size should be 16×20 inches.

- **Purchase pre-cut, acid-free mats.** I find this the easiest and fastest way to mount my photos. You can choose to cut your own mats, of course, but make sure all your materials are acid-free. Acid-free materials help guarantee that your photos will be preserved over long periods of time without the chemical reactions some materials can cause with photographs.

- **Use durable metal or wood frames.** I see a lot of frame kits at a cheap price. Yes, they come with pre-cut mats, but the frames are often made of plastic, and are not of very good quality. Spend the extra money and purchase quality frames and mats from reputable manufacturers such as Neilson Bainbridge. Most art-supply companies carry high-quality frame kits that come with pre-cut mats ready to go.

- **Display your work!** You work hard taking photos and perfecting them in Photoshop. Take the time to print, mat, and frame your photos. Hang them up on the walls of your home, and look into displaying your framed photos at work, school, art associations, or your local bookstore-and-coffee shop.

14

Ten Great Photoshop Filters

M ost of the chapters in this book explain technical stuff — you know, workflows, file management, raw conversion, overall corrections, editing, and printing. Really, it's fun stuff if you're a photographer; we need to do all those things! Once in a while, however, we need to have some fun with our photos. I'm not talking about cheesy hacks like moving body parts around images of politicians downloaded from the Internet (though those can be a hoot), I'm talking about applying some cool effects to use on your own photos, using Photoshop filters.

Some filters — in particular, the Liquify filter — are simply outrageous. You can do some quick morphing of photos of friends and family (and get in a lot of trouble in the process) or focus on bringing out the sensitive artist in you, adding strong or subtle effects to your images. I often use some of the Artistic filters to enhance portraits and landscapes in the direction of fine art. Then sometimes a silly impulse strikes, and . . .

A-Morphing We Will Go

One of the goofiest Photoshop filters (well, actually, maybe the only *really* goofy filter) is the Liquify filter. This is the utility you can use to enlarge ears, shrink eyes, and mess around with other parts of your image. You don't have to use it on photos of people, you can always "morph" other types of photos too. You'll want to be careful though, morphing people can get you in trouble!

But onward: Start out with a decent photo like the portrait shown in Figure 14-1. Then figure out some fiendish ways to mess it around with the Liquify tool. I decided to transform this normally silly guy into a Vulcan, ears and all!

Be sure to create a new layer you can use to apply your filter to the image *before* you choose your filter. If you don't like the effect that the filter applies, you can always delete the layer and create another one to start over.

You can get to the Liquify filter by choosing Filter⇨ Liquify. Figure 14-2 shows the image in the Liquify window. I used both the Forward Warp and Bloat tools to hack away at the eyes, nose, and ears, quickly transforming this normally wacky guy into a seriously troubled Vulcan. (Actually, I think it's a big improvement. Don't tell him I said so.)

Photo courtesy Amy L. Moss

Figure 14-1: Original photo.

Bloat tool

Pucker tool

Trim Clockwise tool

Forward Warp tool   Brush   Restore to original

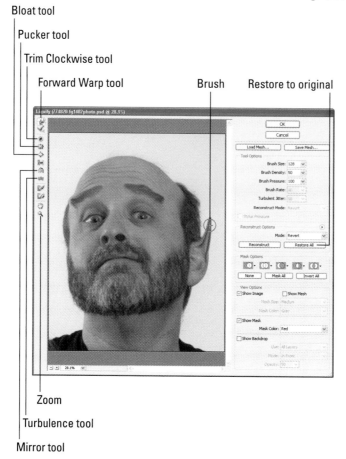

Zoom

Turbulence tool

Mirror tool

Figure 14-2: Liquify filter.

Getting Artsy with the Chalk & Charcoal Filter

Ordinary photos suddenly take on an antique feeling when you apply the Chalk & Charcoal filter. This filter transforms a normal color image to appear drawn with chalk or taken as a nineteenth-century photograph. Figure 14-3 shows an original photo before this filter does its work.

Access the Chalk & Charcoal filter by choosing Filter➪Sketch➪Chalk & Charcoal. Figure 14-4 shows the Chalk & Charcoal filter, with the altered image displayed in the Image Preview area. Adjust the charcoal and chalk effects by moving the Charcoal Area or Chalk Area sliders to the right (to increase the effect), or to the left (to decrease the effect).

Figure 14-3: Original photo.

Increase charcoal effect

Sketch filter choices   Click to save

Image preview   Increase chalk effect

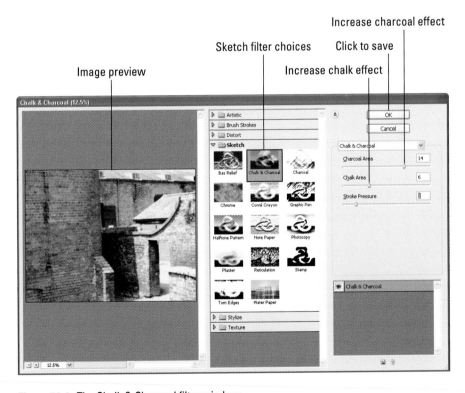

Figure 14-4: The Chalk & Charcoal filter window.

The Sketch filter is one of the few filters that require you to convert your images to 8-bit from 16-bit. (To convert your images to 8-bit mode, choose Image⇨Mode⇨8 Bits/Channel.) Other filters that won't work in 16-bit mode are the Artistic, Brush Strokes, Pixelate, and Texture filters.

Figure 14-5 shows the finished image. I added contrast by applying a Curves adjustment layer, and then darkened some of the highlight areas.

Figure 14-5: Finished image with the Chalk & Charcoal filter applied.

After you've chosen the Chalk & Charcoal filter (or any Sketch filter), you can always change filters by clicking the other icons in the Sketch filter choices.

Creating the Look of a Drawing with the Graphic Pen

Another Sketch filter that transforms a digital image into something that looks more handmade is the Graphic Pen. Like the Chalk & Charcoal filter, it converts the image to black and white, but the Graphic Pen gives your image more of the look of an old-fashioned ink drawing. You can access the Graphic Pen filter by choosing Filter⇨Sketch⇨Graphic Pen. Figure 14-6 shows the Graphic Pen filter window.

For this image, I moved the Stroke Length slider all the way to the right to a setting of 15, and then increased contrast by moving the Light/Dark balance slider slightly to the right. You can choose the stroke direction by clicking Stroke Direction and choosing one of its four options.

Figure 14-7 shows the original image and the image with the Graphic Pen filter applied.

Stroke direction

Light/Dark balance

Stroke length

Image preview   Click to save

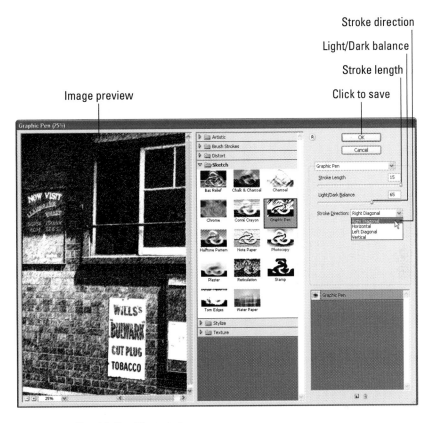

Figure 14-6: Graphic Pen filter window.

Figure 14-7: Original image (left) and the image with the Graphic Pen filter applied.

Adding Artistic Effects with the Glass Filter

One of my favorite special effects for abstracts is the Glass filter. I'll usually apply it to a landscape photo (preferably one with lots of color). Applying the Glass filter adds immediate visual interest, even an artistic or abstract feeling, to the image. You have some unique, glass-inspired looks you can apply when you use this filter — such as an appearance of being viewed through glass blocks or frosted glass — and it's a paneless process. (Sorry.)

Try using an image you normally wouldn't bother using — and apply a filter such as the Glass filter to it. You may be surprised at how readily you can rescue normal "throwaways" and turn them into works of art. The image shown in Figure 14-8 (in the Glass filter window preview) is typical of an image I normally wouldn't bother using in my portfolio. But after I apply effects such as the Glass filter (Filter⇨Distort⇨Glass), a relatively uninteresting or plain photo takes on new life!

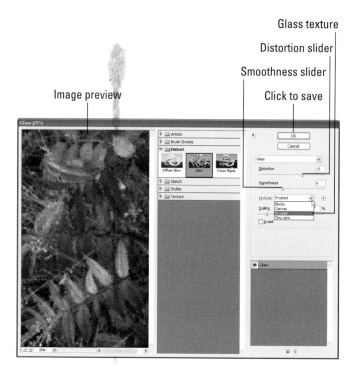

Figure 14-8: The Glass filter.

Figure 14-9 shows an original image (which I was never crazy about as just a straight photo), and the same image processed using the Glass filter with its Frosted texture option. The filter gives the image an entirely new look; it has become an image I'd be proud to print, matte, and frame.

Figure 14-9: Original image (left) and the final image with the Glass filter applied.

Caught Reticulating

The Photoshop Reticulation filter recalls the days of the chemical darkroom; we used to get this effect when developing black-and-white film. We'd develop the film normally, and then soak the film in ice water for 10 minutes. The ice water would cause a small pattern of cracks in the film emulsion; when the film was printed, the images

Figure 14-10: Reticulation filter.

would show a pattern of cracks that could suggest (say) age or wear. The Reticulation filter (see Figure 14-10) does the same thing, only digitally, without any physical cracking of your image!

You can get to the Reticulation filter by choosing Filter⇨Sketch⇨Reticulation. Using the Density setting, you can control how much of this filter's distinctive texture to apply to the image. The example shown in Figure 14-10 has a density setting of 10 — a grainy look that's much like what you'd get with black-and-white film. You can experiment with reticulation by using the Density, Foreground, and Background sliders. The effect isn't to everyone's taste, but it's appropriate for those who want to produce images with a fine-art or old-fashioned look.

To add additional effects to get some really stunning graphic images, experiment with using the different blending modes and opacity adjustments for the layer you have applied the filter to. These settings are available to you on the top portion of the Layer palette.

Figure 14-11 shows an original color image, and the same image with the Reticulation filter applied.

Figure 14-11: Original color image (left) and the same image with reticulation added.

Painting with Brush Stroke Filters

The Brush Stroke filters are especially popular among digital artists. Many photographers use them to take "digital art" to the next level; viewing their images at art shows and galleries, I can tell they're using the Photoshop Brush Stroke filters with success. You can access the Brush Stroke filter dialog box (shown in Figure 14-12) by choosing Filter➪ Brush Stroke.

Figure 14-12: Brush Stroke filter.

The Brush Stroke filter is one of those filters that requires converting your images from 16-bit to 8-bit mode. To do that, choose Image➪Mode➪ 8 Bits/Channel.

There are eight different Brush Stroke filters to choose from, each with unique painting effects you can customize with individual adjustment sliders. Choose a colorful photo, and experiment with each one. I've provided examples of a few in Figure 14-13.

Original image

Cross Hatch

Sprayed Strokes

Accented Edges

Figure 14-13: The results of a few Brush Stroke filters.

Adding Texture to Photos

A great way to add texture to images — a technique many digital artists prefer — is to use the Underpainting filter (shown in Figure 14-14). This is one of the Photoshop Artistic filters; you get to it by choosing Filter⇨Artistic⇨ Underpainting. There are four textures you can add to your photos with this filter: canvas, sandstone, burlap, and brick.

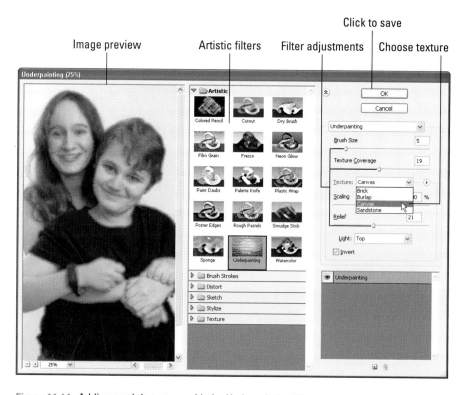

Figure 14-14: Adding a subtle texture with the Underpainting filter.

I find that the canvas and burlap textures work best for portraits, such as the one shown in Figure 14-15. The textures give the photo an appearance of being printed on a textured surface — without having to go through the hassle of having that professionally done. I've seen high-end portrait photographers use a combination of these filters with different papers, with excellent results. If you want to add some classy effects to your photos, the Underpainting filter is a good addition to your bag of tricks!

Figure 14-15: Original (left) and the finished portrait, using the Underpainting filter.

Bring Out the Artist in You with the Watercolor Filter

Photography is an art form — and if you're like me (one who couldn't paint a closet, let alone a watercolor painting), you can still become that artist using yet another artistic filter: Watercolor. Start out by choosing a colorful photo that you'd like to see as a painting, and then choose Filter➪Artistic➪Watercolor. Figure 14-16 shows the Watercolor filter with a colorful photo I've chosen to convert into a virtual watercolor painting.

Figure 14-16: Getting artsy with the Watercolor filter.

As with some photos I apply filters to, I normally wouldn't have used this photo for my portfolio. By applying the Watercolor filter, however, I've given the image an entirely new "feeling" and it becomes more interesting. As photographers, we all have some photos that never make it past Bridge to be processed in Photoshop. We have a tendency to pick the best photographs, and process those — but even the "rejects" have possibilities. Take a look at photos you've skipped over in the past, and apply some Photoshop filters to them. I think you'll be happy with some of the results!

Figure 14-17 shows the original photo, and then the watercolor creation I created with it.

Figure 14-17: Original photo (inset) and the watercolor version of the same image.

Adding Cool Glowing Edges

Want to take an already-abstract photo like the one shown in Figure 14-18, and make it even weirder? The Glowing Edges filter can do just that. It automates that old art-class project where you color solid swaths of color onto a small rectangular piece of cardboard (bearing down on the crayons to leave many layers). Color over the whole thing with black, and then use a sharp object to etch

Figure 14-18: Original photo.

a picture with outlines that expose the solid colors in the layers. I always thought those projects were fun, and they wasted a lot of class time! Well, get ready to take that to the next level.

The Glowing Edges filter, shown in Figure 14-19, is accessible by choosing Filter⇨Stylize⇨Glowing Edges. When your photo is first displayed, it looks transformed into a very black background with some glowing, colored edges around the subjects of the frame. You can adjust the effects of the glowing edges by adjusting the Edge Width, Edge Brightness, and Smoothness sliders. Figure 14-19 shows the Glowing Edges filter and the image with the filter applied.

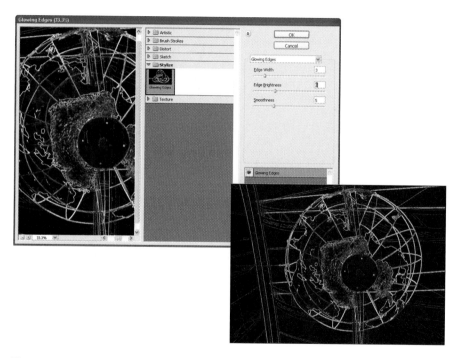

Figure 14-19: The effects of the Glowing Edges filter.

Using the Lighting Effects Filter

One industrial-strength addition to Photoshop is the Lighting Effects filter. This filter, shown in Figure 14-20, can take ordinary photos and apply lighting effects that you just could not duplicate while shooting. After choosing which lighting type and style looks best for your photo, you can click and drag the lighting guides in the image preview to redirect or resize the lighting effect.

Styles

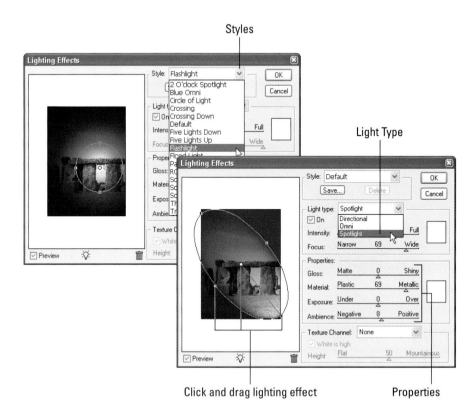

Light Type

Click and drag lighting effect   Properties

Figure 14-20: Lighting Effects filter.

Three light types — Directional, Omni, and Spotlight — are available to you; you can apply a multitude of styles to each one of those light types. The combinations are endless, and you can have a lot of fun experimenting with each until you get the cool lighting effects you want. Figure 14-21 shows the original image, shot at midday (not ideal conditions), and the photo after the Omni light type and Flashlight style were applied.

Photos courtesy Amy L. Moss

Figure 14-21: Original image (left) and the final image with the Lighting Effects filter applied.

Index

• R •